D1230615

WITTGENSTEIN

NOTEBOOKS 1914–1916

NOTEBOOKS 1914–1916

LUDWIG WITTGENSTEIN

Second Edition

Edited by

G. H. von WRIGHT

and

G. E. M. ANSCOMBE

with an English translation by

G. E. M. ANSCOMBE

Index prepared by

E. D. KLEMKE

THE UNIVERSITY OF CHICAGO PRESS

The University of Chicago Press, Chicago 60637
Basil Blackwell, Oxford

Published 1961
Second edition 1979

Library of Congress Cataloging in Publication Data

Wittgenstein, Ludwig, 1889–1951
Notebooks, 1914–1916.

English and German.
Includes index.
1. Logic, Symbolic and mathematical. 2. Languages—Philosophy. I. Wright, Georg Henrick von, 1916– II. Anscombe, Gertrude Elizabeth Margaret. III. Title.
B3376.W563N6 1979 193 79-15686
ISBN 0-226-90429-6

Printed in Great Britain

PREFACE TO THE SECOND EDITION

THE text of this volume has been completely revised for this edition, and a number of misreadings have been corrected. These were mostly very small. The most serious one that I have found was the reading of "u.u." ("und umgekehrt) as "u.U" ("unter Umständen"). The diagram on p. 126 has been corrected in accordance with the MS.

The second appendix, *Notes on Logic* 1913, appears here in a different arrangement from that of the first edition. That edition used the text published in the *Journal of Philosophy* (Vol. LIV (1957), p. 484) by J. J. Costelloe: he reported having got it from Bertrand Russell in 1914. There was a different text which the editors had, and which they had also got from Russell. It was clear that the Costelloe version was a slightly corrected total rearrangement of that text under headings, and we assumed that it had been made by Wittgenstein himself.

A debt of gratitude is owing to Brian McGuinness, not only for having pointed out some errors of transcription in the first edition, but also for having proved that the Costelloe version was constructed by Russell. The other one is therefore closer to Wittgenstein, the first part of it being his own dictation in English and the rest a translation by Russell of material dictated by Wittgenstein in German. Mr. McGuinness' article giving the evidence for this can be found in the *Revue Internationale de Philosophie*, no. 102 (1972).

In the first edition a number of passages of symbolism, in one case with accompanying text, were omitted because nothing could be made of them: they were presumably experimental, but it seemed impossible to interpret them. Nor would it always have been clear what was an exact transcription of them. Photographs of them are printed here as a fourth appendix.

At the 20th of December 1914 there was a rough line of adjacent crayonned patches, using 7 colours. This was treated as a mere doodle in the first edition, and so it may be. But, having regard to the subject matter of meaning and negation, which is the topic of the surrounding text, it is possible that there is here an anticipation of *Philosophical Investigations* § 48. A representation of it is printed on the dust cover of this edition.

22. 8. 14.

Die Logik muß für sich selber sorgen. [*S.* 5.473.]

Wenn sich syntaktische Regeln für Funktionen *überhaupt* aufstellen lassen, dann ist die ganze Theorie der Dinge, Eigenschaften etc. überflüssig. Es ist auch gar zu auffällig, daß weder in den "Grundgesetzen" noch in den "Principia Mathematica" von dieser Theorie die Rede ist. Nochmals: denn die Logik muß für sich selbst sorgen. Ein *mögliches* Zeichen muß auch bezeichnen können. Alles, was überhaupt möglich ist, ist auch legitim (erlaubt). Erinnern wir uns an die Erklärung, warum "Sokrates ist Plato" unsinnig ist. Nämlich darum, weil *wir* eine willkürliche Bestimmung nicht getroffen haben, aber NICHT darum, weil das Zeichen an und für sich etwa illegitim sei! [*Vgl.* 5.473.]

2. 9. 14.

Wir müssen in einem gewissen Sinne uns nicht in der Logik irren können. Dies ist schon teilweise darin ausgedrückt: Die Logik muß für sich selbst sorgen. Dies ist eine ungemein tiefe und wichtige Erkenntnis. [*Vgl.* 5.473.]

Frege sagt: jeder rechtmäßig gebildete Satz muß einen Sinn haben, und ich sage: jeder mögliche Satz ist rechtmäßig gebildet, und wenn er keinen Sinn hat, so kann das nur daran liegen, daß wir einigen seiner Bestandteilen keine Bedeutung *gegeben* haben. Wenn wir auch glauben, es getan zu haben. [*Vgl.* 5.4733.]

3. 9. 14.

Wie ist es mit der Aufgabe der Philosophie vereinbar, daß die Logik für sich selbst sorgen soll? Wenn wir z. B. fragen: ist die und die Tatsache von der Subjekt-Prädikat Form, dann müssen wir doch wissen, was wir unter der "Subjekt-Prädikat Form" verstehen. Wir müssen wissen, *ob* es so eine Form überhaupt gibt. Wie können wir dies wissen? "Aus den Zeichen!" Aber wie? Wir haben ja gar keine *Zeichen* von dieser Form. Wir können zwar sagen: Wir haben Zeichen, die sich so benehmen, wie solche von der Subjekt-Prädikat Form, aber beweist das, daß es wirklich Tatsachen dieser Form geben muß? Nämlich: wenn diese vollständig analysiert sind. Und hier fragt es sich wieder: gibt es so eine vollständige Analyse? *Und wenn nicht*: Was ist denn dann die Aufgabe der Philosophie?!!?

Also können wir uns fragen: Gibt es die Subjekt-Prädikat Form? Gibt es die Relationsform? Gibt es überhaupt irgend eine der Formen,

22.8.14.

Logic must take care of itself. [*See* 5.473.]

If syntactical rules for functions can be set up *at all*, then the whole theory of things, properties, etc., is superfluous. It is also all too obvious that this theory isn't what is in question either in the *Grundgesetze*, or in *Principia Mathematica*. Once more: logic must take care of itself. A *possible* sign must also be capable of signifying. Everything that is possible at all, is also legitimate. Let us remember the explanation why "Socrates is Plato" is nonsense. That is, because *we* have not made an arbitrary specification, NOT because a sign is, shall we say, illegitimate in itself! [*Cf.* 5.473.]

2.9.14.

It must in a certain sense be impossible for us to go wrong in logic. This is already partly expressed by saying: Logic must take care of itself. This is an extremely profound and important insight. [*Cf.* 5.473.]

Frege says: Every well-formed sentence must make sense; and I say: Every possible sentence is well-formed, and if it does not make sense that can only come of our not having *given* any meaning to certain of its parts. Even when we believe we have done so. [*Cf.* 5.4733.]

3.9.14.

How is it reconcilable with the task of philosophy, that logic should take care of itself? If, for example, we ask: Is such and such a fact of the subject-predicate form?, we must surely know what we mean by "subject-predicate form". We must know *whether* there is such a form at all. How can we know this? "From the signs". But how? For we haven't got any *signs* of this form. We may indeed say: We have signs that behave like signs of the subject-predicate form, but does that mean that there really must be facts of this form? That is, when those signs are completely analysed? And here the question arises again: Does such a complete analysis exist? *And if not*: then what is the task of philosophy?!!?

Then can we ask ourselves: Does the subject-predicate form exist? Does the relational form exist? Do any of the forms exist at all that

von denen Russell und ich immer gesprochen haben? (Russell würde sagen: "ja! denn das ist einleuchtend." *Jaha!*)

Also: wenn *alles*, was gezeigt werden braucht, durch die Existenz der Subjekt-Prädikat SÄTZE etc. gezeigt wird, dann ist die Aufgabe der Philosophie eine andere, als ich ursprünglich annahm. Wenn dem aber nicht so ist, so müßte das Fehlende durch eine Art Erfahrung gezeigt werden, und das halte ich für ausgeschlossen.

Die Unklarheit liegt *offenbar* in der Frage, worin eigentlich die logische Identität von Zeichen und Bezeichnetem besteht! Und diese Frage ist (*wieder*) eine Hauptansicht des ganzen philosophischen Problems.

Es sei eine Frage der Philosophie gegeben: etwa die, ob "A ist gut" ein Subjekt-Prädikat Satz sei; oder die, ob "A ist heller als B" ein Relations-Satz sei! *Wie läßt sich so eine Frage überhaupt entscheiden?*! Was für eine Evidenz kann mich darüber beruhigen, daß—*zum Beispiel*—die erste Frage bejaht werden muß? (Dies ist eine ungemein wichtige Frage.) Ist die einzige Evidenz hier wieder *jenes höchst zweifelhafte "Einleuchten"??* Nehmen wir eine ganz ähnliche Frage, die aber einfacher und grundlegender ist; nämlich diese: ist ein Punkt in unserem Gesichtsbild ein *einfacher Gegenstand*, ein *Ding?* Solche Fragen habe ich doch bisher immer als die eigentlichen philosophischen angesehen—und sie sind es auch gewiß in einem Sinne—aber nochmals, welche Evidenz könnte so eine Frage überhaupt entscheiden? Ist hier nicht ein Fehler in der Fragestellung; denn es scheint als leuchtete mir über diese Frage *gar nichts* ein; es scheint als könnte ich mit Bestimmtheit sagen, daß diese Fragen überhaupt nie entschieden werden könnten.

4. 9. 14.

Wenn nicht die Existenz des Subjekt-Prädikat *Satzes* alles Nötige zeigt, dann könnte es doch nur die Existenz irgend einer besonderen Tatsache jener Form zeigen. Und die Kenntnis einer solchen kann nicht für die Logik wesentlich sein.

Gesetzt den Fall, wir hätten ein Zeichen, das *wirklich* von der Subjekt-Prädikat Form wäre, wäre dieses für den Ausdruck von Subjekt-Prädikat Sätzen irgendwie geeigneter als unsere Subjekt-Prädikat Sätze? Es scheint nein! Liegt das an der bezeichnenden Relation?

Wenn sich die Logik ohne die Beantwortung gewisser Fragen abschließen läßt, dann *muß sie ohne* sie abgeschlossen werden.

Die logische Identität von Zeichen und Bezeichnetem besteht darin,

Russell and I were always talking about? (Russell would say: "Yes! that's self-evident." *Ha!*)

Then: if *everything* that needs to be shewn is shewn by the existence of subject-predicate SENTENCES etc., the task of philosophy is different from what I originally supposed. But if that is not how it is, then what is lacking would have to be shewn by means of some kind of experience, and that I regard as out of the question.

The obscurity *obviously* resides in the question: what does the logical identity of sign and thing signified really consist in? And this question is (*once more*) a main aspect of the whole philosophical problem.

Let some philosophical question be given: e.g., whether "A is good" is a subject-predicate proposition; or whether "A is brighter than B" is a relational proposition. *How can such a question be settled at all?* What sort of evidence can satisfy me that—*for example*—the first question must be answered in the affirmative? (This is an extremely important question.) Is the only evidence here once more *that extremely dubious "self-evidence"*? Let's take a question quite like that one, which however is simpler and more fundamental, namely the following: Is a point in our visual field a *simple object*, a *thing*? Up to now I have always regarded such questions as the real philosophical ones: and so for sure they are in some sense—but once more what evidence could settle a question of this sort at all? Is there not a mistake in formulation here, for it looks as if *nothing at all* were self-evident to me on this question; it looks as if I could say definitively that these questions could never be settled at all.

4.9.14.

If the existence of the subject-predicate *sentence* does not show everything needful, then it could surely only be shewn by the existence of some particular fact of that form. And acquaintance with such a fact cannot be essential for logic.

Suppose we had a sign that *actually* was of the subject-predicate form, would this be somehow better suited to express subject-predicate propositions than our subject-predicate sentences are? It seems not! Does this arise from the signifying relation?

If logic can be completed without answering certain questions, then it *must* be completed *without* answering them.

The logical identity between sign and thing signified consists in

daß man im Zeichen nicht mehr und nicht weniger wiedererkennen darf als im Bezeichneten.

Wären Zeichen und Bezeichnetes *nicht* ihrem vollen logischen Inhalte nach identisch, dann müßte es noch etwas Fundamentaleres geben als die Logik.

5. 9. 14.

ϕa. ϕb. aRb = Def ϕ[aRb]

Erinnere dich, daß die Worte "Funktion", "Argument", "Satz" etc. in der Logik nicht vorkommen dürfen!

Von zwei Klassen zu sagen, sie seien identisch, sagt etwas. Von zwei Dingen dies zu sagen, sagt nichts; dies schon zeigt die Unzulässigkeit der Russellschen Definition.

6. 9. 14.

Der letzte Satz ist eigentlich nichts Anderes als der uralte Einwand gegen die Identität in der Mathematik. Nämlich der, daß wenn 2 × 2 wirklich *gleich* 4 wäre, daß dieser Satz dann nicht mehr sagen würde als a = a.

Könnte man sagen: Die Logik kümmert die Analysierbarkeit der Funktionen, mit denen sie arbeitet, *nicht*.

7. 9. 14.

Bedenke, daß auch ein unanalysierter Subjekt-Prädikat Satz etwas *ganz Bestimmtes* klar aussagt.

Kann man nicht sagen: Es kommt nicht darauf an, daß wir es mit nicht analysierbaren Subjekt-Prädikat Sätzen zu tun haben, sondern darauf, daß unsere Subjekt-Prädikat Sätze sich in *jeder* Beziehung so wie solche benehmen, d. h. also, daß die Logik *unserer* Subjekt-Prädikat Sätze dieselbe ist, wie die Logik jener anderen. Es kommt uns ja nur darauf an, die Logik abzuschließen, und unser Haupteinwand gegen die nicht-analysierten Subjekt-Prädikat Sätze war der, daß wir ihre Syntax nicht aufstellen können, solange wir ihre Analyse nicht kennen. Muß aber nicht die Logik eines scheinbaren Subjekt-Prädikat Satzes dieselbe sein wie die Logik eines wirklichen? Wenn eine Definition überhaupt möglich ist, die dem Satz die Subjekt-Prädikat Form gibt . . .?

8. 9. 14.

Das "Einleuchten", von dem Russell so viel sprach, kann nur dadurch in der Logik entbehrlich werden, daß die Sprache selbst jeden logischen Fehler verhindert. Und es ist klar, daß jenes "Einleuchten" immer gänzlich trügerisch ist und war. [*Vgl.* 5.4731.]

its not being permissible to recognize more or less in the sign than in what it signifies.

If sign and thing signified were *not* identical in respect of their total logical content then there would have to be something still more fundamental than logic.

5.9.14.

$$\phi(a).\ \phi(b).\ aRb = \text{Def}\ \phi[aRb]$$

Remember that the words "function", "argument", "sentence" etc. ought not to occur in logic.

To say of two classes that they are identical means something. To say it of two things means nothing. This of itself shews the inadmissibility of Russell's definition.

6.9.14.

The last sentence is really nothing but the old old objection against identity in mathematics. Namely the objection that if 2×2 were really the *same* as 4, then this proposition would say no more than $a = a$.

Could it be said: Logic is *not* concerned with the analysability of the functions with which it works.

7.9.14.

Remember that even an unanalysed subject-predicate proposition is a clear statement of something *quite definite*.

Can't we say: It all depends, not on our dealing with unanalysable subject-predicate sentences, but on the fact that our subject-predicate sentences behave in the same way as such sentences in *every* respect, i.e. that the logic of *our* subject-predicate sentences is the same as the logic of those. The point for us is simply to complete logic, and our objection-in-chief against unanalysed subject-predicate sentences was that we cannot construct their syntax so long as we do not know their analysis. But must not the logic of an apparent subject-predicate sentence be the same as the logic of an actual one? If a definition giving the proposition the subject-predicate form is possible at all. . .?

8.9.14.

The "self-evidence" of which Russell has talked so much can only be dispensed with in logic if language itself prevents any logical mistake. And it is clear that that "self-evidence" is and always was wholly deceptive. [*Cf.* 5.4731.]

19. 9. 14.

Ein Satz wie "dieser Sessell ist braun" scheint etwas enorm Kompliziertes zu sagen, denn wollten wir diesen Satz so aussprechen, daß uns niemand gegen ihn Einwendungen, die aus seiner Vieldeutigkeit entspringen, machen könnte, so würde er endlos lang werden müssen.

20. 9. 14.

Daß der Satz ein logisches Abbild seiner Bedeutung ist, leuchtet dem unbefangenen Auge ein.

Gibt es Funktionen von Tatsachen? Z. B. "Es ist besser, wenn dies der Fall ist, als wenn jenes der Fall ist."

Worin besteht denn die Verbindung zwischen dem Zeichen p und den übrigen Zeichen des Satzes "Es ist gut, daß p der Fall ist"? Worin besteht diese Verbindung??

Der Unbefangene wird sagen: Offenbar in der räumlichen Beziehung des Buchstaben p zu den zwei Nachbarzeichen. Wenn aber die Tatsache "p" eine solche wäre, in welcher keine Dinge vorkommen??

"Es ist gut, *daß* p" kann wohl analysiert werden in "p. es ist gut, *wenn* p".

Wir setzen voraus: p sei NICHT *der Fall*: Was heißt es dann zu sagen, "es ist gut, daß p"? Wir können ganz offenbar sagen, der Sachverhalt p sei gut, ohne zu wissen ob "p" wahr oder falsch ist.

Der Ausdruck der Grammatik: "Ein Wort bezieht sich auf ein anderes" wird hier beleuchtet.

Es handelt sich in den obigen Fällen darum anzugeben, wie Sätze in sich zusammenhängen. Wie der *Satz-Verband* zustande kommt. [*Vgl.* 4.221.]

Wie kann sich eine Funktion *auf einen Satz bezeihen*???? Immer die uralten Fragen!

Nur sich nicht von Fragen überhäufen lassen; nur es sich bequem machen!

"$\phi(\psi x)$": Nehmen wir an, uns sei eine Funktion eines Subjekt-Prädikat Satzes gegeben, und wir wollen die Art der Beziehung der Funktion zum Satz dadurch erklären, daß wir sagen: Die Funktion bezieht sich unmittelbar nur auf das Subjekt des Subjekt-Prädikat Satzes, und was bezeichnet ist das logische Produkt aus dieser Beziehung und dem Subjekt-Prädikat Satzzeichen. Wenn wir das nun sagen, so könnte man fragen: wenn du den Satz so erklären kannst,

19.9.14.

A proposition like "this chair is brown" seems to say something enormously complicated, for if we wanted to express this proposition in such a way that nobody could raise objections to it on grounds of ambiguity, it would have to be infinitely long.

20.9.14.

That a sentence is a logical portrayal of its meaning is obvious to the uncaptive eye.

Are there functions of facts? e.g. "It is better for this to be the case than for that to be the case?"

What, then, is the connexion between the sign p and the rest of the signs of the sentence "that p is the case, is good"? What does this connexion consist in?

The uncaptive judgement will be: Obviously in the spatial relation of the letter p to the two neighbouring signs. But suppose the fact "p" were such as to contain no things?

"It is good *that* p" can presumably be analysed into "p. it is good *if* p".

We assume: *p is* NOT *the case*: now what does it mean to say "that p, is good"? Quite obviously we can say that the situation p is good without knowing whether "p" is true or false.

This throws light on what we say in grammar: "One word refers to another".

That is why the point in the above cases is to say how propositions hang together internally. How the *propositional bond* comes into existence. [*Cf.* 4.221.]

How can a function *refer to a proposition*???? Always the old old questions.

Don't let yourself get overwhelmed with questions; just take it easy.

"$\phi(\psi x)$": Suppose we are given a function of a subject-predicate proposition and we try to explain the way the function refers to the proposition by saying: The function only relates immediately to the subject of the subject-predicate proposition, and what signifies is the logical product of this relation and the subject-predicate propositional sign. Now if we say this, it can be asked: If you can explain the

warum erklärst du dann nicht auch seine Bedeutung auf die analoge Art und Weise? Nämlich "sie sei keine Funktion einer Subjekt-Prädikat Tatsache, sondern das logische Produkt einer solchen und einer Funktion ihres Subjektes"? Muß nicht der Einwand, der gegen diese Erklärung gilt, auch gegen jene gelten?

21. 9. 14.

Es scheint mir jetzt plötzlich in irgend einem Sinne klar, daß eine Eigenschaft eines Sachverhalts immer intern sein muß.

ϕa, ψb, aRb. Man könnte sagen, der Sachverhalt aRb habe immer eine gewisse Eigenschaft, wenn die beiden ersten Sätze wahr sind.

Wenn ich sage: Es ist gut, daß p der Fall ist, dann muß dies eben *in sich* gut sein.

Es scheint mir jetzt klar, daß es keine Funktionen von Sachverhalten geben kann.

23. 9. 14.

Man könnte fragen: wie kann der Sachverhalt p eine Eigenschaft haben, wenn es sich am Ende gar nicht so verhält?

24. 9. 14.

Die Frage, wie ist eine Zuordnung von Relationen möglich, ist identisch mit dem Wahrheits-Problem.

25. 9. 14.

Denn dies ist identisch mit der Frage, wie ist die Zuordnung von Sachverhalten möglich (einem bezeichnenden und einem bezeichneten).

Sie ist nur durch die Zuordnung der Bestandteile möglich; ein Beispiel bietet die Zuordnung von Namen und Benanntem. (Und es ist klar, daß auch eine Zuordnung der Relationen auf irgend eine Weise stattfindet.)

| aRb | ; | a b | ; p = aRb Def

Hier wird ein einfaches Zeichen einem Sachverhalt zugeordnet.

26. 9. 14.

Worauf gründet sich unsere—sicher wohl begründete—Zuversicht, daß wir jeden beliebigen Sinn in unserer zweidimensionalen Schrift werden ausdrücken können?!

27. 9. 14.

Ein Satz kann seinen Sinn ja nur dadurch ausdrücken, daß er dessen logisches Abbild ist!

proposition like that, then why not give an analogous explanation of what it stands for? Namely: "It is not a function of a subject-predicate fact but the logical product of such a fact and of a function of its subject"? Must not the objection to the latter explanation hold against the former too?

21.9.14.

Now it suddenly seems to me in some sense clear that a property of a situation must always be internal.

ϕa, ψb, aRb. It could be said that the situation aRb always has a certain property, if the first two propositions are true.

When I say: It is good for p to be the case, then this must be good *in itself*.

It now seems clear to me that there cannot be functions of situations.

23.9.14.

It could be asked: How can the situation p have a property if it turns out that the situation does not hold at all?

24.9.14.

The question how a correlation of relations is possible is identical with the problem of truth.

25.9.14.

For the latter is identical with the question how the correlation of situations is possible (one that signifies and one that is signified).

It is only possible by means of the correlation of the components; the correlation between names and things named gives an example. (And it is clear that a correlation of relations too takes place somehow.)

$$| \text{aRb} | \quad ; \quad | \text{a b} | \quad ; \quad \text{p} = \text{aRb Def}$$

Here a simple sign is correlated with a situation.

26.9.14.

What is the ground of our—certainly well founded—confidence that we shall be able to express any sense we like in our two-dimensional script?

27.9.14.

A proposition can express its sense *only* by being the logical portrayal of it.

Auffallend ist die Ähnlichkeit zwischen den Zeichen

"aRb"

und "$a\sigma R$. $R\sigma b$".

29. 9. 14.

Der allgemeine Begriff des Satzes führt auch einen ganz allgemeinen Begriff der Zuordnung von Satz und Sachverhalt mit sich: Die Lösung aller meiner Fragen muß *höchst* einfach sein!

Im Satz wird eine Welt probeweise zusammengestellt. (Wie wenn im Pariser Gerichtssaal ein Automobilunglück mit Puppen etc. dargestellt wird.)[1] [*Vgl.* 4.031.]

Daraus muß sich (wenn ich nicht blind wäre) sofort das Wesen der Wahrheit ergeben.

Denken wir an hieroglyphische Schriften, bei denen jedes Wort seine Bedeutung darstellt! Denken wir daran, daß auch *wirkliche* Bilder von Sachverhalten *stimmen* und *nicht stimmen* können. [*Vgl.* 4.016.]

" 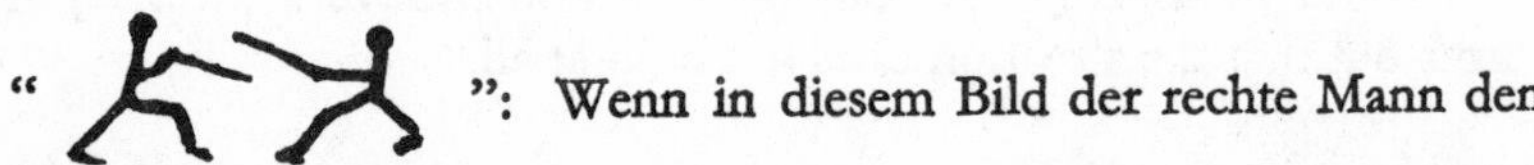 ": Wenn in diesem Bild der rechte Mann den Menschen A vorstellt, und bezeichnet der linke den Menschen B, so könnte etwa das ganze aussagen "A ficht mit B". Der Satz in Bilderschrift kann wahr und falsch sein. Er hat einen Sinn unabhängig von seiner Wahr-oder Falschheit. An ihm muß sich alles Wesentliche demonstrieren lassen.

Man kann sagen, wir haben zwar nicht die Gewißheit, daß wir alle Sachverhalte in Bildern aufs Papier bringen können, wohl aber die Gewißheit, daß wir alle *logischen* Eigenschaften der Sachverhalte in einer zweidimensionalen Schrift abbilden können.

Wir sind hier noch immer sehr an der Oberfläche, aber wohl auf einer guten Ader.

30. 9. 14.

Man kann sagen, in unserem Bilde stellt der Rechte etwas dar und auch der Linke, *aber* selbst wenn dies nicht der Fall wäre, so könnte ihre gegenseitige Stellung etwas darstellen. (Nämlich eine Beziehung.)

[1] Diese Bemerkung weist auf ein Ereignis hin, von dem Wittgenstein später mehreren seiner Freunde erzählt hat. (Vgl. G. H. von Wright, *Ludwig Wittgenstein, a Biographical Sketch* in *The Philosophical Review*, Vol. LXIV, 1955, Ss. 532–533.) Nach den Datierungen des hier gedruckten Textes zu beurteilen, dürfte die Angabe, daß es sich in einem Schützengraben an der Ostfront zugetragen hätte, nicht stichhaltig sein. (Herausg.)

The similarity between these signs is striking:

"aRb"

"aσR . Rσb".

29.9.14.

The general concept of the proposition carries with it a quite general concept of the co-ordination of proposition and situation: The solution to all my questions must be *extremely* simple.

In the proposition a world is as it were put together experimentally. (As when in the law-court in Paris a motor-car accident is represented by means of dolls, etc.[1]) [*Cf.* 4.031.]

This must yield the nature of truth straight away (if I were not blind).

Let us think of hieroglyphic writing in which each word is a representation of what it stands for. Let us think also of the fact that *actual* pictures of situations can be *right* and *wrong*. [*Cf.* 4.016.]

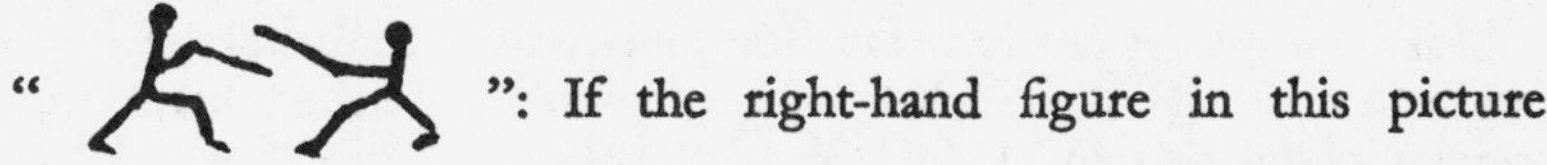

" ": If the right-hand figure in this picture represents the man A, and the left-hand one stands for the man B, then the whole might assert, e.g.: "A is fencing with B". The proposition in picture-writing can be true and false. It has a sense independent of its truth or falsehood. It must be possible to demonstrate everything essential by considering this case.

It can be said that, while we are not certain of being able to turn all situations into pictures on paper, still we are certain that we can portray all *logical* properties of situations in a two-dimensional script.

This is still very much on the surface, but we are on good ground.

30.9.14.

It can be said that in our picture the right-hand figure is a representation of something and also the left-hand one, *but* even if this were not the case, their relative position could be a representation of something. (Namely a relation.)

[1] This remark refers to an incident, about which Wittgenstein later told several of his friends. (Cf. G. H. von Wright, *Ludwig Wittgenstein, a Biographical Sketch* in the *Philosophical Review*, Vol. LXIV, 1955, pp. 532–533.) To judge from the date of the present MS., however, this incident cannot very well have taken place in a trench on the East Front. (*Edd.*)

Ein Bild kann Beziehungen darstellen, die es nicht gibt!!! Wie ist dies möglich?

Jetzt scheint es wieder, als müßten alle Beziehungen logisch sein, damit ihre Existenz durch die des Zeichens verbürgt sei.

2. 10. 14.

Was in "aRb.bSc" a und c verbindet, ist nicht das " . " Zeichen sondern *das Vorkommen desselben Buchstaben* "b" in den beiden einfachen Sätzen.

Man kann geradezu sagen: statt, dieser Satz hat diesen und diesen Sinn: dieser Satz stellt diesen und diesen Sachverhalt dar! [*S.* 4.031.]

Er bildet ihn logisch ab.

Nur so kann *der Satz* wahr oder falsch sein : nur dadurch kann er mit der Wirklichkeit übereinstimmen oder nicht übereinstimmen, daß er *ein Bild* eines Sachverhaltes ist. [*Vgl.* 4.06.]

3. 10. 14.

Nur in *soweit* ist der Satz ein Bild eines Sachverhalts, als er logisch gegliedert ist! (Ein einfaches—ungegliedertes—Zeichen kann weder wahr noch falsch sein.) [*Vgl.* 4.032.]

Der *Name* ist *kein* Bild des Benannten!

Der Satz *sagt nur insoweit etwas aus*, als er *ein Bild* ist! [*S.* 4.03.]

Tautologien sagen nichts aus, sie sind nicht Bilder von Sachverhalten: Sie sind selber logisch vollkommen neutral. (Das logische Produkt einer Tautologie und eines Satzes sagt nicht mehr noch weniger aus als dieser allein.) [*Vgl.* 4.462 *u.* 4.465.]

4. 10. 14.

Es ist klar, daß in "xRy" das bezeichnende Element einer Relation enthalten sein kann, auch wenn "x" und "y" nichts bezeichnen. Und dann ist die Relation das einzige, was in jenem Zeichen bezeichnet wird.

Aber wie ist es dann[1] möglich, daß in einem Code "Kilo" heißt: "es geht mir gut"? Hier sagt doch ein *einfaches Zeichen* etwas aus, und wird benützt, andern etwas mitzuteilen!!——

Kann denn in der vorigen Bedeutung das *Wort* "Kilo" nicht wahr oder falsch sein?!

[1] Bezieht sich auf früher.

A picture can present relations that do not exist! How is that possible?

Now once more it looks as if all relations must be logical in order for their existence to be guaranteed by that of the sign.

2.10.14.

What connects a and c in "aRb.bSc" is not the sign " . " but the occurrence of the same letter "b" in the two simple sentences.

We can say straight away: Instead of: this proposition has such and such a sense: this proposition represents such and such a situation. [*See* 4.031.]

It portrays it logically.

Only in this way can *the proposition* be true or false: It can only agree or disagree with reality by being *a picture* of a situation. [*See* 4.06.]

3.10.14.

The proposition is a picture of a situation only in *so far* as it is logically articulated. (A simple—non-articulated—sign can be neither true nor false.) [*Cf.* 4.032.]

The *name* is *not* a picture of the thing named!

The proposition *only says something in so far* as it is *a picture*! [*See* 4.03.]

Tautologies say nothing, they are not pictures of situations: they are themselves logically completely neutral. (The logical product of a tautology and a proposition says neither more nor less than the latter by itself.) [*See* 4.462 and 4.465.]

4.10.14.

It is clear that "xRy" can contain the signifying element of a relation even if "x" and "y" do not stand for anything. And in that case the relation is the only thing that is signified in that sign.

But in that case,[1] how is it possible for "kilo" in a code to mean: "I'm all right"? Here surely *a simple sign* does assert something and is used to give information to others.——

For can't the *word* "kilo", with that meaning, be true or false?

[1] Referring back.

5. 10. 14.

Jedenfalls kann man doch ein einfaches Zeichen dem Sinne eines Satzes zuordnen.——

Nur die Wirklichkeit interessiert die Logik. Also die Sätze NUR in soweit sie *Bilder* der Wirklichkeit sind.

Wie aber KANN EIN *Wort* wahr oder falsch sein? Es kann jedenfalls nicht den *Gedanken* ausdrücken, der mit der Wirklichkeit übereinstimmt oder nicht übereinstimmt. Der muß doch gegliedert sein!

Ein Wort kann nicht wahr oder falsch sein in *dem* Sinne, daß es nicht mit der Wirklichkeit übereinstimmen kann, oder das Gegenteil.

6. 10. 14.

Der allgemeine Begriff zweier Komplexe, von denen der eine das logische Bild des andern sein kann, also in *einem* Sinne *ist*.

Die Übereinstimmung zweier Komplexe ist offenbar *intern* und kann daher nicht ausgedrückt sondern nur gezeigt werden.

"p" ist wahr, sagt nichts Anderes aus als p!

" 'p' ist wahr" ist—nach dem obigen—nur ein Scheinsatz, wie alle jene Zeichenverbindungen die scheinbar etwas sagen was nur gezeigt werden kann.

7. 10. 14.

Wenn ein Satz ϕa gegeben ist, so sind mit ihm auch *schon* alle seine logischen Funktionen (~ ϕa etc.) mitgegeben! [*Vgl.* 5.442.]

8. 10. 14.

Vollständige und unvollständige Abbildung eines Sachverhaltes. (Funktion und Argument wird durch Funktion und Argument abgebildet.)

Der Ausdruck "nicht mehr weiter zerlegbar" ist auch einer der mit "Funktion", "Ding" etc. auf dem Index stehenden; wie aber wird das *gezeigt*, was wir durch ihn ausdrücken wollen?

(Man kann natürlich weder von einem Ding noch von einem Komplex sagen, sie seien nicht mehr weiter zerlegbar.)

9. 10. 14.

Wenn es eine unmittelbare Zuordnung von Relationen gäbe, so wäre die Frage: wie sind dann die Dinge zu einander zugeordnet, die in diesen Relationen stehen? Gibt es eine direkte Zuordnung von Relationen ohne Rücksicht auf ihren *Sinn*?

5.10.14.

At any rate it is surely possible to correlate a simple sign with the sense of a sentence.——

Logic is interested only in reality. And thus in sentences ONLY in so far as they are *pictures* of reality.

But how CAN a SINGLE *word* be true or false? At any rate it cannot express the *thought* that agrees or does not agree with reality. That *must* be articulated.

A single word cannot be true or false in *this* sense: it cannot agree with reality, or the opposite.

6.10.14.

The general concept of two complexes of which the one can be the logical picture of the other, and so in one sense *is* so.

The agreement of two complexes is obviously *internal* and for that reason cannot be expressed but can only be shewn.

"p" is true, says nothing else but p.

" 'p' is true" is—by the above—only a pseudo-proposition like all those connexions of signs which apparently say something that can only be shewn.

7.10.14.

If a proposition ϕa is given, then all its logical functions ($\sim \phi a$, etc.) are *already* given with it! [*Cf.* 5.442.]

8.10.14.

Complete and incomplete portrayal of a situation. (Function plus argument is portrayed by function plus argument.)

The expression "not further analysable" too is one of those which, together with "function", "thing" etc. are on the Index; but how does what we try to express by means of it get *shewn*?

(Of course it cannot be said either of a thing or of a complex that it is not further analysable.)

9.10.14.

If there were such a thing as an immediate correlation of relations, the question would be: How are the things that stand in these relations correlated with one another in this case? Is there such a thing as a direct correlation of relations without consideration of their *direction*?

Ob wir zu der Annahme von "Beziehungen zwischen Beziehungen" nicht nur irregeführt werden, durch die scheinbare Analogie zwischen den Ausdrücken:

"Beziehungen zwischen Dingen"
und "Beziehungen zwischen Beziehungen"?

Ich mache bei allen diesen Überlegungen irgendwo irgend einen GRUNDLEGENDEN FEHLER.

Die Frage nach der Möglichkeit von Existenzsätzen steht nicht in der Mitte sondern am Uranfang der Logik.

Alle Probleme, die das "Axiom of Infinity" mit sich bringt, sind schon im Satze "(∃x)x = x" zu lösen! [*Vgl.* 5.535.]

10. 10. 14.

Oft macht man eine Bemerkung und sieht erst später, *wie* wahr sie ist.

11. 10. 14.

Unsere Schwierigkeit liegt jetzt darin, daß in der Sprache allem Anscheine nach die Analysierbarkeit oder das Gegenteil nicht wiedergespiegelt wird. Das heißt: wir können, wie es scheint, aus der Sprache allein *nicht* entnehmen, ob es z. B. wirkliche Subjekt-Prädikat Tatsachen gibt oder nicht. Wie aber KÖNNTEN wir diese Tatsache oder ihr Gegenteil *ausdrücken*? *Dies muß gezeigt* werden!

Wie aber, wenn wir uns um die Frage der Zerlegbarkeit gar nicht kümmerten? (Wir würden dann mit Zeichen arbeiten, die nichts bezeichnen, sondern nur durch ihre logischen Eigenschaften ausdrücken *helfen*.) Denn auch der unzerlegte Satz spiegelt ja logische Eigenschaften seiner Bedeutung wieder. Wie also, wenn wir sagten: daß ein Satz weiter zerlegbar ist, das zeigt sich, wenn wir ihn durch Definitionen weiter zerlegen, und wir arbeiten mit ihm in jedem Fall gerade so, als wäre er unanalysierbar.

Bedenke, daß die "Sätze von den *unendlichen* Anzahlen" alle mit *endlichen* Zeichen dargestellt sind!

Aber brauchen wir—wenigstens nach Freges Methode—nicht hundert millionen Zeichen, um die Zahl 100.000.000 zu definieren? (Kommt es hier nicht darauf an, ob sie auf Klassen oder Dinge angewandt wird?)

Die Sätze, die von den unendlichen Zahlen handeln, können wie *alle* Sätze der Logik dadurch erhalten werden, daß man die Zeichen selber berechnet (denn es tritt zu den ursprünglichen Urzeichen ja an

Are we misled into assuming "relations between relations" merely through the apparent analogy between the expressions:

"relations between things"
and "relations between relations"?

In all these considerations I am somewhere making some sort of FUNDAMENTAL MISTAKE.

The question about the possibility of existence propositions does not come in the middle but at the very first beginning of logic.

All the problems that go with the Axiom of Infinity have already to be solved in the proposition "$(\exists x)x = x$". [*Cf.* 5.535.]

10.10.14.

One often makes a remark and only later sees *how* true it is.

11.10.14.

Our difficulty now lies in the fact that to all appearances analysability, or its opposite, is not reflected in language. That is to say: We can *not*, as it seems, gather from language alone whether for example there are real subject-predicate facts or not. But how COULD we *express* this fact or its opposite? *This must* be *shewn.*

But suppose that we did not bother at all about the question of analysability? (We should then work with signs that do not stand for anything but merely *help* to express by means of their logical properties.) For even the unanalysed proposition mirrors logical properties of its meaning. Suppose then we were to say: The fact that a proposition is further analysable is shewn in our further analysing it by means of definitions, and we work with it in every case exactly as if it were unanalysable.

Remember that the "propositions about *infinite* numbers" are all represented by means of *finite* signs.

But do we not—at least according to Frege's method—need 100 million signs in order to define the number 100,000,000? (Doesn't this depend on whether it is applied to classes or to things?)

The propositions dealing with infinite numbers, like *all* propositions of logic, can be got by calculating the signs themselves (for at no point does a foreign element get added to the original primitive signs). So

keiner Stelle ein fremdes Element hinzu), also müssen auch hier die Zeichen alle logischen Eigenschaften des Dargestellten selber haben.

12. 10. 14.

Die triviale Tatsache, daß ein vollkommen analysierter Satz ebensoviel Namen enthält als seine Bedeutung Dinge, diese Tatsache ist ein Beispiel der allumfassenden Darstellung der Welt durch die Sprache.

Man müßte jetzt einmal genauer die Definitionen der Kardinalzahlen untersuchen, um den eigentlichen Sinn von Sätzen wie dem "Axiom of Infinity" zu verstehen.

13. 10. 14.

Die Logik sorgt für sich selbst; wir müssen ihr nur zusehen, wie sie es macht. [*Vgl.* 5. 473.]

Betrachten wir den Satz: "Es gibt eine Klasse mit nur einem Glied". Oder, was auf dasselbe hinauskommt, den Satz:

$$(\exists\phi):.(\exists x):\phi x:\phi y.\phi z.\supset_{y,z}.y = z$$

Bei "$(\exists x)x = x$" könnte man verstehen, daß er tautologisch sei, da er überhaupt nicht hingeschrieben werden könnte, wenn er falsch wäre, aber hier! *Dieser* Satz kann an Stelle des "Axiom of Infinity" untersucht werden!

Ich weiß, daß die folgenden Sätze, wie sie stehen, unsinnig sind: Kann man von den Zahlen reden, wenn es nur Dinge gibt? Wenn also z. B. die Welt nur aus einem Dinge bestünde und aus sonst nichts, könnte man sagen, es gäbe EIN Ding? Russell würde wahrscheinlich sagen: wenn es ein Ding gibt, dann gibt es auch die Funktion $(\exists x)\,\hat{\xi} = x$. Aber!——

Wenn es diese Funktion nicht tut, dann kann von der 1 nur die Rede sein, wenn es eine materielle Funktion gibt, die nur von einem Argument befriedigt wird.

Wir verhält es sich mit Sätzen wie:

$$(\exists\phi).(\exists x).\phi(x)$$

und: $(\exists\phi).(\exists x).\sim\phi(x)$.

Ist einer von diesen eine Tautologie? Sind dies Sätze einer Wissenschaft d. h., sind dies überhaupt *Sätze*?

Erinnern wir uns aber, daß die *Variable* und *nicht* die Allgemeinheitsbezeichnung die Logik charakterisiert!

14. 10. 14.

Gibt es denn eine Wissenschaft der vollständig verallgemeinerten Sätze? Dies klingt höchst unwahrscheinlich.

here, too, the signs must themselves possess all the logical properties of what they represent.

12.10.14.

The trivial fact that a completely analysed proposition contains just as many names as there are things contained in its reference; this fact is an example of the all-embracing representation of the world through language.

It would be necessary to investigate the definitions of the cardinal numbers more exactly in order to understand the real sense of propositions like the Axiom of Infinity.

13.10.14.

Logic takes care of itself; all we have to do is to look and see how it does it. [*Cf.* 5.473.]

Let us consider the proposition: "there is a class with only one member". Or, what comes to the same thing, the proposition:

$$(\exists\phi):.(\exists x):\phi x:\phi y.\phi z. \supset_{y,z} .y = z$$

If we take "$(\exists x)x = x$" it might be understood to be tautological since it could not get written down at all if it were false, but here! *This* proposition can be investigated in place of the Axiom of Infinity.

I know that the following sentences as they stand are nonsensical: Can we speak of numbers if there are only things? I.e. if for example the world only consisted of one thing and of nothing else, could we say that there was ONE thing? Russell would probably say: If there is one thing then there is also a function $(\exists x)\ \hat{\xi} = x$. But!——

If this function does not do it then we can only talk of 1 if there is a material function which is satisfied only by one argument.

How is it with propositions like:

$$(\exists\phi).(\exists x).\phi(x).$$
$$\text{and } (\exists\phi).(\exists x).\sim\phi(x).$$

Is one of these a tautology? Are these propositions of some science, i.e. are they *propositions* at all?

But let us remember that it is the *variables* and *not* the sign of generality that are characteristic of logic.

14.10.14.

For is there such a thing as a science of completely generalized propositions? This sounds extremely improbable.

Das ist klar: Wenn es völlig verallgemeinerte *Sätze* gibt, dann hängt ihr Sinn von keiner willkürlichen Zeichengebung mehr ab! Dann aber kann eine solche Zeichenverbindung die Welt nur durch ihre eigenen logischen Eigenschaften darstellen d. h., sie kann nicht falsch, und nicht wahr sein. Also gibt es keine vollständig verallgemeinerten SÄTZE. Aber jetzt die Anwendung!

Nun aber die Sätze: "$(\exists\phi,x).\phi x$"
und "$\sim(\exists\phi,x).\phi x$".
Welcher von ihnen ist tautologisch, welcher kontradiktorisch?

Immer wieder entsteht das Bedürfnis nach einer vergleichenden Zusammenstellung von Sätzen, die in internen Beziehungen stehen. Man könnte zu diesem Buch geradezu Bildertafeln anlegen.

(Die Tautologie *zeigt*, was sie zu *sagen* scheint, die Kontradiktion zeigt *das Gegenteil* von dem, was sie zu sagen scheint.)

Es ist klar, daß wir alle überhaupt möglichen völlig allgemeinen Sätze bilden können, sobald uns nur *eine Sprache* gegeben ist. Und darum ist es doch kaum zu glauben, daß solche Zeichenverbindungen wirklich etwas über die Welt aussagen sollten.—— Andererseits aber dieser graduelle Übergang vom elementaren Satz zum völlig allgemeinen!!

Man kann sagen: die völlig allgemeinen Sätze kann man alle *a priori* bilden.

15. 10. 14.

Es scheint doch, als könnte die bloße Existenz der in "$(\exists x,\phi).\phi x$" enthaltenen Formen die Wahr- oder Falschheit dieses Satzes *allein nicht* bestimmen! Es scheint also nicht *undenkbar*, daß, z. B., die Verneinung keines Elementarsatzes wahr sei. Aber würde diese Aussage nicht schon den SINN *der Verneinung* betreffen?

Offenbar können wir jeden ganz allgemeinen Satz auffassen als die Bejahung oder Verneinung der Existenz irgend einer Art von Tatsachen. Aber gilt dies nicht von allen Sätzen?

Jede Zeichenverbindung, die etwas über ihren eigenen Sinn auszusagen scheint, ist ein Scheinsatz (wie alle Sätze der Logik).

Der Satz soll einen Sachverhalt logisch vorbilden. Das kann er aber doch nur dadurch, daß seinen Elementen willkürlich Gegenstände zugeordnet wurden. Wenn dies nun im ganz allgemeinen

This is clear: If there are completely generalized *propositions*, then their sense does not depend on any arbitrary formation of signs! In that case, however, such a connexion of signs can represent the world only by means of its own logical properties, i.e. it can not be false, and not be true. So there are no completely generalized *propositions*. But now the application!

But now the propositions: "$(\exists\phi,x).\phi x$"
and "$\sim(\exists\phi,x).\phi x$".
Which of these is tautological, which contradictory?

We keep on needing a comparative arrangement of propositions standing in internal relations. This book might well be equipped with diagrams.

(The tautology *shews* what it appears to *say*, the contradiction shews the *opposite* of what it appears to say.)

It is clear that we can form all the completely general propositions that are possible at all as soon as we are merely given *a language*. And that is why it is scarcely credible that such connexions of signs should really say anything about the world.——On the other hand, however, this gradual transition from the elementary proposition to the completely general one!

We can say: The completely general propositions can all be formed *a priori*.

15.10.14.

Yet it does *not* look as if the mere existence of the forms contained in "$(\exists x,\phi).\phi x$" could *by itself* determine the truth or falsehood of this proposition! So it does not appear *unthinkable* that, e.g., the negation of no elementary proposition should be true. But would not this statement itself touch the SENSE *of negation*?

Obviously we can conceive every quite general proposition as the affirmation or negation of the existence of some kind of facts. But does this not hold of all propositions?

Every connexion of signs which appears to say something about its own sense is a pseudo-proposition (like all propositions of logic).

The proposition is supposed to give a logical model of a situation. It can surely only do this, however, because objects have been arbitrarily correlated with its elements. Now if this is not the case in the

Satz nicht der Fall ist, so ist nicht einzusehen, wie er etwas außerhalb ihm darstellen soll.

Im Satze stellen wir—sozusagen—*zur Probe* die Dinge zusammen, wie sie sich in Wirklichkeit aber *nicht* zu verhalten brauchen, wir können aber nicht etwas *Unlogisches* zusammenstellen, denn dazu müßten wir in der Sprache aus der Logik heraus können.—Wenn aber der ganz allgemeine Satz *nur* "*logische* Konstante" enthält, so kann er für uns nicht mehr sein als—einfach—ein logisches Gebilde, und kann nicht mehr tun als uns seine eigenen logischen Eigenschaften zu zeigen.——Wenn es ganz allgemeine Sätze gibt,—*was* stellen wir in ihnen probeweise zusammen?? [*Vgl.* 4.031 *u.* 3.03.]

Wenn man sich vor der Wahrheit fürchtet (wie ich jetzt), so ahnt man nie die *volle* Wahrheit.

Ich habe hier die Beziehungen der Satz-Elemente zu ihren Bedeutungen gleichsam als Fühler betrachtet, durch welche der Satz mit der Außenwelt in Berührung steht; und das Verallgemeinern eines Satzes gleicht dann dem Einziehen der Fühler; bis endlich der ganz allgemeine Satz ganz isoliert ist. Aber stimmt dieses Bild? (Ziehe ich wirklich einen Fühler ein, wenn ich statt ϕa, $(\exists x).\phi x$ sage? [*Vgl.* 2.1515.]

16. 10. 14.

Nun scheint es aber, als sprächen genau dieselben Gründe, die ich anführte, um zu zeigen, daß "$(\exists x,\phi).\phi x$" nicht falsch sein *könne*, als sprächen diese Gründe auch dafür, daß "$\sim (\exists x,\phi).\phi x$" nicht falsch sein könne; und hier zeigt sich ein grundlegender Fehler. Denn es ist gar nicht einzusehen, warum gerade der erste Satz und nicht der zweite eine Tautologie sein soll. Vergiß doch nicht, daß auch die Kontradiktion "$p. \sim p$" etc. etc. nicht wahr sein kann und doch selbst ein logisches Gebilde ist.

Angenommen, daß keine Verneinung eines Elementarsatzes wahr ist, hat in diesem Falle "Verneinung" nicht einen anderen Sinn als im entgegengesetzten Falle?

"$(\exists\phi):(x).\phi x$"—von diesem Satz scheint es fast gewiß, daß er weder eine Tautologie noch eine Kontradiktion ist. Hier spitzt sich das Problem unerhört zu.

17. 10. 14.

Wenn es ganz allgemeine Sätze gibt, so scheint es also, als wären solche Sätze probeweise Zusammenstellungen "logischer Konstanten". (!)

quite general proposition, then it is difficult to see how it should represent anything outside itself.

In the proposition we—so to speak—arrange things *experimentally*, as they do *not* have to be in reality; but we cannot make any *unlogical* arrangement, for in order to do that we should have to be able to get outside logic *in* language.—But if the quite general proposition contains *only* "*logical* constants", then it cannot be anything more to us than—simply—a logical structure, and cannot do anything more than shew us its own logical properties.——If there are quite general propositions—*what* do we arrange experimentally in them? [*Cf.* 4.031 and 3.03.]

When one is frightened of the truth (as I am now) then it is never the *whole* truth that one has an inkling of.

Here I regarded the relations of the elements of the proposition to their meanings as feelers, so to say, by means of which the proposition is in contact with the outer world; and the generalization of a proposition is in that case like the drawing in of feelers; until finally the completely general proposition is quite isolated. But is this picture right? (Do I really draw a feeler in when I say $(\exists x).\phi x$ instead of ϕa?) [*Cf.* 2.1515.]

16.10.14.

Now, however, it looks as if exactly the same grounds as those I produced to shew that "$(\exists x,\phi).\phi x$" *could* not be false would be an argument shewing that "$\sim (\exists x,\phi).\phi x$" could not be false; and here a fundamental mistake makes its appearance. For it is quite impossible to see why just the first proposition and not the second is supposed to be a tautology. But do not forget that the contradiction "$p . \sim p$" etc. etc. cannot be true and is nevertheless itself a logical structure.

Suppose that no negation of an elementary proposition is true, has not "negation" another sense in this case than in the opposite case?

"$(\exists \phi):(x).\phi x$"—of this proposition it appears almost certain that it is neither a tautology nor a contradiction. Here the problem becomes extremely sharp.

17.10.14.

If there are quite general propositions, then it looks as if such propositions were experimental combinations of "logical constants". (!)

Kann man denn aber nicht die ganze Welt vollständig mit ganz allgemeinen Sätzen beschreiben? (Das Problem zeigt sich von allen Seiten.)

Ja, man könnte die Welt vollständig durch ganz allgemeine Sätze beschreiben, also ganz ohne irgend einen Namen oder sonst ein bezeichnendes Zeichen zu verwenden. Und um auf die gewöhnliche Sprache zu kommen, brauchte man Namen etc. nur dadurch einführen, indem man nach einem "$(\exists x)$" sagte "und dieses x ist A" u.s.w. [*Vgl.* 5.526.]

Man kann also ein Bild der Welt entwerfen, ohne zu sagen, was was darstellt.

Nehmen wir z. B. an, die Welt bestünde aus den Dingen A und B und der Eigenschaft F, und es wäre F(A) der Fall und nicht F(B). Diese Welt könnten wir auch durch die folgenden Sätze beschreiben:

$$(\exists x,y).(\exists \phi).x \neq y.\phi x. \sim \phi y : \phi u.\phi z. \supset_{u,z} .u = z$$

$$(\exists \phi).(\psi).\psi = \phi$$

$$(\exists x,y).(z).z = x \vee z = y$$

Und hier braucht man auch Sätze von der Art der letzten zwei, um die Gegenstände identifizieren zu können.

Aus alledem folgt natürlich, daß es *ganz allgemeine Sätze gibt*!

Genügt oben nicht der erste Satz $(\exists x,y,\phi)\phi x.\sim\phi y.x \neq y)$? Die Schwierigkeit der Identifizierung kann man dadurch wegschaffen, indem man die ganze Welt in *einem* allgemeinen Satz beschreibt, welcher anfängt: "$(\exists x,y,z \ldots \phi,\psi \ldots R,S \ldots)$" und nun folgt ein logisches Produkt, etc.

Wenn wir sagen "ϕ ist eine Einheitsfunktion und $(x).\phi x$", so heißt das soviel wie: "es gibt nur ein Ding"! (Wir sind hiermit *scheinbar* um den Satz "$(\exists x)(y).y = x$" herumgekommen.)

18. 10. 14.

Mein Fehler liegt offenbar in einer falschen Auffassung der logischen Abbildung durch den Satz.

Eine Aussage kann nicht den logischen Bau der Welt betreffen, denn damit eine Aussage überhaupt möglich sei, damit ein Satz SINN haben KANN, muß die Welt schon den logischen Bau haben, den sie eben hat. Die Logik der Welt ist aller Wahr- und Falschheit primär.

But is it not possible to describe the whole world completely by means of completely general propositions? (The problem crops up on all sides.)

Yes, the world could be completely described by completely general propositions, and hence without using any sort of names or other denoting signs. And in order to arrive at ordinary language one would only need to introduce names, etc. by saying, after an "$(\exists x)$", "and this x is A" and so on. [*Cf.* 5.526.]

Thus it is possible to devise a picture of the world without saying what is a representation of what.

Let us suppose, e.g., that the world consisted of the things A and B and the property F, and that F(A) were the case and not F(B). This world could also be described by means of the following propositions:

$$(\exists x,y).(\exists \phi).x \neq y.\phi x. \sim \phi y:\phi u.\phi z.\supset_{u,z} .u = z$$

$$(\exists \phi).(\psi).\psi = \phi$$

$$(\exists x,y).(z).z = x \vee z = y$$

And here one also needs propositions of the type of the last two, only in order to be able to identify the objects.

From all this, of course, it follows that *there are completely general propositions!*

But isn't the first proposition above enough: $(\exists x,y,\phi)\phi x.\sim\phi y.x \neq y$? The difficulty of identification can be done away with by describing the whole world in a single general proposition beginning: "$(\exists x,y, z \ldots \phi,\psi \ldots R,S \ldots)$" and now follows a logical product, etc.

If we say "ϕ is a unit function and $(x).\phi x$", that is as much as to say: There is only one thing! (By this means we have *apparently* got round the proposition $(\exists x)(y).y = x$".)

18.10.14.

My mistake obviously lies in a false conception of logical portrayal by the proposition.

A statement cannot be concerned with the logical structure of the world, for in order for a statement to be possible at all, in order for a proposition to be CAPABLE of making SENSE, the world must already have just the logical structure that it has. The logic of the world is prior to all truth and falsehood.

Beiläufig gesprochen: bevor irgend ein Satz überhaupt Sinn haben kann, müssen die logischen Konstanten Bedeutung haben.

19. 10. 14.

Die Beschreibung der Welt durch Sätze ist nur dadurch möglich, daß das Bezeichnete nicht sein eigenes Zeichen ist! Anwendung—.

Beleuchtung von Kants Frage "Wie ist reine Mathematik möglich?" durch die Theorie der Tautologien!

Es leuchtet ein, daß man den Bau der Welt ohne irgend welche *Namen* zu *nennen* beschreiben können muß. [*Vgl.* 5.526.]

20. 10. 14.

Aus dem Satz muß man den logischen Bau des Sachverhaltes ersehen, der ihn wahr oder falsch macht. (Wie ein Bild zeigen muß, in welchen räumlichen Beziehungen die darauf wiedergegebenen Dinge stehen müssen, wenn das Bild richtig (wahr) ist.)

Die Form eines Bildes könnte man dasjenige nennen, worin das Bild mit der Wirklichkeit stimmen MUSS (um sie überhaupt abbilden zu können). [*Vgl.* 2.17 *u.* 2.18.]

Die Theorie der logischen Abbildung durch die Sprache gibt als erste einen Aufschluß über das Wesen der Wahrheits-Beziehung.

Die Theorie der logischen Abbildung durch die Sprache sagt—ganz allgemein: Damit es möglich ist, daß ein Satz wahr oder falsch sei—daß er mit der Wirklichkeit übereinstimme oder nicht—dazu muß im Satze etwas mit der Wirklichkeit *identisch* sein. [*Vgl.* 2.18.]

Das, was in "∼p" verneint, ist nicht das "∼" vor dem "p" sondern dasjenige, was allen Zeichen, die in dieser Notation mit "∼p" gleichbedeutend sind, gemeinsam ist; also das Gemeinsame von

∼p	}	und dasselbe
∼∼∼p		gilt für die
∼pv∼p		Allgemeinheits-
∼p. ∼p		bezeichnung etc.
etc. etc.		

[*Vgl.* 5.512.]

Roughly speaking: before any proposition can make sense at all the *logical* constants must have reference.[1]

19.10.14.

The description of the world by means of propositions is only possible because what is signified is not its own sign! Application—.

Light on Kant's question "How is pure mathematics possible?" through the theory of tautologies.

It is obvious that we must be able to describe the structure of the world without mentioning any *names*. [*Cf.* 5.526.]

20.10.14.

The proposition must enable us to see the logical structure of the situation that makes it true or false. (As a picture must shew the spatial relation in which the things represented in it must stand if the picture is correct (true).)

The form of a picture might be called that in which the picture MUST agree with reality (in order to be capable of portraying it at all). [*Cf.* 2.17 and 2.18.]

The first thing that the theory of logical portrayal by means of language gives us is a piece of information about the nature of the truth-relation.

The theory of logical portrayal by means of language says—quite generally: In order for it to be possible that a proposition should be true or false—agree with reality or not—for this to be possible something in the proposition must be *identical* with reality. [*Cf.* 2.18.]

What negates in "p" is not the "$\sim$" in front of the "p", but is what is common to all the signs that have the same meaning as "$\sim$p" in this notation; and therefore what is common in

$\sim$p
$\sim\sim\sim$p
$\sim$p v $\sim$p
$\sim$p. $\sim$p
etc. etc.

and the same holds for the generality notation, etc.

[Cf. 5.512.]

[1] I render 'Bedeutung', here and elsewhere, by 'reference' in order to bring it especially to the reader's attention, (*a*) that Wittgenstein was under the influence of Frege in his use of 'Sinn' ('sense') and 'Bedeutung' ('reference' or 'meaning' in the sense 'what a word or sentence *stands for*') and (*b*) that there is a great contrast between his ideas at this stage of the *Notebooks* and those of the *Tractatus*, where he denies that logical constants or sentences have 'Bedeutung'. (*Translator*.)

Scheinsätze sind solche, die, wenn analysiert, das, was sie *sagen* sollten, doch nur wieder *zeigen*.

Das Gefühl, daß der Satz einen Komplex auf die Art der Russellschen Beschreibungen beschreibe, rechtfertigt sich jetzt: Der Satz beschreibt den Komplex durch seine logischen Eigenschaften.

Der Satz konstruiert eine Welt mit Hilfe seines logischen Gerüstes, und darum kann man am Satz auch sehen, wie sich alles Logische verhielte, wenn er wahr wäre: man kann aus einem falschen Satz *Schlüsse ziehen* etc. (So kann ich sehen daß, wenn "$(x,\phi).\phi x$" wahr wäre, dieser Satz im Widerspruch stünde mit einem Satze "ψa".) [*Vgl.* 4.023.]

Daß sich von materiellen Sätzen auf ganz allgemeine Sätze schließen läßt—daß diese zu jenen in *bedeutungsvollen* internen Beziehungen stehen können—zeigt, daß die ganz allgemeinen Sätze logische Konstruktionen von Sachverhalten sind.

21. 10. 14.

Ist die Russellsche Definition der Null nicht unsinnig? Kann man von einer Klasse $\hat{x}\,(x \neq x)$ überhaupt reden?—Kann man denn von einer Klasse $\hat{x}\,(x = x)$ reden? Ist denn $x \neq x$ oder $x = x$ eine Funktion von x??—Muß nicht die Null definiert werden durch die *Hypothese* $(\exists\phi)$: $(x){\sim}\phi x$? Und Analoges würde von allen anderen Zahlen gelten. Dies nun wirft ein Licht auf die ganze Frage nach der Existenz von Anzahlen von Dingen.

$$0 = \hat{\alpha}\{(\exists\phi):(x) \sim\phi x.\ \alpha = \hat{u}(\phi u)\}\ \text{Def.}$$

$$1 = \hat{\alpha}\{(\exists\phi)::(\exists x).\phi x:\ \phi y.\phi z.\ \supset_{y,z}\ y = z : \alpha = \hat{u}(\phi u)\}\ \text{Def.}$$

[Das Gleichheitszeichen in der geschweiften Klammer könnte man *vermeiden*, wenn man schriebe

$$0 = \widehat{\hat{u}\ (\phi u)}\{(x){\sim}\phi x\}.$$[1]]

Der Satz muß die *Möglichkeit seiner Wahrheit enthalten* (und so zeigen). Aber nicht mehr als die *Möglichkeit*. [*Vgl.* 2.203 *u.* 3.02 *u.* 3.13.]

Nach meiner Definition der Klassen ist $(x).{\sim}\hat{x}(\phi x)$ die Aussage, daß $\hat{x}(\phi x)$ null ist, und die Definition der Null ist dann $0 = \hat{\alpha}\ [(x).\ {\sim}\alpha]$ Def.

[1] Gesprochen: Die Klasse aller derjenigen Klassen der Elemente *u*, für welche *φu*, für welche kein Element *φ* ist. (Herausg.)

Pseudo-propositions are such as, when analysed, turn out after all only to *shew* what they were supposed to *say*.

Here we have a justification for the feeling that the proposition describes a complex in the kind of way that Russellian descriptions do: the proposition describes the complex by means of its logical properties.

The proposition constructs a world by means of its logical scaffolding, and that is why we can actually see in the proposition how everything logical would stand if it were true: we can *draw conclusions* from a false proposition, etc. (In this way I can see that if "$(x,\phi).\phi x$" were true, this proposition would contradict a proposition "ψa".) [*Cf* 4.023.]

The possibility of inferring completely general propositions from material propositions—the fact that the former are capable of standing in *meaningful* internal relations with the latter—shews that the completely general propositions are logical constructions from situations.

21.10.14.

Isn't the Russellian definition of nought nonsensical? Can we speak of a class $\hat{x}\,(x \neq x)$ at all?—Can we speak of a class $\hat{x}\,(x = x)$ either? For is $x \neq x$ or $x = x$ a function of x?—Must not 0 be defined by means of the *hypothesis* $(\exists\phi):(x)\sim\phi x$? And something analogous would hold of all other numbers. Now this throws light on the whole question about the existence of numbers of things.

$$0 = \hat{\alpha}\{(\exists\phi):(x) \sim \phi x.\alpha = \hat{u}(\phi u)\}\ \text{Def.}$$
$$1 = \hat{\alpha}\{(\exists\phi)::(\exists x).\phi x:\phi y.\phi z \supset_{y,z} y = z:\alpha = \hat{u}(\phi u)\}\ \text{Def.}$$

[The sign of equality in the curly brackets could be *avoided* if we were to write:

$$0 = \widehat{\hat{u}\,(\phi u)}\,\{(x) \sim \phi\, x\}.^{1}]$$

The proposition must *contain* (and in this way shew) the *possibility of its truth*. But not more than the *possibility*. [*Cf.* 2.203 and 3.02 and 3.13.]

By my definition of classes $(x).\sim \hat{x}(\phi x)$ is the assertion that $\hat{x}(\phi x)$ is null and the definition of 0 is in that case $0 = \hat{\alpha}[(x). \sim \alpha]$ Def.

[1] To be read as: the class of all classes of elements u such that ϕu, such that nothing is ϕ. (*Edd.*)

Ich dachte, die Möglichkeit der Wahrheit eines Satzes $\phi(a)$ ist an die Tatsache $(\exists x,\phi).\phi x$ gebunden. Aber es ist nicht einzusehen, warum ϕa nur dann möglich sein soll, wenn es einen anderen Satz derselben Form gibt. ϕa braucht doch keinen Präzedenzfall. (Denn angenommen, es gäbe nur die beiden Elementarsätze "ϕa" und "ψa" und "ϕa" sei falsch: warum soll dieser Satz nur dann einen Sinn haben, wenn "ψa" wahr ist?!)

22. 10. 14

Im Satz muß etwas mit seiner Bedeutung identisch sein, der Satz darf aber nicht mit seiner Bedeutung identisch sein, also muß etwas in ihm mit seiner Bedeutung *nicht* identisch sein. (Der Satz ist ein Gebilde mit den logischen Zügen des Dargestellten und mit noch anderen Zügen, diese nun werden willkürlich sein und in verschiedenen Zeichensprachen verschieden.) Es muß also verschiedene Gebilde mit denselben logischen Zügen geben; das Dargestellte wird eines von diesen sein, und es wird sich bei der Darstellung darum handeln, dieses von anderen Gebilden mit denselben logischen Zügen zu unterscheiden (da ja sonst die Darstellung nicht eindeutig wäre). Dieser Teil der Darstellung (die Namengebung) muß nun durch willkürliche Bestimmungen geschehen. Es muß darnach also jeder Satz Züge mit willkürlich bestimmten Bedeutungen enthalten.

Versucht man dies auf die ganz allgemeinen Sätze anzuwenden so scheint es, daß darin irgend ein grundlegender Fehler ist.

Die Allgemeinheit des ganz allgemeinen Satzes ist die zufällige. Er handelt von allen Dingen, die es zufälligerweise gibt. Und darum ist er ein materieller Satz.

23. 10. 14.

Einerseits scheint meine Theorie der logischen Abbildung die einzig mögliche, andererseits scheint in ihr ein unlöslicher Widerspruch zu sein!

Wenn der ganz allgemeine Satz nicht ganz entmaterialisiert ist, so wird ein Satz durch die Verallgemeinerung wohl überhaupt nicht entmaterialisiert, wie ich glaubte.

Ob ich von einem bestimmten Ding oder von allen Dingen, die es gibt, etwas aussage, die Aussage ist gleich materiell.

I thought that the possibility of the truth of the proposition ϕa was tied up with the fact $(\exists x,\phi).\phi x$. But it is impossible to see why ϕa should only be possible if there is another proposition of the same form. ϕa surely does not need any precedent. (For suppose that there existed only the two elementary propositions "ϕa" and "ψa" and that "ϕa" were false: Why should this proposition only make sense if "ψa" is true?)

22.10.14.

There must be something in the proposition that is identical with its reference, but the proposition cannot be identical with its reference, and so there must be something in it that is *not* identical with the reference. (The proposition is a formation with the logical features of what it represents and with other features besides, but these will be arbitrary and different in different sign-languages.) So there must be different formations with the same logical features; what is represented will be one of these, and it will be the business of the representation to distinguish this one from other formations with the same logical features. (Since otherwise the representation would not be unambiguous.) This part of the representation (the assignment of names) must take place by means of arbitrary stipulations. Every proposition must accordingly contain features with arbitrarily determined references.

If one tries to apply this to a completely generalized proposition, it appears that there is some fundamental mistake in it.

The generality of the completely general proposition is accidental generality. It deals with all the things that there chance to be. And that is why it is a material proposition.

23.10.14.

On the one hand my theory of logical portrayal seems to be the only possible one, on the other hand there seems to be an insoluble contradiction in it!

If the completely generalized proposition is not completely dematerialized, then a proposition does not get dematerialized at all through generalization, as I used to think.

Whether I assert something of a particular thing or of all the things that there are, the assertion is equally material.

"Alle Dinge", das ist sozusagen eine Beschreibung statt "a und b und c".

Wie, wenn unsere Zeichen ebenso unbestimmt wären, wie die Welt, welche sie spiegeln?

Um das Zeichen im Zeichen zu erkennen, muß man auf den Gebrauch achten. [*Vgl.* 3.326.]

Wollten wir dasjenige, welches wir durch "(x).ϕx" ausdrücken, durch das Vorsetzen eines Index vor "ϕx" ausdrücken, etwa so "Alg. ϕx", es würde nicht genügen (wir wüßten nicht, was verallgemeinert wurde).

Wollten wir es durch einen Index am "x" anzeigen, etwa so $\phi(x_A)$, es würde auch nicht genügen (wir wüßten auf diese Weise nicht den Bereich der Allgemeinheit).

Wollten wir es durch Einfüllen einer Marke in die leeren Argumentstellen versuchen, etwa so "(A, A). ψ (A, A)", es würde nicht genügen (wir könnten die Identität der Variablen nicht feststellen).

Alle diese Bezeichnungsweisen genügen nicht, *weil sie nicht die notwendigen logischen Eigenschaften haben.* Alle jene Zeichenverbindungen vermögen den gewünschten Sinn—auf die vorgeschlagene Weise—nicht abzubilden.
[*Vgl.* 4.0411.]

24. 10. 14.

Um überhaupt eine Aussage machen zu können, müssen wir—in einem Sinne—wissen, wie es sich verhält, wenn die Aussage wahr ist (und dies bilden wir eben ab). [*Vgl.* 4.024.]

Der Satz *drückt aus*, was ich nicht weiß, was ich aber doch wissen muß, um ihn überhaupt aussagen zu können, das *zeige ich in ihm.*

Die Definition ist eine Tautologie und zeigt interne Relationen zwischen ihren beiden Gliedern!

25. 10. 14.

Warum aber untersuchst du nie ein einzelnes spezielles Zeichen auf die Art und Weise hin, wie es logisch abbildet?

Der vollkommen analysierte Satz muß seine Bedeutung vorstellen.

Man könnte auch sagen, unsere Schwierigkeit läuft da hinaus, daß der ganz allgemeine Satz nicht zusammengesetzt zu sein scheint.——
Er scheint nicht, wie alle anderen Sätze, aus willkürlich bezeichnenden Bestandteilen zu bestehen, die in einer logischen Form vereinigt sind. Er scheint keine Form zu HABEN, sondern selbst eine in sich abgeschlossene Form zu sein.

"All things"; that is, so to speak, a description taking the place of "a and b and c".

Suppose our signs were just as indeterminate as the world they mirror?

In order to recognize the sign in the sign we have to attend to the use. [*Cf.* 3.326.]

If we were to try and express what we express by means of "(x).ϕx" by prefixing an index to "ϕx", e.g., like this: "Gen. ϕx", it would not be adequate (we should not know what was being generalized).

If we tried to shew it by means of an index to the "x", e.g., like this: ϕ (x_G), it would still not be adequate (in this way we should not know the scope of generality).

If we thought of trying to do it by inserting a mark in the empty argument places, e.g., like this: "(G,G).ψ(G,G)" it would not be adequate (we could not settle the identity of the variables).

All these methods of symbolizing are inadequate *because they do not have the necessary logical properties*. All those collections of signs lack the power to portray the requisite sense—in the proposed way. [*Cf.* 4.0411.]

24.10.14.

In order to be able to frame a statement at all, we must—in some sense—know how things stand if the statement is true (and that is just what we portray). [*Cf.* 4.024.]

The proposition *expresses* what I do not know; but what I must know in order to be able to say it at all, *I shew in it*.

A definition is a tautology and shews internal relations between its two terms!

25.10.14.

But why do you never investigate an individual particular sign in order to find out how it is a logical portrayal?

The completely analysed proposition must image its reference.

We might also say that our difficulty starts from the completely generalized proposition's not appearing to be complex.——

It does not appear, like all other propositions, to consist of arbitrarily symbolizing component parts which are united in a logical form. It appears not to HAVE a form but itself to be a form complete in itself.

Man braucht bei den logischen Konstanten nie nach ihrer Existenz zu fragen, sie können ja auch *verschwinden*!

Warum soll "$\phi(\hat{x})$" nicht vorstellen, wie $(x).\phi x$ ist? Kommt es da nicht *nur* darauf an, *wie*—auf welche Art und Weise—jenes Zeichen etwas vorstellt?

Angenommen, ich wollte vier Paare kämpfender Männer darstellen, könnte ich es nicht so machen, daß ich nur eines darstelle und sage: "So sehen alle viere aus"? (Durch diesen Nachsatz bestimme ich die Art und Weise der Darstellung.) (Ähnlich stelle ich $(x).\phi x$ durch "$\phi(\hat{x})$" dar.)

Bedenke aber, daß es keine hypothetischen internen Beziehungen gibt. Ist eine Struktur gegeben und eine strukturelle Beziehung an ihr, dann muß es eine andere Struktur geben, die jene Beziehung zu der ersten hat. (Dies liegt ja im Wesen der strukturellen Beziehungen.) Und dies spricht für die Richtigkeit der obigen Bemerkung, sie wird hierdurch zu keiner—Ausflucht.

26. 10. 14.

Es scheint also, als wäre nicht die logische *Identität* von Zeichen und Bezeichnetem nötig, sondern nur *eine* interne, *logische* Relation zwischen beiden. (Das Bestehen einer solchen schließt in gewissem Sinne das Bestehen einer Art grundlegender—interner—Identität mit ein.)

Es handelt sich ja nur darum, daß das Logische des Bezeichneten durch das Logische des Zeichens und der Bezeichnungsweise allein vollständig bestimmt ist. Man könnte sagen: Zeichen und Bezeichnungsweise *zusammen* müssen mit dem Bezeichneten logisch identisch sein.

Der Sinn des Satzes ist das, was er vorstellt. [*Vgl.* 2.221.]

27. 10. 14.

"$x = y$" ist *keine* Satzform. (Folgen.)

Es ist ja klar, daß "aRa" gleichbedeutend wäre mit "$aRb.a = b$". Man kann also den Scheinsatz "$a = b$" durch eine ganz analysierte Notation zum Verschwinden bringen. Bester Beweis für die Richtigkeit der obigen Bemerkung.

Die Schwierigkeit vor meiner Theorie der logischen Abbildung war die, einen Zusammenhang zwischen den Zeichen auf Papier und einem Sachverhalt draußen in der Welt zu finden.

With the logical constants one need never ask whether they exist, for they can even *vanish*!

Why should "$\phi(\hat{x})$" not image how (x).ϕx is the case? Doesn't it all depend here *only* on *how*—in what kind of way—that sign images something?

Suppose that I wanted to represent four pairs of men fighting; could I not do so by representing only one and saying: "That is how they all four look"? (By means of this appendix I determine the kind of representation.) (Similarly I represent (x).ϕx by means of "$\phi(\hat{x})$".)

Remember that there are no hypothetical internal relations. If a structure is given and a structural relation to it, then there must be another structure with that relation to the first one. (This is involved in the nature of structural relations.)

And this speaks for the correctness of the above remark: it stops it from being—an evasion.

26.10.14.

So it looks as if the logical *identity* between sign and things signified were not necessary, but only *an* internal, *logical*, relation between the two. (The holding of such a relation incorporates in a certain sense the holding of a kind of fundamental—internal—identity.)

The point is only that the logical part of what is signified should be completely determined just by the logical part of the sign and the method of symbolizing: sign and method of symbolizing *together* must be logically identical with what is signified.

The sense of the proposition is what it images. [*Cf.* 2.221.]

27.10.14.

"x = y" is *not* a propositional form. (Consequences.)

It is clear that "aRa" would have the same reference as "aRb.a = b". So we can make the pseudo-proposition "a = b" disappear by means of a completely analysed notation. The best proof of the correctness of the above remark.

The difficulty of my theory of logical portrayal was that of finding a connexion between the signs on paper and a situation outside in the world.

Ich sagte immer, die Wahrheit ist eine Beziehung zwischen dem Satz und dem Sachverhalt, konnte aber niemals eine solche Beziehung ausfindig machen.

Die Darstellung der Welt durch ganz allgemeine Sätze könnte man die unpersönliche Darstellung der Welt nennen.

Wie geschieht die unpersönliche Darstellung der Welt?

Der Satz ist ein Modell der Wirklichkeit, so wie wir sie uns denken. (*S.* 4.01.)

28.10.14.

Was der Scheinsatz "es gibt n Dinge" ausdrücken will, zeigt sich in der Sprache durch das Vorhandensein von n Eigennamen mit verschiedener Bedeutung. (Etc.)

Das, was die ganz allgemeinen Sätze beschreiben, sind allerdings in gewissem Sinne strukturelle Eigenschaften der Welt. Dennoch können diese Sätze noch immer wahr oder falsch sein. Auch nachdem sie *Sinn haben*, bleibt der Welt noch immer jener Spielraum.

Schließlich verändert ja die Wahr- oder Falschheit *jedes* Satzes etwas an der allgemeinen *Struktur* der Welt. Und der Spielraum, der ihrer Struktur durch die GESAMTHEIT aller Elementarsätze gelassen wird, ist eben derjenige, welchen die ganz allgemeinen Sätze begrenzen. [*Vgl.* 5.5262.]

29. 10. 14.

Denn, wenn ein Elementarsatz wahr ist, so ist doch jedenfalls *ein* Elementarsatz *mehr* wahr, u.u. [*S.* 5.5262.]

Damit ein Satz wahr sei, muß er vor allem wahr sein *können*, und nur das geht die Logik etwas an.

Der Satz muß zeigen, was er sagen will.——Er muß sich zu seiner Bedeutung ähnlich verhalten, wie eine Beschreibung zu ihrem Gegenstand.

Die logische Form des Sachverhaltes aber, läßt sich nicht beschreiben.——[*Vgl.* 4. 12 *u.* 4. 121.]

Die interne Relation zwischen dem Satz und seiner Bedeutung, die Bezeichnungsweise—ist das System von Koordinaten, das den Sachverhalt in dem Satz abbildet. Der Satz entspricht den Grundkoordinaten.

Man könnte zwei Koordinaten a_P und b_P als einen Satz auffassen der aussagt, der materielle Punkt P befinde sich im Ort (ab). Und damit

I always said that truth is a relation between the proposition and the situation, but could never pick out such a relation.

The representation of the world by means of completely generalized propositions might be called the impersonal representation of the world.

How does the impersonal representation of the world take place?

The proposition is a model of reality as we imagine it. (*See* 4.01.)

28.10.14.

What the pseudo-proposition "There are n things" tries to express shews in language by the presence of n proper names with different references. (Etc.)

What the completely general propositions describe are indeed in a certain sense structural properties of the world. Nevertheless these propositions can still be true or false. According as they *make sense* the world still has that permanent range.

In the end the truth or falsehood of *every* proposition makes some difference to the general *structure* of the world. And the range which is left to its structure by the TOTALITY of all elementary propositions is just the one that is bounded by the completely general propositions. [*Cf.* 5.5262.]

29.10.14.

For, if an elementary proposition is true, then at any rate *one more* elementary proposition is true, and conversely. [*See* 5.5262.]

In order for a proposition to be true it must first and foremost be *capable* of truth, and that is all that concerns logic.

The proposition must shew what it is trying to say.——Its relation to its reference must be like that of a description to its subject.

The logical form of the situation, however, cannot be described.——[*Cf.* 4.12 and 4.121.]

The internal relation between the proposition and its reference, the method of symbolizing—is the system of co-ordinates which projects the situation into the proposition. The proposition corresponds to the fundamental co-ordinates.

We might conceive two co-ordinates a_P and b_P as a proposition stating that the material point P is to be found in the place (ab). For

diese Aussage möglich sei, müssen also die Koordinaten a und b wirklich einen Ort bestimmen. Damit eine Aussage möglich ist, müssen die logischen Koordinaten wirklich einen logischen Ort bestimmen!

(Der Gegenstand, von welchem die allgemeinen Sätze handeln, ist recht eigentlich die Welt; die in ihnen durch eine logische Beschreibung eintritt.——Und darum kommt die Welt eigentlich doch nicht in ihnen vor, so wie ja auch der Gegenstand der Beschreibung nicht in dieser vorkommt.)

Daß in gewissem Sinne die logische Form von p vorhanden sein muß, auch wenn p nicht der Fall ist, das zeigt sich symbolisch dadurch, daß "p" in "$\sim$ p" vorkommt.

Die Schwierigkeit ist die : wie kann es die Form von p geben, wenn es keinen Sachverhalt dieser Form gibt. Und worin besteht diese Form dann eigentlich?!

Analytische *Sätze* gibt es nicht.

30. 10. 14.

Könnte man sagen : in "$\sim \phi(x)$" stellt "$\phi(x)$" vor, wie es sich *nicht* verhält?

Man könnte auch auf einem Bild eine negative Tatsache darstellen, indem man darstellt, was *nicht* der Fall ist.

Wenn wir aber diese Darstellungsmethoden einräumen, was ist dann eigentlich charakteristisch für die Beziehung des *Darstellens*?

Kann man nicht sagen: Es gibt eben verschiedene logische Koordinatensysteme!

Es gibt eben verschiedene Darstellungsweisen, auch durch das Bild, und das Darstellende ist nicht nur das Zeichen oder Bild, sondern auch die Methode der Darstellung. *Aller Darstellung ist gemeinsam*, *daß sie stimmen oder nicht stimmen*, *wahr oder falsch sein kann.*

Denn, Bild *und Darstellungsweise* sind ganz außerhalb des Dargestellten!

Beide zusammen sind wahr oder falsch, nämlich *das Bild auf eine bestimmte Art und Weise*. (Dies gilt natürlich auch vom Elementarsatz!)

Jeder Satz kann verneint werden. Und dies zeigt, daß für alle Sätze "Wahr" und "Falsch" dasselbe bedeuten. (Dies ist von allerhöchster Wichtigkeit.) (Im Gegensatz zu Russell.)

this statement to be possible the co-ordinates a and b must really determine a place. For a statement to be possible the logical co-ordinates must really determine a logical place!

(The subject-matter of general propositions is really the world; which makes its appearance in them by means of a logical description. ——And that is why the world does not really occur in them, just as the subject of the description does not occur in it.)

The fact that in a certain sense the logical form of p must be present even if p is not the case, shews symbolically through the fact that "p" occurs in "$\sim$p".

This is the difficulty: How can there be such a thing as the form of p if there is no situation of this form? And in that case, what does this form really consist in?

There are no such things as analytic *propositions*.

30. 10. 14.

Could we say: In "$\sim \phi(x)$" "$\phi(x)$" images how things are *not*?

Even in a picture we could represent a negative fact by representing what is *not* the case.

If, however, we admit these methods of representation, then what is really characteristic of the relation of *representing*?

Can't we say: It's just that there are different logical co-ordinate-systems!

There are different ways of giving a representation, even by means of a picture, and what represents is not merely the sign or picture but also the method of representation. *What is common to all representation is that they can be right or wrong, true or false.*

Then—picture *and way of representing* are completely outside what is represented!

The two together are true or false, namely *the picture, in a particular way*. (Of course this holds for the elementary proposition too!)

Any proposition can be negated. And this shews that "true" and "false" mean the same for all propositions. (This is of the greatest possible importance.) (In contrast to Russell.)

Die Bedeutung des Satzes muß durch *ihn und seine Darstellungsweise* auf ja oder nein fixiert sein. [*Vgl.* 4. 023.]

In der Logik gibt es kein Nebeneinander, kann es keine Klassifikation geben! [*S.* 5.454.]

31. 10. 14.

Ein Satz wie "(∃x,ϕ).ϕx" ist gerade so gut zusammengesetzt wie ein elementarer; dies zeigt sich darin, daß wir in der Klammer "ϕ" und "x" *extra* erwähnen müssen. Beide stehen—unabhängig—in bezeichnenden Beziehungen zur Welt, gerade wie im Falle eines Elementarsatzes "ψa". [*Vgl.* 5.5261.]

Verhält es sich nicht so: Die logischen Konstanten charakterisieren die Darstellungsweise der Elementarformen des Satzes?

Die Bedeutung des Satzes muß durch ihn und seine Darstellungsweise auf ja oder nein fixiert sein. Dazu muß sie durch ihn vollständig beschrieben sein. [*Vgl.* 4.023.]

Die Darstellungsweise bildet *nicht* ab; nur der Satz ist Bild.

Die Darstellungsweise bestimmt, wie die Wirklichkeit mit dem Bild verglichen werden muß.

Vor allem muß die Elementarsatzform abbilden, alle Abbildung geschieht durch diese.

1. 11. 14.

Sehr nahe liegt die Verwechslung zwischen der darstellenden Beziehung des Satzes zu seiner Bedeutung und der Wahrheitsbeziehung. Jene ist für verschiedene Sätze verschieden, diese ist eine und für alle Sätze die Gleiche.

Es scheint als wäre "(x,ϕ).ϕx" die Form einer Tatsache ϕa.ψb. θc etc. (Ähnlich wäre (∃x).ϕx die Form von ϕa, wie ich auch wirklich glaubte.)

Und hier muß eben mein Fehler liegen.

Untersuche doch den Elementarsatz: welches ist denn die Form von "ϕa" und wie verhält sie sich zu "$\sim\phi$(a)".

Jener Präzedenzfall, auf den man sich immer berufen möchte, muß schon im Zeichen selber liegen. [*Vgl.* 5.525.]

The reference of the proposition must be fixed, as confirming or contradicting it, through it *together with its method of representation.* [*Cf.* 4.023.]

In logic there is no side by side, there cannot be any classification. [*See* 5.454.]

31.10.14.

A proposition like "(∃x,ϕ).ϕx" is just as complex as an elementary one. This comes out in our having to mention "ϕ" and "x" *explicitly* in the brackets. The two stand—independently—in symbolizing relations to the world, just as in the case of an elementary proposition "ψ(a)". [*Cf.* 5.5261.]

Isn't it like this: The logical constants signalise the way in which the elementary forms of the proposition represent?

The reference of the proposition must be fixed as confirming or contradicting it, by means of it and its way of representing. To this end it must be completely described by the proposition. [*Cf.* 4.023.]

The way of representing does not portray; only the proposition is a picture.

The way of representing determines how the reality has to be compared with the picture.

First and foremost the elementary propositional form must portray; all portrayal takes place through it.

1.11.14.

We readily confuse the representing relation which the proposition has to its reference, and the truth relation. The former is different for different propositions, the latter is one and the same for all propositions.

It looks as if "(x,ϕ).ϕx" were the form of a fact ϕa.ψb.θc etc. (Similarly (∃x).ϕx would be the form of ϕa, as I actually thought.)

And this must be where my mistake is.

Examine the elementary proposition: What is the form of "ϕa" and how is it related to "∼ϕ(a)"?

That precedent to which we should always like to appeal must be involved in the sign itself. [*Cf.* 5.525.]

Die logische Form des Satzes muß schon durch die Formen seiner Bestandteile gegeben sein. (Und diese haben nur mit dem *Sinn* der Sätze, nicht mit ihrer Wahr- und Falschheit zu tun.)

In der Form des Subjekts und des Prädikats liegt schon die Möglichkeit des Subjekt-Prädikat Satzes etc.; aber—wie billig—nichts über seine Wahr- oder Falschheit.

Das Bild hat die Relation zur Wirklichkeit, die es nun einmal hat. Und es kommt darauf an: wie soll es darstellen. Dasselbe Bild wird mit der Wirklichkeit übereinstimmen oder nicht übereinstimmen je nachdem, wie es darstellen soll.

Analogie zwischen Satz und Beschreibung: *Der Komplex*, *welcher* mit diesem Zeichen kongruent ist. (Genau so in der graphischen Darstellung.)

Nur kann man eben nicht *sagen*, dieser Komplex ist mit jenem kongruent (oder dergleichen), sondern dies zeigt sich. Und daher nimmt auch die Beschreibung einen anderen Charakter an. [*Vgl.* 4.023.]

Es muß ja die Abbildungsmethode vollkommen bestimmt sein ehe man überhaupt die Wirklichkeit mit dem Satze vergleichen kann um zu sehen, ob er wahr oder falsch ist. Die Vergleichsmethode muß mir gegeben sein, ehe ich vergleichen kann.

Ob ein Satz wahr oder falsch ist, muß sich zeigen.
Wir müssen aber im voraus wissen, *wie* es sich zeigen wird.

Daß zwei Leute nicht kämpfen, kann man darstellen indem man sie nicht-kämpfend darstellt und auch so, indem man sie kämpfend darstellt und sagt, das Bild zeige, wie es sich *nicht* verhält. Man *könnte* mit negativen Tatsachen ebensogut darstellen wie mit positiven——. Wir aber wollen bloß die Principe der Darstellung *überhaupt* untersuchen.

Der Satz " 'p' ist wahr" ist gleichbedeutend mit dem logischen Produkt von 'p' und einen Satz " 'p' ", der den Satz 'p' beschreibt, und einer Zuordnung der Bestandteile der beiden Sätze.—Die internen Beziehungen von Satz und Bedeutung werden durch die internen Beziehungen zwischen 'p' und " 'p' " abgebildet. (Schlechte Bemerkung.)

Nur sich nicht in Teilfragen verstricken, sondern immer dort hinaus flüchten, wo man freien Überblick über das ganze *eine* große Problem hat, wenn auch dieser Überblick noch unklar ist!

The logical form of the proposition must already be given by the forms of its component parts. (And these have to do only with the *sense* of the propositions, not with their truth and falsehood.)

In the form of the subject and of the predicate there already lies the possibility of the subject-predicate proposition, etc.; but—fair enough—nothing about its truth or falsehood.

The picture has whatever relation to reality it does have. And the point is how it is supposed to represent. The same picture will agree or fail to agree with reality according to how it is supposed to represent.

Analogy between proposition and description: *The complex which* is congruent with this sign. (Exactly as in representation in a map.) Only it just cannot be *said* that this complex is congruent with that (or anything of the kind), but this shews. And for this reason the description assumes a different character. [*Cf.* 4.023.]

The method of portrayal must be completely determinate before we can compare reality with the proposition at all in order to see whether it is true or false. The method of comparison must be given me before I can make the comparison.

Whether a proposition is true or false is something that has to appear. We must however know in advance *how* it will appear.

That two people are not fighting can be represented by representing them as not fighting and also by representing them as fighting and saying that the picture shews how things are *not*. We *could* represent by means of negative facts just as much as by means of positive ones ——. However, all we want is to investigate the principles of representing *as such*.

The proposition " 'p' is true" has the same reference as the logical product of 'p', and a proposition " 'p' " which describes the proposition 'p', and a correlation of the components of the two propositions.—The internal relations between proposition and reference are portrayed by means of the internal relations between 'p' and " 'p' ". (Bad remark.)

Don't get involved in partial problems, but always take flight to where there is a free view over the whole *single* great problem, even if this view is still not a clear one.

"Ein Sachverhalt ist denkbar" ("vorstellbar") heißt: Wir können uns ein Bild von ihm machen. [3.001.]

Der Satz muß einen logischen Ort bestimmen.

Die Existenz dieses logischen Orts ist durch die Existenz der Bestandteile allein verbürgt, durch die Existenz des sinnvollen Satzes.

Wenn auch kein Komplex in dem logischen Ort ist, so ist doch Einer: nicht in dem logischen Ort. [*Vgl.* 3.4.]

2. 11. 14.

In der Tautologie heben die Bedingungen der Übereinstimmung mit der Welt (die Wahrheitsbedingungen)—die darstellenden Beziehungen—einander auf, sodaß sie in keiner darstellenden Beziehung zur Wirklichkeit steht (nichts sagt.). [*Vgl.* 4.462.]

$a = a$ ist nicht in demselben Sinne eine Tautologie wie $p \supset p$.

Daß ein Satz wahr ist, besteht nicht darin, daß er eine *bestimmte* Beziehung zur Wirklichkeit hat, sondern darin, daß er zu ihr eine bestimmte Beziehung wirklich *hat*.

Verhält es sich nicht so: Der falsche Satz hat, wie der wahre und unabhängig von seiner Falsch- oder Wahrheit, einen Sinn, aber keine Bedeutung? (Ist hier nicht ein besserer Gebrauch des Wortes "Bedeutung"?)

Könnte man sagen: sobald mir Subjekt und Prädikat gegeben sind, so ist mir eine Relation gegeben, die zwischen einem Subjekt-Prädikat Satz und seiner Bedeutung *bestehen* oder nicht *bestehen* wird. Sobald ich nur Subjekt und Prädikat kenne, kann ich auch um jene Relation wissen, die ja auch für den Fall, daß der Subjekt-Prädikat Satz falsch ist, eine unumgängliche Voraussetzung ist.

3. 11. 14.

Damit es den negativen Sachverhalt geben kann, muß es das Bild des positiven geben. [*Vgl.* 5.5151.]

Die Kenntnis der darstellenden Relation *darf* sich ja auch nur auf die Kenntnis der Bestandteile des Sachverhalts gründen!

Könnte man also sagen: Die Kenntnis des Subjekt-Prädikat Satzes und von Subjekt und Prädikat gibt uns die Kenntnis einer internen Relation etc.?

Auch dies ist streng genommen nicht richtig, da wir kein bestimmtes Subjekt oder Prädikat zu kennen brauchen.

'A situation is thinkable' ('imaginable') means: We can make ourselves a picture of it. [3.001.]

The proposition must determine a logical place.

The existence of this logical place is guaranteed by the existence of the component parts alone, by the existence of the significant proposition.

Supposing there is no complex in the logical place, there is one then that is: not in that logical place. [*Cf.* 3.4.]

2.11.14.

In the tautology the conditions of agreement with the world (the truth-conditions)—the representing relations—cancel one another out, so that it does not stand in any representing relation to reality (says nothing). [*Cf.* 4.462.]

$a = a$ is not a tautology in the same sense as $p \supset p$.

For a proposition to be true does not consist in its having a *particular* relation to reality but in its really *having* a particular relation.

Isn't it like this: the false proposition makes sense like the true and independently of its falsehood or truth, but it has no reference? (Is there not here a better use of the word "reference"?)

Could we say: As soon as I am given subject and predicate I am given a relation which will *exist* or not *exist* between a subject-predicate proposition and its reference. As soon as I really know subject and predicate, I can also know about the relation, which is an indispensable presupposition even for the case of the subject-predicate proposition's being false.

3.11.14.

In order for it to be possible for a negative situation to exist, the picture of the positive situation must exist. [*Cf.* 5.5151.]

The knowledge of the representing relation *must* be founded only on the knowledge of the component parts of the situation!

Then would it be possible to say: the knowledge of the subject-predicate proposition and of subject and predicate gives us the knowledge of an internal relation, etc.?

Even this is not strictly correct since we do not need to know any particular subject or predicate.

Offenbar, daß wir den Elementarsatz als das Bild eines Sachverhalts empfinden.—Wie geht das zu? [*Vgl.* 4.012.]

Muß nicht die Möglichkeit der darstellenden Beziehung durch den Satz *selbst* gegeben sein?

Der Satz *selber* scheidet das mit ihm Kongruierende von dem nicht Kongruierenden.

Zum Beispiel: ist also der Satz gegeben und Kongruenz, dann ist der Satz wahr, wenn der Sachverhalt mit ihm kongruent IST, oder es sind gegeben der Satz und Nicht-Kongruenz, dann ist der Satz wahr, wenn der Sachverhalt mit ihm nicht kongruent ist.

Wie aber wird uns die Kongruenz oder Nicht-Kongruenz oder dergleichen gegeben?

Wie kann mir *mitgeteilt* werden, *wie* der Satz darstellt? Oder kann mir das Überhaupt nicht *gesagt* werden? Und wenn dem so ist, kann ich es "*wissen*"? Wenn es mir gesagt werden sollte, so müßte dies durch einen Satz geschehen; der könnte es aber nur zeigen.

Was gesagt werden kann, kann mir durch einen Satz gesagt werden, also kann nichts, was zum Verständnis *aller* Sätze nötig ist, gesagt werden.

Jene willkürliche Zuordnung von Zeichen und Bezeichnetem, die die Möglichkeit der Sätze bedingt, und die ich in den ganz allgemeinen Sätzen vermißte, geschieht dort durch die Allgemeinheitsbezeichnung geradeso wie beim Elementarsatz durch Namen (denn die Allgemeinheitsbezeichnung gehört nicht zum *Bild*). Daher empfand man auch immer, daß die Allgemeinheit ganz wie ein Argument auftritt. [*Vgl.* 5.523.]

Verneinen kann man nur einen fertigen Satz. (Ähnliches gilt von allen ab-Funktionen.[1]) [*Vgl.* 4.064 *u.* 4.0641.]

Der Satz ist das logische Bild eines Sachverhaltes.

Die Verneinung bezieht sich auf den *fertigen* Sinn des verneinten Satzes und nicht auf dessen Darstellungsweise. [*Vgl.* 4.064 *u.* 4.0641.]

Wenn ein Bild auf die vorhin erwähnte Weise darstellt was-nicht-der-Fall-ist, so geschieht dies auch nur dadurch, daß es *dasjenige* darstellt, das nicht der Fall *ist*.

Denn das Bild sagt gleichsam: "*so* ist es *nicht*", und auf die Frage "*wie* ist es nicht?" ist eben die Antwort der positive Satz.

[1] ab-Funktionen sind die Wahrheitsfunktionen. S. Appendix I. (Herausg.)

It is *evident* that we feel the elementary proposition as the picture of a situation.—How is this? [*Cf.* 4.012.]

Must not the possibility of the representing relation be given by the proposition *itself*?

The proposition *itself* sunders what is congruent with it from what is not congruent.

For example: if the proposition is given, and congruence, then the proposition is true if the situation IS congruent with it. Or: the proposition is given and non-congruence; then the proposition is true if the situation is not congruent with it.

But how is congruence or non-congruence or the like given us?

How can I be *told how* the proposition represents? Or can this not be *said* to me at all? And if that is so can I "*know*" it? If it was supposed to be said to me, then this would have to be done by means of a proposition; but the proposition could only shew it.

What can be said can only be said by means of a proposition, and so nothing that is necessary for the understanding of *all* propositions can be said.

That arbitrary correlation of sign and thing signified which is a condition of the possibility of the propositions, and which I found lacking in the completely general propositions, occurs there by means of the generality notation, just as in the elementary proposition it occurs by means of names. (For the generality notation does not belong to the *picture*.) Hence the constant feeling that generality makes its appearance quite like an argument. [*Cf.* 5.523.]

Only a finished proposition can be negated. (And similarly for all ab-functions.)[1] [*Cf.* 4.064 and 4.0641.]

The proposition is the logical picture of a situation.

Negation refers to the *finished* sense of the negated proposition and not to its way of presenting. [*Cf.* 4.064 and 4.0641.]

If a picture presents what-is-not-the-case in the forementioned way, this only happens through its presenting *that* which *is* not the case.

For the picture says, as it were: "*This* is how it is *not*", and to the question "*How* is it not?" just the positive proposition is the answer.

[1] ab-functions are the truth-functions. Cf. Appendix I. [*Edd.*]

Man könnte sagen: Die Verneinung bezieht sich schon auf den logischen Ort, den der verneinte Satz bestimmt. [*S.* 4.0641.]

Nur den festen Grund, auf dem man einmal gestanden ist, nicht verlieren!

Der verneinende Satz bestimmt einen *anderen* logischen Ort als der verneinte. [*S.* 4.0641.]

Der verneinte Satz zieht nicht nur die Grenzlinie zwischen dem verneinten Gebiet und dem übrigen, sondern er deutet auch schon auf das verneinte Gebiet.

Der verneinende Satz bestimmt seinen logischen Ort mit Hilfe des logischen Ortes des verneinten Satzes. Indem er jenen als den außerhalb diesem liegenden beschreibt. [*S.* 4.0641.]

Der Satz ist wahr, wenn es das gibt, was er vorstellt.

4. 11. 14.

Wie bestimmt der Satz den logischen Ort?

Wie repräsentiert das Bild einen Sachverhalt?

Selbst ist es doch nicht der Sachverhalt, ja dieser braucht gar nicht der Fall zu sein.

Ein Name repräsentiert ein Ding, ein anderer ein anderes Ding und selbst sind sie verbunden; so stellt das Ganze—wie ein lebendes Bild—den Sachverhalt vor. [*Cf.* 4.0311.]

Die logische Verbindung muß natürlich unter den repräsentierten Dingen möglich sein, und dies wird immer der Fall sein, wenn die Dinge wirklich repräsentiert sind. Wohlgemerkt, jene Verbindung ist keine Relation, sondern nur das *Bestehen* einer Relation.

5. 11. 14.

So stellt der Satz den Sachverhalt gleichsam auf eigene Faust dar.

Wenn ich aber sage: Die Verbindung der Satzbestandteile muß für die repräsentierten Dinge möglich sein: liegt nicht hierin das ganze Problem! Wie kann eine Verbindung zwischen Gegenständen möglich sein, die nicht ist?

Die Verbindung muß möglich sein, heißt: der Satz und die Bestandteile des Sachverhalts müssen in einer bestimmten Relation stehen.

It might be said: The negation refers to the very logical place which is determined by the negated proposition. [*See* 4.0641.]

Only don't lose the solid ground on which you have just been standing!

The negating proposition determines a *different* logical place from the negated proposition. [*See* 4.0641.]

The negated proposition not only draws the boundary between the negated domain and the rest; it actually points to the negated domain.

The negating proposition uses the logical place of the negated proposition to determine its own logical place. By describing the latter as the place that is outside the former. [*See* 4.0641.]

The proposition is true when what it images exists.

4.11.14.

How does the proposition determine the logical place?

How does the picture present a situation?

It is after all itself not the situation, which need not be the case at all.

One name is representative of one thing, another of another thing, and they themselves are connected; in this way—like a *tableau vivant*—the whole images the situation. [*Cf.* 4.0311.]

The logical connexion must, of course, be one that is possible as between the things that the names are representatives of, and this will always be the case if the names really are representatives of the things. N.B. that connexion is not a relation but only the *holding* of a relation.

5.11.14.

In this way the proposition represents the situation—as it were off its own bat.

But when I say: the connexion of the propositional components must be possible for the represented things—does this not contain the whole problem? How can a non-existent connexion between objects be possible?

"The connexion must be possible" means: The proposition and the components of the situation must stand in a particular relation.

Damit also ein Satz einen Sachverhalt darstelle, ist nur nötig, daß seine Bestandteile die des Sachverhalts repräsentieren und daß jene in einer für diese möglichen Verbindung stehen.

Das Satzzeichen verbürgt die Möglichkeit der Tatsache, welche es darstellt (nicht, daß diese Tatsache wirklich der Fall ist), das gilt auch für die allgemeinen Sätze.

Denn, wenn die positive Tatsache ϕa gegeben ist, dann ist auch die *Möglichkeit* für $(x).\phi x$, $\sim(\exists x).\phi x$, $\sim\phi a$ etc. etc. gegeben. (Alle logischen Konstanten sind bereits im Elementarsatz enthalten.) [*Vgl.* 5.47.]

So entsteht das Bild.——
Um mit dem Bilde einen logischen Ort zu bezeichnen, müssen wir zu ihm eine Bezeichnungsweise setzen (die positive, negative, etc.).

Man könnte z. B. mittelst fechtenden Puppen zeigen, wie man *nicht* fechten solle.

6. 11. 14.

Und der Fall ist hier ganz der gleiche, wie bei $\sim\phi a$, obwohl das Bild von dem handelt, was nicht geschehen *soll*, statt von dem, was nicht geschieht.

Daß man den verneinten Satz wieder verneinen kann, zeigt, daß das, was verneint wird, schon ein Satz und nicht erst die Vorbereitung zu einem Satz ist. [*S.* 4.0641.]

Könnte man sagen: Hier ist das Bild, aber ob es stimmt oder nicht, kann man nicht sagen, ehe man weiß, was damit gesagt sein soll?

Das Bild muß nun wieder seinen Schatten auf die Welt werfen.

7. 11. 14.

Der räumliche und der logische Ort stimmen darin überein, daß beide die Möglichkeit einer Existenz sind. [*Vgl.* 3.411.]

8. 11. 14.

Was sich in den Sätzen über Wahrscheinlichkeit durch das Experiment bestätigen läßt, kann unmöglich Mathematik sein! [*Vgl.* 5.154.]

Wahrscheinlichkeitssätze sind Auszüge naturwissenschaftlicher Gesetze. [*Vgl.* 5.156.]

Sie sind Verallgemeinerungen und drücken eine unvollständige Kenntnis jener Gesetze aus. [*Vgl.* 5.156.]

Then in order for a proposition to present a situation it is only necessary for its component parts to represent those of the situation and for the former to stand in a connexion which is possible for the latter.

The propositional sign guarantees the possibility of the fact which it presents (not, that this fact is actually the case)—this holds for the general propositions too.

For if the positive fact ϕa is given then so is the *possibility* of $(x).\phi x$, $\sim(\exists x).\phi x$, $\sim\phi a$ etc. etc. (All logical constants are already contained in the elementary proposition.) [*Cf.* 5.47.]

That is how the picture arises.——

In order to designate a logical place with the picture we must attacn a way of symbolizing to it (the positive, the negative, etc.).

We might, e.g., shew how *not* to fence by means of fencing puppets.

6.11.14.

And it is just the same with this case as with $\sim\phi a$, although the picture deals with what *should* not happen instead of with what does not happen.

The possibility of negating the negated proposition in its turn shews that what is negated is already a proposition and not merely the preliminary to a proposition. [*See* 4.0641.]

Could we say: Here is the picture, but we cannot tell whether it is right or not until we know what it is supposed to say.

The picture must now in its turn cast its shadow on the world.

7.11.14.

Spatial and logical place agree in both being the possibility of an existence. [*Cf.* 3.411.]

8.11.14.

What can be confirmed by experiment, in propositions about probability, cannot possibly be mathematics. [*Cf.* 5.154.]

Probability propositions are abstracts of scientific laws. [*Cf.* 5.156.]

They are generalizations and express an incomplete knowledge of those laws. [*Cf.* 5.156.]

Wenn ich z. B. schwarze und weiße Ballen aus einer Urne ziehe, so kann ich nicht vor einem Zug sagen, ob ich einen weißen oder schwarzen Ballen ziehen werde, da ich hierzu die Naturgesetze nicht genau genug kenne; aber *das weiß ich doch*, daß, im Falle gleich viel schwarze und weiße Ballen vorhanden sind, die Zahl der gezogenen schwarzen sich der der weißen bei fortgesetztem Ziehen nähern wird, *so* genau kenne ich die Naturgesetze eben *doch*. [*Vgl.* 5.154.]

9. 11. 14.

Was ich nun in den Wahrscheinlichkeitssätzen kenne, sind gewisse allgemeine Eigenschaften der unverallgemeinerten naturwissenschaftlichen Sätze, wie z. B. ihre Symmetrie in gewissen Beziehungen, ihre Asymmetrie in anderen etc. [*Vgl.* 5.156.]

Vexierbilder und das Sehen von Sachverhalten. [*Vgl.* 5.5423.]

Es war das, was ich mein starkes scholastisches Gefühl nennen möchte, was die Ursache meiner besten Entdeckungen war.

"Nicht p" und "p" widersprechen einander, beide können nicht wahr sein; aber doch kann ich beide aussprechen, *beide Bilder gibt es*. Sie liegen nebeneinander.

Oder vielmehr "p" und "$\sim$p" sind wie ein Bild und die unendliche Ebene außerhalb dieses Bildes (logischer Ort).
Den unendlichen Raum außerhalb kann ich nur mit Hilfe des Bildes herstellen, indem ich ihn durch dieses begrenze.

10. 11. 14.

Wenn ich sage "p ist möglich", heißt das '"p" hat einen Sinn'? Redet jener Satz von der Sprache, sodaß also für seinen Sinn die Existenz eines Satzzeichens ("p") wesentlich ist? (Dann wäre er ganz unwichtig.) Aber will er nicht vielmehr das sagen, was "p v $\sim$ p" zeigt?

Entspricht nicht mein Studium der Zeichensprache dem Studium der Denkprozesse, welches die Philosophen für die Philosophie der Logik immer für so wesentlich hielten?—Nur verwickelten sie sich immer in unwesentliche psychologische Untersuchungen und eine analoge Gefahr gibt es auch bei meiner Methode. [*S.* 4.1121.]

11. 11. 14.

Da "a = b" kein Satz, "x = y" keine Funktion ist, so ist eine "Klasse $\hat{x}$ (x = x)" ein Unding und ebenso die sogenannte Nullklasse. (Man hatte übrigens immer schon das Gefühl, daß überall da, wo

If, e.g., I take black and white balls out of an urn I cannot say before taking one out whether I shall get a white or a black ball, since I am not well enough acquainted with the natural laws for that, but *all the same I do know* that if there are equally many black and white balls there, the numbers of black balls that are drawn will approach the number of white ones if the drawing is continued; I do know the natural laws as accurately as *this*. [*Cf.* 5.154]

9.11.14.

Now what I know in probability statements are certain general properties of ungeneralized propositions of natural science, such as, e.g., their symmetry in certain respects, and asymmetry in others, etc. [*Cf.* 5.156.]

Puzzle pictures and the seeing of situations. [*Cf.* 5.5423.]

It has been what I should like to call my strong scholastic feeling that has occasioned my best discoveries.

"Not p" and "p" contradict one another, both cannot be true; but I can surely express both, *both pictures exist*. They are to be found side by side.

Or rather "p" and "∼ p" are like a picture and the infinite plane outside this picture. (Logical place.)
I can construct the infinite space outside only by using the picture to bound that space.

10.11.14.

When I say "p is possible", does that mean that " 'p' makes sense"? Is the former proposition about language, so that the existence of a propositional sign ("p") is essential for its sense? (In that case it would be quite unimportant.) But does it not rather try to say what "pv ∼ p" shews?

Does not my study of sign language correspond to the study of the processes of thought, which philosophers have always taken as so essential for philosophy of logic?—Only they always got involved in inessential psychological investigations, and there is an analogous danger with my method too. [*See* 4.1121.]

11.11.14.

Since "a=b" is not a proposition, nor "x=y" a function, a "class $\hat{x}$ (x=x)" is a chimera, and so equally is the so-called null class. (One

man sich in Satzkonstruktionen mit $x = x$, $a = a$, etc. half, daß es sich in allen solchen Fällen um ein sich-heraus-schwindeln handelte; so wenn man sagte "a existiert", heißt "$(\exists x)x = a$".)

Dies ist falsch: da die Definition der Klassen selbst die Existenz der wirklichen Funktionen verbürgt.

Wenn ich nun eine Funktion von der Nullklasse auszusagen scheine, so sage ich, daß diese Funktion von allen Funktionen wahr ist, welche null sind—und dies kann ich auch dann sagen, wenn *keine* Funktion null ist.

Ist $x \neq x. \equiv_x. \phi x$ identisch mit
$(x).\sim\phi x$? Gewiß!

Der Satz deutet auf die Möglichkeit, daß es sich so und so verhält.

12. 11. 14.

Die Verneinung ist im selben Sinne *eine Beschreibung* wie der Elementarsatz selbst.

Man könnte die Wahrheit eines Satzes möglich, die einer Tautologie gewiß, und die einer Kontradiktion unmöglich nennen. Hier tritt schon das Anzeichen einer Gradation auf, die wir in der Wahrscheinlichkeitsrechnung brauchen. [*Vgl.* 4.464.]

In der Tautologie bildet der Elementarsatz selbstverständlich noch immer ab, aber er ist mit der Wirklichkeit so lose verbunden, daß diese unbeschränkte Freiheit hat. Die Kontradiktion wieder setzt solche Schranken, daß keine Wirklichkeit in ihnen existieren kann.

Es ist, als projizierten die logischen Konstanten das Bild des Elementarsatzes auf die Wirklichkeit—die dann mit dieser Projektion stimmen oder nicht-stimmen kann.

Obwohl im einfachen Satz bereits alle logischen Konstanten vorkommen, so *muß* in ihm doch auch sein eigenes Urbild ganz und unzerlegt vorkommen!

Ist also etwa nicht der einfache Satz das Bild sondern vielmehr sein Urbild, welches in ihm vorkommen muß?

Dieses Urbild ist dann wirklich kein Satz, (hat aber die Gestalt eines Satzes) und *es* könnte der Fregeschen "Annahme" entsprechen.

did indeed always have the feeling that wherever $x=x$, $a=a$, etc. were used in the construction of sentences, in all such cases one was only getting out of a difficulty by means of a swindle; as though one said "a exists" means "$(\exists x)x=a$".)

This is wrong: since the definition of classes itself guarantees the existence of the real functions.

When I appear to assert a function of the null class, I am saying that this function is true of all functions that are null—and I can say that even if *no* function is null.

Is $x \neq x. \equiv_x. \phi x$ identical with
$(x).\sim\phi x$? Certainly!

The proposition points to the possibility that such and such is the case.

12.11.14.

The negation is *a description* in the same sense as the elementary proposition itself.

The truth of the proposition might be called possible, that of a tautology certain, and that of a contradiction impossible. Here we already get the hint of a gradation that we need in the probability calculus. [*Cf.* 4.464.]

In the tautology the elementary proposition does, of course, still portray, but it is so loosely connected with reality that reality has unlimited freedom. Contradiction in its turn imposes such constraints that no reality can exist under them.

It is as if the logical constants projected the picture of the elementary proposition on to reality—which may then accord or not accord with this projection.

Although all logical constants must already occur in the simple proposition, its own peculiar proto-picture *must* surely also occur in it whole and undivided.

Then is the picture perhaps not the simple proposition, but rather its prototype which must occur in it?

Then, this prototype is not actually a proposition (though it has the Gestalt of a proposition) and it might correspond to Frege's "assumption".

Der Satz bestünde dann aus Ur*bildern*, die auf die Welt projiziert wären.

13. 11. 14.

Bei dieser Arbeit lohnt es sich mehr als bei jeder anderen, Fragen, die man für gelöst hält, immer wieder von neuen Seiten als ungelöst zu betrachten.

14. 11. 14.

Denke an die Darstellung *negativer* Tatsachen, durch Modelle etwa: So und so dürfen zwei Eisenbahnzüge nicht auf den Gleisen stehen. Der Satz, das Bild, das Modell sind—im negativen Sinn—wie ein fester Körper, der die Bewegungsfreiheit der anderen beschränkt, im positiven Sinne, wie der von fester Substanz begrenzte Raum, worin ein Körper Platz hat. [*Vgl.* 4. 463.]

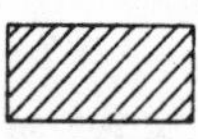

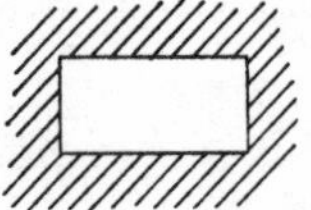

Diese Vorstellung ist *sehr* deutlich und müßte zur Lösung führen.

15. 11. 14.

Projektion des Bildes auf die Wirklichkeit

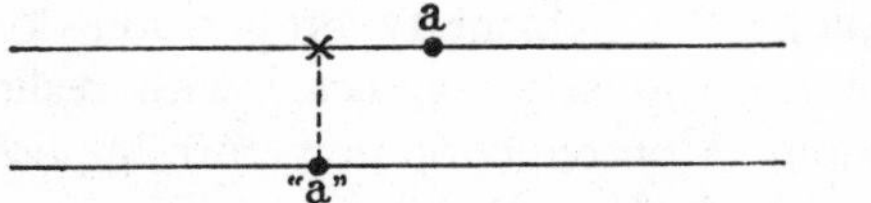

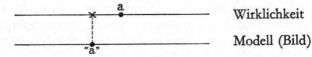

(Maxwell's Methode der mechanischen Modelle.)

Nur sich nicht um das kümmern, was man einmal geschrieben hat! Nur immer von frischem anfangen zu denken, als ob noch gar nichts geschehen wäre!

Jener Schatten, welchen das Bild gleichsam auf die Welt wirft: Wie soll ich ihn exakt fassen?

Hier ist ein tiefes Geheimnis.

Es ist das Geheimnis der Negation : Es verhält sich nicht so, und doch können wir sagen, *wie* es sich *nicht* verhält.——

Der Satz ist eben nur die *Beschreibung* eines Sachverhalts. (Aber das ist alles noch an der Oberfläche.) [*Vgl.* 4.023.]

In that case the proposition would consist of proto-*pictures*, which were projected on to the world.

13.11.14.

In this work more than any other it is rewarding to keep on looking at questions, which one considers solved, from another quarter, as if they were unsolved.

14.11.14.

Think of the representation of *negative* facts by means of models. E.g.: two railway trains must not stand on the rails in such-and-such a way. The proposition, the picture, the model are—in the negative sense—like a solid body restricting the freedom of movement of others; in the positive sense, like the space bounded by solid substance, in which there is room for a body. [*Cf.* 4.463.]

This image is *very* clear and must lead to the solution.

15.11.14.

Projection of the picture on to reality.

(Maxwell's method of mechanical models.)

Don't worry about what you have already written. Just keep on beginning to think afresh as if nothing at all had happened yet.

That shadow which the picture as it were casts upon the world: How am I to get an exact grasp of it?

Here is a deep mystery.

It is the mystery of negation: This is not how things are, and yet we can say *how* things are *not*.——

For the proposition is only the *description* of a situation. (But this is all still only on the surface.) [*Cf.* 4.023.]

Eine Einsicht am Ursprung ist mehr wert als noch so viele irgendwo in der Mitte.

16. 11. 14.

Einführung des Zeichens "o" um die Dezimalnotation möglich zu machen: Die logische Bedeutung dieses Vorgehens.

17. 11. 14.

Angenommen "ϕa" ist wahr: Was heißt es zu sagen $\sim\phi$a ist möglich?

(ϕa ist selber gleichbedeutend mit $\sim(\sim\phi$a).)

18. 11. 14.

Es handelt sich da immer nur um die Existenz des logischen Orts.

Was—zum Teufel—ist aber dieser "logische Ort"!?

19. 11. 14.

Der Satz und die logischen Koordinaten: das ist der logische Ort. [*Vgl.* 3.41.]

20. 11. 14.

Die Realität, die dem Sinne des Satzes entspricht, kann doch nichts Anderes sein, als seine Bestandteile, da wir doch *alles* Andere nicht *wissen*.

Wenn die Realität in noch etwas Anderem besteht, so kann dies jedenfalls weder bezeichnet noch ausgedrückt werden, denn im ersten Fall wäre es noch ein Bestandteil, im zweiten wäre der Ausdruck ein Satz für den wieder dasselbe Problem bestünde, wie für den ursprünglichen.

21. 11. 14.

Was weiß ich eigentlich, wenn ich den Sinn von "ϕa" verstehe, aber nicht weiß, ob es wahr oder falsch ist? Dann weiß ich doch nicht mehr als ϕa v $\sim\phi$a; und das heißt, ich *weiß* nichts.

Da die Realitäten, die dem Sinn des Satzes entsprechen, nur seine Bestandteile sind, so können sich auch die logischen Koordinaten nur auf jene beziehen.

22. 11. 14.

An dieser Stelle versuche ich wieder etwas auszudrücken, was sich nicht ausdrücken läßt.

23. 11. 14.

Obwohl der Satz nur auf einen Ort des logischen Raumes deuten darf, so muß doch durch ihn *schon* der ganze logische Raum gegeben

A single insight at the start is worth more than ever so many somewhere in the middle.

16.11.14.

The introduction of the sign "o" in order to make the decimal notation possible: the logical significance of this procedure.

17.11.14.

Suppose "ϕa" is true: what does it mean to say ~ϕa is possible? (ϕa is itself equivalent in meaning with ~(~ϕa).)

18.11.14.

It is all simply a matter of the existence of the logical place.

But what the devil is this "logical place"?!

19.11.14.

The proposition and the logical co-ordinates: that is the logical place. [*Cf.* 3.41.]

20.11.14.

The reality that corresponds to the sense of the proposition can surely be nothing but its component parts, since we are surely *ignorant* of *everything* else.

If the reality consists in anything else as well, this can at any rate neither be denoted nor expressed; for in the first case it would be a further component, in the second the expression would be a proposition, for which the same problem would exist in turn as for the original one.

21.11.14.

What do I really know when I understand the sense of "ϕa" but do not know whether it is true or false? In that case I surely know no more than ϕa v~ϕa; and that means I *know* nothing.

As the realities corresponding to the sense of a proposition are only its component parts, the logical co-ordinates too can only refer to these.

22.11.14.

At this point I am again trying to express something that cannot be expressed.

23.11.14.

Although the proposition must only point to a region of logical space, still the whole of logical space must *already* be given by means of it.——

sein.——Sonst würden durch Verneinung, Disjunkiton etc. immer *neue* Elemente—und zwar in Koordination—eingeführt, was natürlich nicht geschehen darf. [*Vgl.* 3. 42.]

24. 11. 14.

Satz und Sachverhalt verhalten sich zueinander, wie der Meterstab zu der zu messenden Länge.

Daß man aus dem *Satz* "(x).ϕx" auf den *Satz* " ϕa" schließen kann, das zeigt, wie die Allgemeinheit auch im *Zeichen* "(x).ϕx" vorhanden ist.

Und das Gleiche gilt natürlich für die Allgemeinheitsbezeichnung überhaupt.

Im Satze legen wir ein Urbild an die Wirklichkeit an.

(Immer wieder ist es Einem bei der Untersuchung der negativen Tatsachen, als ob sie die Existenz des Satzzeichens voraussetzten.)

Muß das Zeichen des negativen Satzes mit dem Zeichen des positiven gebildet werden? (Ich glaube, ja!)

Warum sollte man den negativen Satz nicht durch eine negative Tatsache ausdrücken können?! Es ist, wie wenn man statt des Meterstabes den Raum außerhalb des Meterstabes als Vergleichsobjekt nähme. [*Vgl.* 5.5151.]

Wie widerspricht eigentlich der *Satz* "$\sim$p" dem *Satze* "p"? Die internen Relationen der beiden Zeichen müssen Widerspruch bedeuten.

Freilich muß nach jedem negativen Satz gefragt werden können: *Wie* verhält es sich *nicht*; aber die Antwort hierauf ist ja nur wieder ein Satz. (Diese Bemerkung unvollständig.)

25. 11. 14.

Jener negative Tatbestand, der als Zeichen dient, kann doch wohl bestehen ohne einen Satz der ihn wiederum ausdrückt.

Immer wieder ist es bei der Untersuchung dieser Probleme, als wären sie schon gelöst, und diese Täuschung kommt daher, daß die Probleme oft ganz unseren Blicken entschwinden.

Daß $\sim\phi$a der Fall ist, kann ich durch die Beobachtung von $\phi\hat{x}$ und a allein ersehen.

Die Frage ist hier: Ist die positive Tatsache primär, die negative sekundär, oder sind sie gleichberechtigt? Und wenn so, wie ist es dann mit den Tatsachen p v q, p $\supset$ q etc., sind diese nicht mit $\sim$p

Otherwise *new* elements—and in co-ordination—would keep on being introduced by means of negation, disjunction, etc.; which, of course, must not happen. [*Cf.* 3.42.]

24.11.14.

Proposition and situation are related to one another like the yard-stick and the length to be measured.

That the *proposition* "ϕa" can be inferred from the *proposition* "(x).ϕx" shews how generality is present even in the *sign* "(x).ϕx". And the same thing, of course, holds for any generality notation.

In the proposition we hold a proto-picture up against reality.

(When investigating negative facts one keeps on feeling as if they presupposed the existence of the propositional sign.)

Must the sign of the negative proposition be constructed by means of the sign of the positive one? (I believe so.)
Why shouldn't one be able to express the negative proposition by means of a negative fact? It's as if one were to take the space outside the yardstick as the object of comparison instead of the yardstick. [*Cf.* 5.5151.]

How does the *proposition* "$\sim$ p" really contradict the *proposition* "p"? The internal relations of the two signs must mean contradiction.

Of course it must be possible to ask whenever we have a negative proposition: *What* is it that is *not* the case? But the answer to this is, of course, in its turn only a proposition. (This remark incomplete.)

25.11.14.

That negative state of affairs that serves as a sign can, of course, perfectly well exist without a proposition that in turn expresses it.

In investigating these problems it's constantly as if they were already solved, an illusion which arises from the fact that the problems often quite disappear from our view.

I can see that $\sim\phi$a is the case just by observing $\phi\hat{x}$ and a.

The question here is: Is the positive fact primary, the negative secondary, or are they on the same level? And if so, how is it with the facts pvq, p $\supset$ q, etc.? Aren't these on the same level as $\sim$ p? But then

gleichberechtigt? Aber *müssen* denn nicht *alle Tatsachen* gleichberechtigt sein? Die Frage ist eigentlich die: Gibt es Tatsachen außer den positiven? (Es ist nämlich schwer, das was nicht der Fall ist, nicht zu verwechseln mit dem was stattdessen der Fall *ist*.)

Es ist ja klar, daß alle die ab-Funktionen nur so viele verschiedene Meßmethoden der Wirklichkeit sind.—Und gewiß haben die Meßmethoden durch p und ~p etwas Besonderes allen anderen voraus.——

Es ist der *Dualismus*, positive und negative Tatsachen, der mich nicht zur Ruhe kommen läßt. So einen Dualismus kann es ja nicht geben. Aber wie ihm entgehen?

Alles das würde sich von selbst lösen durch ein Verständnis des Wesens des Satzes!

26. 11. 14.

Wenn von einem Dinge alle positiven Aussagen gemacht sind, sind doch nicht schon alle negativen auch gemacht! Und darauf kommt alles an!

Der gefürchtete Dualismus von positiv und negativ besteht nicht denn (x).ϕx etc., etc. sind weder positiv noch negativ.

Wenn schon der positive Satz nicht im negativen vorkommen *muß*, muß nicht in jedem Fall das Urbild des positiven Satzes im negativen vorkommen?

Indem wir—und zwar in jeder möglichen Notation—zwischen ~aRb und ~bRa unterscheiden, setzen wir in einer jeden eine bestimmte Zuordnung von Argument und Argumentstelle im negativen Satz voraus; die ja das Urbild des verneinten positiven Satzes ausmacht.

Ist also nicht jene Zuordnung der Bestandteile des Satzes, mit welcher noch nichts *gesagt* ist, das eigentliche Bild im Satze?

Ob nicht meine Unklarheit auf dem Unverständnis des Wesens der Relationen beruht?

Kann man denn ein *Bild* verneinen? Nein. Und darin liegt der Unterschied zwischen Bild und Satz. Das Bild kann als Satz dienen. Dann tritt aber etwas zu ihm hinzu, was macht, daß es nun etwas *sagt*. Kurz: Ich kann nur verneinen, daß das Bild stimmt, aber das *Bild* kann ich nicht verneinen.

Dadurch, daß ich den Bestandteilen des Bildes Gegenstände zuordne, *dadurch* stellt es nun einen Sachverhalt dar und stimmt nun entweder

must not *all facts* be on the same level? The question is really this: Are there facts besides the positive ones? (For it is difficult not to confuse what is not the case with what *is* the case instead of it.)

It is clear that all the ab-functions are only so many different methods for measuring reality.—And certainly the methods of measurement by means of p and ~p have some special advantage over all others.——

It is the *dualism*, positive and negative facts, that gives me no peace. For such a dualism can't exist. But how to get away from it?

All this would get solved of itself if we understood the nature of the proposition.

26.11.14.

If all the positive statements about a thing are made, aren't all the negative ones already made too? And that is the whole point.

The dualism of positive and negative that I feared does not exist, for (x).ϕx, etc. etc. are neither positive nor negative.

If the positive proposition does not *have* to occur in the negative, mustn't at any rate the proto-picture of the positive proposition occur in the negative one?

By making a distinction—as we do in any possible notation—between ~aRb and ~bRa we presuppose in any notation a particular correlation between argument and argument-place in the negative proposition; the correlation gives the prototype of the negated positive proposition.

Then is that correlation of the components of the proposition by means of which nothing is yet *said* the real picture in the proposition?

Doesn't my lack of clarity rest on a lack of understanding of the nature of relations?

Can one negate a *picture*? No. And in this lies the difference between picture and proposition. The picture can serve as a proposition. But in that case something gets added to it which brings it about that now it *says* something. In short: I can only deny that the picture is right, but the *picture* I cannot deny.

By my correlating the components of the picture with objects, it

oder stimmt nicht. (Z. B. stellt ein Bild das Innere eines Zimmers dar etc.)

27. 11. 14.

"$\sim$p" ist wahr, wenn p falsch ist. Also, in dem wahren Satz "$\sim$p" ist der Teil ein falscher Satz. Wie kann ihn nun den Haken "$\sim$" mit der Wirklichkeit zum Stimmen bringen? Wir haben freilich schon gesagt, daß es nicht der Haken "$\sim$" allein ist, sondern alles, was den verschiedenen Verneinungszeichen gemeinsam ist. Und was diesen allen gemeinsam ist, muß offenbar aus der Bedeutung der Verneinung selbst hervorgehen. Und so muß sich also in dem Negationszeichen doch seine eigene Bedeutung spiegeln. [*Vgl.* 5.512.]

28. 11. 14.

Die Negation vereinigt sich mit den ab-Funktionen des elementaren Satzes. Und die logischen Funktionen des Elementarsatzes müssen ebenso wie alle anderen ihre Bedeutung wiederspiegeln.

29. 11. 14.

Die ab-Funktion bleibt nicht *vor* dem Elementarsatz stehen, sondern sie durchdringt ihn.

Was gezeigt werden *kann*, kann nicht gesagt werden. [4.1212.]

Ich glaube, man könnte das Gleichheitszeichen ganz aus unserer Notation entfernen und die Gleichheit immer nur durch die Gleichheit der Zeichen (u.u.) andeuten. Es wäre dann freilich ϕ(a,a) kein spezieller Fall von (x,y).ϕ(x,y) und ϕa keiner von ($\exists$x,y).ϕx.ϕy. Dann aber könnte man statt $\phi x.\phi y \supset_{x,y} x = y$ einfach schreiben $\sim$($\exists$x,y).ϕx.ϕy. [*Vgl.* 5.53 *u.* 5.533.]

Durch diese Notation verlören auch der Scheinsatz (x)x = a oder ähnliche allen Schein von Berechtigung. [*Vgl.* 5.534.]

1. 12. 14.

Der Satz sagt gleichsam: Dieses Bild kann auf diese Weise keinen (oder kann einen) Sachverhalt darstellen.

2. 12. 14.

Es kommt eben darauf an, das festzusetzen, was den Satz vom bloßen Bild unterscheidet.

4. 12. 14.

Sehen wir uns z. B. die Gleichung $\sim\sim$p = p an: diese bestimmt mit anderen das Zeichen für p, da sie besagt, daß es etwas sei, was "p"

comes to represent a situation and to be right or wrong. (E.g., a picture represents the inside of a room, etc.)

27.11.14.

"$\sim$ p" is true when p is false. So part of the true proposition "$\sim$ p" is a false proposition. How can the mere twiddle " $\sim$ " bring it into agreement with reality? We have, of course, already said that it is not the twiddle " $\sim$ " alone but everything that is common to the different signs of negation. And what is common to all these must obviously proceed from the meaning of negation itself. And so in this way the sign of negation must surely mirror its own reference. [*Cf.* 5.512.]

28.11.14.

Negation combines with the ab-functions of the elementary proposition. And the logical functions of the elementary proposition must mirror their reference, just as much as all the others.

29.11.14.

The ab-function does not stop short of the elementary proposition but penetrates it.

What *can* be shewn cannot be said. [4.1212.]

I believe that it would be possible wholly to exclude the sign of identity from our notation and always to indicate identity merely by the identity of the signs (and conversely). In that case, of course, $\phi(a,a)$ would not be a special case of $(x,y).\phi(x,y)$, and ϕa would not be a special case of $(\exists x,y).\phi x.\phi y$. But then instead of $\phi x.\phi y \supset_{x,y} x = y$ one could simply write $\sim(\exists x,y).\phi x.\phi y$. [*Cf.* 5.53 and 5.533.]

By means of this notation the pseudo-proposition $(x)x = a$ or the like would lose all appearances of justification. [*Cf.* 5.534.]

1.12.14.

The proposition says as it were: This picture cannot (or can) present a situation in this way.

2.12.14.

It all depends on settling what distinguishes the proposition from the mere picture.

4.12.14.

Let us look at the identity $\sim\sim p = p$: this, together with others, determines the sign for p, since it says that there is something that "p"

und "~~p" gemein haben. Dadurch erhält jenes Zeichen Eigenschaften, die wiederspiegeln, daß die doppelte Verneinung eine Bejahung ist.

5. 12. 14.

Wie sagt "pv ~ p" nichts?

6. 12. 14.

Die Newtonsche Mechanik bringt die Weltbeschreibung auf eine einheitliche Form. Denken wir uns eine weiße Fläche, auf der unregelmäßige schwarze Flecken wären. Wir sagen nun: Was immer für ein Bild hierdurch entsteht, immer werde ich seiner Beschreibung beliebig nahe kommen können, indem ich die Fläche mit einem entsprechend feinem quadratischen Netzwerk bedecke und nun von jedem Quadrat sage, daß es weiß oder schwarz ist. Ich werde auf diese Weise die Beschreibung dieser Fläche auf eine einheitliche Form gebracht haben. Diese Form ist beliebig, denn ich hätte mit dem gleichen Erfolge ein dreieckiges oder sechseckiges Netz verwenden können. Es kann sein, daß die Beschreibung mit Hilfe eines dreieckigen Netzes einfacher geworden wäre, d. h., daß wir die Fläche mit einem gröberen Dreiecksnetz genauer beschreiben könnten als mit einem feineren quadratischen (oder umgekehrt) etc. Den verschiedenen Netzen entsprechen verschiedene Systeme der Weltbeschreibung. Die Mechanik bestimmt die Form der Weltbeschreibung, indem sie sagt: Alle Sätze der Weltbeschreibung müssen aus einer Anzahl gegebener Sätze—den mechanischen Axiomen—auf eine gegebene Art und Weise erhalten werden können. Hierdurch liefert sie die Bausteine zum Bau des wissenschaftlichen Gebäudes und sagt: Welches Gebäude du immer aufführen willst, jedes mußt du irgendwie mit diesen und nur diesen Bausteinen zusammenbringen.

Wie man mit dem Zahlensystem jede beliebige Anzahl muß hinschreiben können, so muß man mit dem System der Mechanik jeden beliebigen Satz der Physik hinschreiben können.

[6.341.]

Und hier sehen wir nun die gegenseitige Stellung von Logik und Mechanik.

(Man könnte das Netz auch aus verschiedenartigen Figuren bestehen lassen.)

Daß sich ein Bild, wie das vorhin erwähnte, durch ein Netz von gegebener Form beschreiben läßt, sagt über das Bild nichts aus (denn dies gilt für jedes solche Bild). Das aber charakterisiert das Bild, daß es sich durch ein bestimmtes Netz von *bestimmter* Feinheit beschreiben läßt. So auch sagt es nichts über die Welt aus, daß sie sich durch die Newtonsche Mechanik beschreiben läßt; aber wohl, daß

and "$\sim\sim$p" have in common. Through this that sign acquires properties which mirror the fact that double negation is an affirmation.

5.12.14.

How does "pv $\sim$ p" say nothing?

6.12.14.

Newtonian mechanics brings the description of the world into a unitary form. Let us imagine a white surface with irregular black spots on it. We now say: Whatever sort of picture arises in this way, I shall always be able to approximate as close as I like to its description by covering the surface with a suitably fine square network and saying of each square that it is white or is black. In this way I shall have brought the description of this surface into a unitary form. This form is arbitrary, for I could with equal success have used a triangular or hexagonal net. It may be that the description by means of a triangular net would have been simpler, i.e. that we could have given a more accurate description of the surface with a coarser triangular net than with a finer square one (or vice versa), etc. Different systems of describing the world correspond to the different nets. Mechanics determines the form of description of the world by saying: All propositions in a description of the world must be capable of being got in a given way from a number of given propositions—the axioms of mechanics. In this way it supplies the stones for building up natural science and says: Whatever building you want to erect you must construct it somehow with these and only these stones.

Just as it must be possible to write down any arbitrary number by means of the system of numbers, so it must be possible to write down any arbitrary proposition of physics by means of the system of mechanics.

[6.341.]

And here we see the relative position of logic and mechanics.

(One might also allow the net to consist of a variety of figures.)

The fact that a configuration like that mentioned above can be described by means of a net of a given form asserts nothing about the configuration (for this holds for any such configuration). What does characterize the configuration however is that it can be described by means of a particular net of a *particular* degree of fineness. In this way too it tells us nothing about the world that it can be described by means of Newtonian mechanics; but it does tell us something that it can be

sie sich so durch jene beschreiben läßt, wie dies eben der Fall ist. (Dies habe ich schon seit *langer* Zeit gefühlt).——Auch das sagt etwas von der Welt, daß sie sich durch die eine Mechanik einfacher beschreiben läßt, als durch die andere.

[*Vgl.* 6.342.]

Die Mechanik ist *ein* Versuch, alle Sätze, welche wir zur Weltbeschreibung benötigen, nach *einem* Plan zu konstruieren. (Die unsichtbaren Massen Hertz's.) [*Vgl.* 6.343.]

Die unsichtbaren Massen Hertz's sind *eingestandenermaßen* Scheingegenstände.

7\. 12. 14.

Die logischen Konstanten des Satzes sind die Bedingungen seiner Wahrheit.

8\. 12. 14.

Hinter unseren Gedanken, wahren und falschen, liegt immer wieder ein dunkler Grund, den wir erst später ins Licht ziehen und als einen Gedanken aussprechen können.

12\. 12. 14.

p. Taut = p; d. h. Taut sagt nichts! [*Vgl.* 4.465.]

13\. 12. 14.

Erschöpft es das Wesen der Negation, daß sie eine Operation ist, die sich selbst aufhebt? Dann müßte χ die Negation bedeuten, wenn $\chi\chi p = p$ vorausgesetzt daß $\chi p \neq p$.

Das ist einmal sicher, daß nach diesen beiden Gleichungen χ nicht mehr die Bejahung ausdrücken kann!

Und zeigt nicht die Fähigkeit des Verschwindens dieser Operationen, daß sie logische sind?

15\. 12. 14.

Es ist offenbar: wir können als Schriftzeichen der ab-Funktionen einführen, welche wir wollen, das eigentliche Zeichen wird sich automatisch bilden. Und welche Eigenschaften werden sich hierbei von selbst herausbilden?

Das logische Gerüst um das Bild (des Satzes) herum bestimmt den logischen Raum. [*Vgl.* 3.42.]

16\. 12. 14.

Der Satz muß den ganzen logischen Raum durchgreifen. [*Vgl.* 3.42.]

described by means of Newtonian mechanics in the way that it actually can. (This I have felt for a *long* time.)——It also asserts something about the world, that it can be described more simply by means of one mechanics than by means of another.

[*Cf.* 6.342.]

Mechanics is *one* attempt to construct all the propositions that we need for the description of the world according to a *single* plan. (Hertz's invisible masses.) [*Cf.* 6.343.]

Hertz's invisible masses are admittedly pseudo-objects.

7.12.14.

The logical constants of the proposition are the conditions of its truth.

8.12.14.

Behind our thoughts, true and false, there is always to be found a dark background, which we are only later able to bring into the light and express as a thought.

12.12.14.

p. Taut = p, i.e. Taut says nothing. [*Cf.* 4.465.]

13.12.14.

Does it exhaust the nature of negation that it is an operation cancelling itself? In that case χ would have to stand for negation if $\chi\chi p = p$, assuming that $\chi p \neq p$.

This for one thing is certain, that according to these two equations χ can no longer express affirmation.

And does not the capacity which these operations have of vanishing shew that they are logical?

15.12.14.

It is obvious that we can introduce whatever we like as the written signs of the ab-function, the real sign will form itself automatically. And when this happens what properties will be formed of themselves?

The logical scaffolding surrounding the picture (in the proposition) determines logical space. [*Cf.* 3.42.]

16.12.14.

The proposition must reach out through the whole of logical space. [*Cf.* 3.42.]

17. 12. 14.

Die ab-Funktionszeichen sind nicht materiell, sonst könnten sie nicht verschwinden. [*Vgl.* 5.44 *u.* 5.441.]

18. 12. 14.

Am eigentlichen Satzzeichen muß geradesoviel zu unterscheiden sein, als am Sachverhalt zu unterscheiden ist. Darin besteht ihre Identität. [*Vgl.* 4.04.]

20. 12. 14.

In "p" ist nicht mehr und nicht weniger zu erkennen als in "~p".

Wie kann ein Sachverhalt mit "p" übereinstimmen und mit "~p" nicht übereinstimmen?

Man könnte auch so fragen: Wenn ich zum Zweck der Verständigung mit einem Anderen *Die Sprache* erfinden wollte, was für Regeln müßte ich mit ihm über unseren Ausdruck vereinbaren?

23. 12. 14.

Charakteristisches Beispiel zu meiner Theorie der Bedeutung der physikalischen Naturbeschreibung: die beiden Wärmetheorien, einmal die Wärme als ein Stoff, ein andermal als eine Bewegung aufgefaßt.

25. 12. 14.

Der Satz sagt etwas, ist identisch mit: Er hat ein bestimmtes Verhältnis zur Wirklichkeit, *was immer diese sein mag.* Und wenn *sie* gegeben ist und jenes Verhältnis, so ist der Sinn des Satzes bekannt. "pvq" hat ein anderes Verhältnis zur Wirklichkeit als "p.q", etc.

Die Möglichkeit des Satzes basiert natürlich auf dem Prinzip der VERTRETUNG von Gegenständen durch Zeichen. [*Vgl.* 4.0312.]

Im Satz haben wir also die Vertretung von etwas durch *etwas Anderes.*

Aber auch das *gemeinsame* Bindemittel.

Mein Grundgedanke ist, daß die logischen Konstanten nicht vertreten. Daß sich die *Logik* der Tatsache nicht vertreten *läßt.* [*S.* 4.0312.]

29. 12. 14.

Im Satze vertritt den Gegenstand der Name. [3.22.]

11. 1. 15.

Ein Meterstab sagt nicht, daß ein zu messendes Objekt einen Meter lang sei.

17.12.14.

The signs of the ab-function are not material, otherwise they could not vanish. [*Cf.* 5.44 and 5.441.]

18.12.14.

It must be possible to distinguish just as much in the real propositional sign as can be distinguished in the situation. This is what their identity consists in. [*Cf.* 4.04.]

20.12.14.

In "p" neither more nor less can be recognized than in "$\sim$p".

How can a situation agree with "p" and not agree with "$\sim$p"?

The following question might also be asked: If I were to try to invent *Language* for the purpose of making myself understood to someone else, what sort of rules should I have to agree on with him about our expression?

23.12.14.

A characteristic example for my theory of the significance of descriptions in physics: The two theories of heat; heat conceived at one time as a stuff, at another time as a movement.

25.12.14.

The proposition says something, is identical with: It has a particular relation to reality, *whatever this may be*. And if this *reality* is given and also that relation, then the sense of the proposition is known. "pvq" has a different relation to reality from "p.q", etc.

The possibility of the proposition is, of course, founded on the principle of signs as GOING PROXY for objects. [*Cf.* 4.0312.]

Thus in the proposition something has *something else* as its proxy.

But there is also the *common cement*.

My fundamental thought is that the logical constants are not proxies. That the *logic* of the fact cannot have anything as its proxy. [*See* 4.0312.]

29.12.14.

In the proposition the name goes proxy for the object. [3.22.]

11.1.15.

A yardstick does not say that an object that is to be measured is one yard long.

Auch dann nicht, wenn wir wissen, daß er zum Messen dieses *bestimmten* Objektes dienen soll.

Könnte man nicht fragen: Was muß zu jenem Meterstab dazukommen, damit es etwas über die Länge des Objektes *aussagt*?

(Der Meterstab ohne diesen Zusatz wäre die "Annahme".)

15. 1. 15.

Das Satzzeichen "p v q" stimmt, wenn p der Fall ist, wenn q der Fall ist, und wenn beide der Fall sind, anderenfalls stimmt es nicht: dies scheint unendlich einfach zu sein; und *so* einfach wird die Lösung sein.

16. 1. 15.

Der Satz ist einem hypothetischen Sachverhalt zugeordnet.

Dieser Sachverhalt ist durch seine Beschreibung gegeben.

Der Satz ist die Beschreibung eines Sachverhalts. [*S*. 4.023.]

Wie die Beschreibung eines Gegenstandes nach seinen externen Eigenschaften, so beschreibt der Satz die Tatsache nach ihren internen Eigenschaften. [*S*. 4.023.]

Die Beschreibung stimmt, wenn der Gegenstand die besagten Eigenschaften hat: Der Satz stimmt, wenn der Sachverhalt die durch den Satz angegebenen internen Eigenschaften hat.

17. 1. 15.

Der Sachverhalt p.q *fällt unter* den Satz "pvq".

Zu dem Netz-Gleichnis der Physik: Obwohl die Flecke geometrische Figuren sind, so kann uns doch selbstverständlich die Geometrie gar nichts über ihre Form und Lage sagen. Das Netz aber ist *rein* geometrisch, alle seine Eigenschaften können a priori angegeben werden. [*S*. 6.35.]

18. 1. 15.

Der Vergleich zwischen Satz und Beschreibung ist rein logisch und *muß* daher weiter geführt werden.

20. 1. 15.

Wieso ist *Alle* ein logischer Begriff?

Wieso ist *Alle* ein Begriff der Form? ?

Wie kommt es, daß *Alle* in jedem Satz vorkommen kann?

Not even when we know that it is supposed to serve for the measurement of this *particular* object.

Could we not ask: What has to be added to that yardstick in order for it to *assert* something about the length of the object?

(The yardstick without this addition would be the "assumption".)

15.1.15.

The propositional sign "pvq" is right if p is the case, if q is the case and if both are the case, otherwise it is wrong. This seems to be infinitely simple; and the solution will be *as* simple as this.

16.1.15.

The proposition is correlated with a hypothetical situation.

This situation is given by means of its description.

The proposition is the description of a situation. [*See* 4.023.]

As the description of an object describes it by its external properties, so the proposition describes the fact by its internal properties. [*See* 4.023.]

The description is right if the object has the asserted property: the proposition is right if the situation has the internal properties given by the proposition.

17.1.15.

The situation p.q *falls under* the proposition "pvq".

On the analogy of the net for physics: although the spots are geometrical figures, all the same geometry can, of course, say nothing at all about their form and position. The net, however, is *purely* geometrical, all its properties can be given *a priori*. [*See* 6.35.]

18.1.15.

The comparison between proposition and description is purely logical and for that reason *must* be carried farther.

20.1.15.

How is it that *all* is a logical concept?

How is it that *all* is a concept of form?

How does it come about that *all* can occur in any proposition?

Denn dies ist das Charakteristikum des Formbegriffs!

Alle SCHEINT dem Inhalt des Satzes näher zu stehen als der Form.

Alle: Dinge, Alle: Funktionen, Alle: Beziehungen: Es ist als ob Alle ein Binde*glied* zwischen dem Begriff des Dinges, der Funktion etc. und dem einzelnen Ding, der einzelnen Funktion sei.

Die Allgemeinheit ist wesentlich mit der Elementar-FORM verbunden.

Das erlösende Wort—?!

21. 1. 15.

Der Übergang von der allgemeinen Betrachtung der Satzform: *Unendlich schwierig, fabelhaft.*

22. 1. 15.

Meine *ganze* Aufgabe besteht darin, das Wesen des Satzes zu erklären.

Das heißt, das Wesen aller Tatsachen anzugeben, deren Bild der Satz *ist*.

Das Wesen alles Seins angeben.

(Und hier bedeutet Sein nicht existieren—dann wäre es unsinnig.)

23. 1. 15.

Die Verneinung ist eine Operation. [*Vgl.* 5.2341.]

Eine Operation bezeichnet eine Operation.

Das Wort ist eine Sonde, manches reicht tief; manches nur wenig tief.

Eine Operation sagt natürlich nichts aus, nur ihr Resultat; und dies hängt von ihrem Gegenstand ab. [*Vgl.* 5.25.]

24. 1. 15.

Die logischen Scheinfunktionen *sind* Operationen.

Nur Operationen können verschwinden! [*Vgl.* 5.254.]

Der negative Satz schließt die Wirklichkeit aus.

Wie kann die allumfassende, weltspiegelnde Logik so spezielle Haken und Manipulationen gebrauchen?! Nur, indem sich alle diese zusammen zu einem *unendlich* feinen Netzwerk, zu dem großen Spiegel verknüpfen! [5.511.]

For that is the characteristic mark of the concept of a form.

All APPEARS to be nearer to the content of the proposition than to the form.

All: things, All: functions, All: relations: it is as if All were a connecting *term* between the concept of the thing, of functions, etc., and the individual thing, the individual functions.

Generality is essentially connected with the elementary FORM.

The key word—?

21.1.15.

The transition from the general consideration of the propositional form: *infinitely difficult*, *fantastic*.

22.1.15.

My *whole* task consists in explaining the nature of the proposition.

That is to say, in giving the nature of all facts, whose picture the proposition *is*.

In giving the nature of all being.

(And here Being does not mean existing—in that case it would be nonsensical.)

23.1.15.

Negation is an operation. [*Cf.* 5.2341.]

An operation denotes an operation.

Words are probes; some reach very deep; some only to a little depth.

An operation, of course, does not say anything, only its result does; and this depends on its object. [*Cf.* 5.25.]

24.1.15.

The logical pseudo-functions *are* operations.

Only operations can vanish!

The negative proposition excludes reality.

How can the all-embracing world-mirroring logic make use of such special twiddles and manipulations? Only by all these being linked together to form one *infinitely* fine network, to form the great mirror. [5.511.]

25. 1. 15.

Man kann auch sagen: $\sim$p ist falsch, wenn p wahr ist.

29. 1. 15.

Die Sprache ist artikuliert. [*Vgl.* 3.141.]

7. 2. 15.

Die musikalischen Themen sind in gewissem Sinne Sätze. Die Kenntnis des Wesens der Logik wird deshalb zur Kenntnis des Wesens der Musik führen.

14. 2. 15.

Gäbe es mathematische Gegenstände—logische Konstante—so wäre der Satz "ich esse 5 Pflaumen" ein Satz der Mathematik. Und er ist auch kein Satz der angewandten Mathematik.

Der Satz muß seine Bedeutung *vollständig* beschreiben. [*Vgl.* 4.023.]

4. 3. 15.

Die Melodie ist eine Art Tautologie, sie ist in sich selbst abgeschlossen; sie befriedigt sich selbst.

5. 3. 15.

Die Menschheit hat immer geahnt, daß es ein Gebiet von Fragen geben muß, worin die Antworten — a priori — symmetrisch und zu einem abgeschlossenen, regelmäßigen Gebilde vereint—liegen. [*S.* 5.4541.]

(Je älter ein Wort ist, desto tiefer reicht es.)

6. 3. 15.

Die Probleme der Verneinung, der Disjunktion, von Wahr und Falsch—sind nur Spiegelbilder des einen, großen Problems, in den verschieden gestellten großen und kleinen Spiegeln der Philosophie.

7. 3. 15.

Wie $\sim\xi$, $\sim\xi \vee \sim\xi$ etc. dieselbe Funktion ist, so ist auch $\sim\eta \vee \eta$, $\eta \supset \eta$, etc. dieselbe—nämlich die tautologische—Funktion. Wie die anderen, so kann auch sie—und vielleicht mit Vorteil—untersucht werden.

8. 3. 15.

Meine Schwierigkeit ist nur eine—enorme—Schwierigkeit des Ausdrucks.

18. 3. 15.

Es ist klar, daß die genaueste Untersuchung des Satzzeichens nicht ergeben kann, was es aussagt—wohl aber, was es aussagen *kann*.

25.1.15.

We can also say: $\sim$ p is false, when p is true.

29.1.15.

Language is articulated. [*Cf.* 3.141.]

7.2.15.

Musical themes are in a certain sense propositions. Knowledge of the nature of logic will for this reason lead to knowledge of the nature of music.

14.2.15.

If there were mathematical objects—logical constants—the proposition "I am eating five plums" would be a proposition of mathematics. And it is not even a proposition of applied mathematics.

The proposition must describe its reference *completely*. [*Cf.* 4.023.]

4.3.15.

A tune is a kind of tautology, it is complete in itself; it satisfies itself.

5.3.15.

Mankind has always had an inkling that there must be a sphere of questions where the answers must—*a priori*—be arranged symmetrically, and united into a complete regular structure. [*See* 5.4541.]

(The older a word, the deeper it reaches.)

6.3.15.

The problems of negation, of disjunction, of true and false, are only reflections of the one great problem in the variously placed great and small mirrors of philosophy.

7.3.15.

Just as $\sim\xi$, $\sim\xi \vee \sim\xi$ etc. are the same function, so too are $\sim\eta \vee \eta$, $\eta \supset \eta$, etc. the same—that is, the tautological—function. Just as the others can be investigated, so can it—and perhaps with advantage.

8.3.15.

My difficulty is only an—enormous—difficulty of expression.

18.3.15.

It is clear that the closest examination of the propositional sign cannot yield what it asserts—what it can yield is what it is *capable* of asserting.

27. 3. 15.

Das Bild kann eine Beschreibung ersetzen.

29. 3. 15.

Das Kausalitätsgesetz ist kein Gesetz, sondern die Form *eines* Gesetzes. [*Vgl.* 6.32.]

"Kausalitätsgesetz", das ist ein Gattungsname. Und wie es in der Mechanik—sagen wir—Minimumgesetze gibt—etwa der kleinsten Wirkung—so gibt es in der Physik EIN Kausalitätsgesetz, ein Gesetz von der Kausalitätsform. [*Vgl.* 6.321.]

Wie die Menschen ja auch eine Ahnung davon gehabt haben, daß es *ein* "Gesetz der kleinsten Wirkung" geben müsse, ehe sie genau wußten, wie es lautete.

(Hier, wie so oft, stellt sich das Aprioristische als etwas rein Logisches heraus.)
[*Vgl.* 6.3211.]

3. 4. 15.

Der Satz ist ein Maß der Welt.

Dies ist das Bild eines Vorgangs und stimmt nicht. Wie kann es dann noch immer das Bild jenes Vorgangs sein?

Daß "a" a vertreten *kann* und "b" b vertreten *kann*, wenn "a" in der Relation "R" zu "b" steht, darin eben besteht jene gesuchte POTENTIELLE interne Relation.

5. 4. 15.

Der Satz ist kein Wörtergemisch. [*S.* 3.141.]

11. 4. 15.

Auch die Melodie ist kein Tongemisch, wie alle Unmusikalischen glauben. [*Vgl.* 3.141.]

12. 4. 15.

Ich *kann* von dem Wesen des Satzes *nicht* auf die einzelnen logischen Operationen kommen!!!

15. 4. 15.

Ich kann eben nicht herausbringen, inwiefern der Satz das *Bild* des Sachverhaltes ist!

Beinahe bin ich bereit, alle Bemühungen aufzugeben.——— ———

16. 4. 15.

Die Beschreibung ist auch sozusagen eine Operation, deren Basis ihre Hilfsmittel, und deren Resultat der beschriebene Gegenstand ist.

27.3.15.

The picture can replace a description.

29.3.15.

The law of causality is not a law but the form of *a* law. [*Cf.* 6.32.]

"Law of causality" is a class name. And just as in mechanics—let us say—there are minimum laws—e.g., that of least action—so in physics there is A law of causality, a law of the causality form. [*Cf.* 6.321.]

Just as men also had an inkling of the fact that there must be *a* "law of least action", before precisely knowing how it ran.

(Here, as so often happens, the *a priori* turns out to be something purely logical.)

[*Cf.* 6.3211.]

3.4.15.

The proposition is a measure of the world.

This is the picture of a process and is wrong. In that case how can it still be a picture of that process?

"a" *can* go proxy for a and "b" *can* go proxy for b when "a" stands in the relation "R" to "b": this is what that POTENTIAL internal relation that we are looking for consists in.

5.4.15.

The proposition is not a blend of words. [*See* 3.141.]

11.4.15.

Nor is a tune a blend of notes, as all unmusical people think. [*Cf.* 3.141.]

12.4.15.

I *cannot* get from the nature of the proposition to the individual logical operations!!!

15.4.15.

That is, I cannot bring out how far the proposition is the *picture* of the situation.

I am almost inclined to give up all my efforts.——— ———

16.4.15.

Description is also, so to speak, an operation with the means of description as its basis, and with the described object as its result.

Das Zeichen "Nicht" ist die Klasse aller verneinenden Zeichen.

17. 4. 15.

Das subjektive Universum.

Statt die logischen Operationen im Satz an dessen Teilsätzen zu vollziehen, können wir diesen auch *Marken* zuordnen und mit ihnen operieren. Dann ist *einem* Satzbild ein mit ihm in kompliziertester Weise zusammenhängendes Markensternbild zugeordnet.

$$(aRb,\ cSd,\ \phi e)\ ((p \vee q).r : \supset : q.r\ . \equiv .\ p \vee r)$$
$$\quad p \quad q \quad r$$

18. 4. 15.

Für die Operation der Verneinung ist der Übergang von p auf $\sim p$ *nicht* charakteristisch. (Der beste Beweis: sie führt auch von $\sim p$ zu p.)——————.

19. 4. 15.

Was sich in der Sprache spiegelt, kann ich nicht mit ihr ausdrücken. [*Vgl.* 4.121.]

23. 4. 15.

Wir glauben nicht a priori an ein Erhaltungsgesetz, sondern wir *wissen* a priori die Möglichkeit seiner logischen Form. [6.33.]

Alle jene a priori gewissen Sätze, wie der Satz vom Grunde, von der Kontinuität in der Natur, etc., etc., alle diese sind aprioristische Einsichten bezüglich der möglichen Formgebung der Sätze der Wissenschaft. [*Vgl.* 6.34.]

"Occams Devise" ist *natürlich* keine willkürliche oder durch ihren praktischen Erfolg gerechtfertigte Regel. Sie besagt, daß unnötige Zeichen-Einheiten nichts bedeuten. [*S.* 5.47321.]

Es ist klar, daß Zeichen, die denselben Zweck erfüllen, logisch identisch sind. Das rein Logische *ist* eben das, was *alle* diese leisten können. [*Vgl.* 5.47321.]

24. 4. 15.

In der Logik (Mathematik) sind Prozeß und Resultat gleichwertig. (Darum keine Überraschungen.) [6.1261.]

25. 4. 15.

Da die Sprache in *internen* Relationen zur Welt steht, so bestimmt *sie* und diese Relationen die logische Möglichkeit der Tatsachen.

The sign "not" is the class of all negating signs.

17.4.15.

The subjective universe.

Instead of performing the logical operations in the proposition upon its component propositions, we can correlate *marks* with these and operate with them. In that case a single propositional formation has correlated with it a constellation of marks which is connected with it in a most complicated way.

(aRb, cSd, ϕe) ((pvq).r : $\supset$: q.r. $\equiv$. pvr)
p q r

18.4.15.

The transition from p to $\sim$p is *not* what is characteristic of the operation of negation. (The *best proof* of this: negation also leads from $\sim$p to p.)——————.

19.4.15.

What is mirrored in language I cannot use language to express. [*Cf.* 4.121.]

23.4.15.

We do not believe *a priori* in a law of conservation, we *know a priori* the possibility of its logical form. [6.33.]

All those propositions which are known *a priori*, like the principle of sufficient reason, of continuity in nature, etc., etc., all these are *a priori* insights relating to the possible ways of forming the propositions of natural science. [*Cf.* 6.34.]

"Ockham's razor" is, *of course*, not an arbitrary rule or one justified by its practical success. What it says is that unnecessary sign-units mean nothing. [*See* 5.47321.]

It is clear that signs fulfilling the same purpose are logically identical. The purely logical thing just *is* what *all* of these are capable of accomplishing. [*Cf.* 5.47321.]

24.4.15.

In logic (mathematics) process and result are equivalent. (Hence no surprises.) [6.1261.]

25.4.15.

Since language stands in *internal* relations to the world, *it* and these relations determine the logical possibility of facts. If we have a signifi-

Haben wir ein bedeutungsvolles Zeichen, so muß es in einer bestimmten internen Relation zu einem Gebilde stehen. Zeichen und Relation bestimmen eindeutig die logische Form des Bezeichneten.

Aber kann nicht irgend ein so genanntes Ding mit irgend einem solchen auf ein und dieselbe Weise zugeordnet werden?
Es ist z. B. ganz klar, daß wir die Wörter der Sprache als mit einander logisch äquivalente Einheiten—empfinden und—gebrauchen.

Es scheint immer, als ob es etwas gäbe, was man *als Ding betrachten könne*, *andererseits* wirkliche einfache Dinge.

Es ist klar: Weder ein Bleistiftstrich noch ein Dampfschiff sind einfach: Besteht zwischen diesen beiden wirklich eine logische Äquivalenz?

"Gesetze", wie der Satz vom Grunde etc., handeln vom Netz, nicht von dem, was das Netz beschreibt. [*S.* 6.35.]

26. 4. 15.

Durch die Allgemeinheit mußen die gebräuchlichen Sätze ihr einfaches Gepräge kriegen.

Wir müßen erkennen, *wie* die Sprache für sich selbst sorgt.

Der Satz, welcher vom "Komplex" handelt, steht in interner Beziehung zum Satze, welcher von dessen Bestandteil handelt. [*S.* 3.24.]

27. 4. 15.

Die Willensfreiheit besteht darin, daß zukünftige Ereignisse jetzt nicht GEWUSST werden *können*. Nur dann könnten wir sie wissen, wenn die Kausalität eine INNERE Notwendigkeit wäre—wie etwa die des logischen Schlusses.—Der Zusammenhang von Wissen und Gewußtem ist *der* der logischen Notwendigkeit. [*S.* 5.1362.]

Ich darf mich nicht um die Sprache kümmern brauchen.

Das Nicht-Stimmen ist ähnlich wie die Nicht-Identität.

28. 4. 15.

Die Operation des Verneinens besteht nicht etwa im Vorsetzen von $\sim$, sondern in der Klasse aller verneinenden Operationen.

Was für Eigenschaften hat aber dann eigentlich diese ideale verneinende Operation?

Wie zeigt es sich, wenn sich zwei Aussagen miteinander vertragen?
Wenn man in $p \vee q$ statt q p setzt, so wird die Aussage zu p!

cant sign it must stand in a particular internal relation to a structure. Sign and relation determine unambiguously the logical form of the thing signified.

But cannot any so-called thing be correlated in one and the same way with any other such?

It is, for example, quite clear that the separate words of language are —experienced and—used as logically equivalent units.

It always seems as if there were something that one *can regard as a thing*, and *on the other hand* real simple things.

It is clear that neither a pencil-stroke nor a steamship is simple. Is there really a logical equivalence between these two?

"Laws" like the law of sufficient reason, etc. deal with the network not with what the network describes. [*See* 6.35.]

26.4.15.

It must be through generality that ordinary propositions get their stamp of simplicity.

We must recognize *how* language takes care of itself.

The proposition that is about a complex stands in internal relation to the proposition about its component part. [*See* 3.24.]

27.4.15.

The freedom of the will consists in the fact that future events *cannot* be KNOWN now. It would only be possible for us to know them, if causality were an INNER necessity—like, say, that of logical inference. —The connexion between knowledge and thing known is *the* connexion of logical necessity. [*See* 5.1362.]

I cannot need to worry about language.

Non-truth is like non-identity.

28.4.15.

The operation of negating does not consist in, say, putting down a ~, but in the class of all negating operations.

But in that case what really are the properties of this ideal negating operation?

How does it come out that two assertions are compatible?

If one puts p instead of q in pvq the statement turns into p.

Gehört das Zeichen p.q auch unter diejenigen, welche p bejahen?— Ist p eins von den Zeichen für p v q ?

Kann man so sagen?: Alle Zeichen, welche p *nicht* bejahen, *nicht* von p bejaht werden und p *nicht* als Tautologie oder Kontradiktion enthalten, alle diese Zeichen verneinen p.

29. 4. 15.

Das heißt: alle Zeichen, die von p abhängig sind, und die weder p bejahen noch von p bejaht werden.

30. 4. 15.

Das Vorkommen einer *Operation* kann *natürlich* allein nichts besagen!

p wird von allen Sätzen bejaht, aus denen es folgt. [5.124.]
Jeder Satz, der p widerspricht, verneint p. [*S.* 5.1241.]

1. 5. 15.

Daß p.~p eine Kontradiktion ist, zeigt, daß ~p p widerspricht. [*Vgl.* 6.1201.]

Skeptizismus ist *nicht* unwiderleglich sondern *offenbar unsinnig*, wenn er bezweifeln will, wo nicht gefragt werden kann. [*S.* 6.51.]

Denn Zweifel kann nur bestehen, wo eine Frage besteht; eine Frage kann nur bestehen, wo eine Antwort besteht, und diese nur, wo etwas *gesagt* werden *kann*. [*S.* 6.51.]

Alle Theorien, die besagen: "Es *muß* sich doch so verhalten, sonst könnten wir ja nicht philosophieren" oder "sonst könnten wir doch nicht leben" etc., etc., müssen natürlich verschwinden.

Meine Methode ist es nicht, das Harte vom Weichen zu scheiden, sondern die Härte des Weichen zu sehen.

Es ist eine Hauptkunst des Philosophen, sich nicht mit Fragen zu beschäftigen, die ihn nichts angehen.

Russells Methode in seiner "Scientific Method in Philosophy" ist geradezu ein Rückschritt von der Methode der Physik.

2. 5. 15.

Die Klasse aller Zeichen, die sowohl p als auch q bejahen, ist das Zeichen für p.q. Die Klasse aller Zeichen, die entweder p oder q bejahen, ist der Satz "p v q". [*Vgl.* 5.513.]

Does the sign p.q also belong among those which assert p?—Is p one of the signs for pvq?

Can one say the following?: All signs that do *not* assert p, are *not* asserted by p and do *not* contain p as tautology or contradiction does—all these signs negate p.

29.4.15.

That is to say: All signs that are dependent on p and that neither assert p nor are asserted by p.

30.4.15.

The occurrence of an *operation* cannot, *of course*, have any import by itself.

p is asserted by all propositions from which it follows. [5.124.]
Every proposition that contradicts p negates p. [*See* 5.1241.]

1.5.15.

The fact that p. ∼ p is a contradiction shews that ∼ p contradicts p. [*Cf.* 6.1201.]

Scepticism is *not* irrefutable, but *obvious nonsense* if it tries to doubt where no question can be asked. [*See* 6.51.]

For doubt can only exist where a question exists; a question can only exist where an answer exists, and this can only exist where something *can* be *said*. [*See* 6.51.]

All theories that say: "This is how it must be, otherwise we could not philosophize" or "otherwise we surely could not live", etc. etc., must of course disappear.

My method is not to sunder the hard from the soft, but to see the hardness of the soft.

It is one of the chief skills of the philosopher not to occupy himself with questions which do not concern him.

Russell's method in his "Scientific method in philosophy" is simply a retrogression from the method of physics.

2.5.15.

The class of all signs that assert both p and q is the sign for p.q. The class of all signs which assert either p or q is the proposition "pvq". [*Cf.* 5.513.]

3. 5. 15.

Man kann nicht sagen, daß sowohl Tautologien als Kontradiktionen *nichts* sagen in dem Sinne, daß sie etwa beide Nullpunkte in der Skala der Sätze wären. Denn zum Mindesten sind sie *entgegengesetzte* Pole.

Kann man sagen: Zwei Sätze sind einander entgegengesetzt, wenn es kein Zeichen gibt, das sie beide bejaht—was eigentlich heißt: wenn sie kein gemeinsames Glied haben. [*Vgl.* 5.1241.]

Man stellt sich also die Sätze als Klassen von Zeichen vor—die Sätze "p" und "q" haben das Glied "p.q" gemeinsam—und zwei Sätze sind einander entgegengesetzt, wenn sie ganz außerhalb einander liegen. [*Vgl.* 5.513.]

4. 5. 15.

Das sogenannte Gesetz der Induktion kann jedenfalls kein logisches Gesetz sein, denn es ist offenbar ein Satz. [*S.* 6.31.]

Die Klasse aller Sätze von der Form Fx ist der Satz (x)ϕx.

5. 5. 15.

Gibt es die allgemeine Satzform?

Ja, wenn darunter die eine "logische Konstante" verstanden ist! [*Vgl.* 5.47.]

Immer wieder scheint die Frage einen Sinn zu haben: "Gibt es einfache Dinge?" Und doch muß diese Frage unsinnig sein!——

6. 5. 15.

Man würde sich vergeblich bemühen, den Scheinsatz "gibt es einfache Dinge?" in Zeichen der Begriffsschrift auszudrücken.

Es ist doch klar, daß ich einen Begriff vom Ding, von der einfachen Zuordnung vor mir habe, wenn ich über diese Sache denke.

Wie stelle ich mir aber das Einfache vor? Da kann ich immer nur sagen " 'x' hat Bedeutung". — Hier ist ein großes Rätsel!

Als Beispiele des Einfachen denke ich immer an Punkte des Gesichtsbildes. (Wie mir als typisch "zusammengesetzte Gegenstände" immer Teile des Gesichtsbildes vorschweben).

7. 5. 15.

Ist räumliche Zusammengesetztheit auch logische Zusammengesetztheit? Es scheint doch, ja!

Aus was besteht aber z. B. ein gleichförmig gefärbter Teil meines Gesichtsbildes? Aus minima sensibilia? Wie sollte man denn den Ort eines jeden solchen bestimmen?

3.5.15.

We cannot say that both tautology and contradiction say *nothing* in the sense that they are both, say, zero points in a scale of propositions. For at least they are *opposite* poles.

Can we say: two propositions are opposed to one another when there is no sign that asserts them both—which really means: when they have no common member? [*Cf.* 5.1241.]

Thus propositions are imagined as classes of signs—the propositions "p" and "q" have the member "p.q" in common—and two propositions are opposed to one another when they lie quite outside one another. [*Cf.* 5.513.]

4.5.15.

The so-called law of induction cannot at any rate be a logical law, for it is evidently a proposition. [*See* 6.31.]

The class of all propositions of the form Fx is the proposition (x) ϕx.

5.5.15.

Does the general form of proposition exist?
Yes, if by that is understood the single "logical constant". [*Cf.* 5.47.]

It keeps on looking as if the question "Are there simple things?" made sense. And surely this question must be nonsense!——

6.5.15.

It would be vain to try and express the pseudo-sentence "Are there simple things?" in symbolic notation.

And yet it is clear that I have before me a concept of a thing, of simple correlation, when I think about this matter.
But how am I imagining the simple? Here all I can say is always " 'x' has reference".—Here is a great riddle!

As examples of the simple I always think of points of the visual field (just as parts of the visual field always come before my mind as typical composite objects).

7.5.15.

Is spatial complexity also logical complexity? It surely seems to be.

But what is a uniformly coloured part of my visual field composed of? Of *minima sensibilia*? How should the place of one such be determined?

Auch wenn die von uns gebrauchten Sätze alle Verallgemeinerungen enthalten, so müssen in ihnen doch die Urbilder der Bestandteile ihrer Spezialfälle vorkommen. Also bleibt die Frage bestehen, wie wir zu jenen kommen.

8. 5. 15.

Daß es keine Zeichen eines bestimmten Urbilds gibt, zeigt nicht, daß jenes Urbild nicht vorhanden ist. Die zeichensprachliche Abbildung geschieht nicht so, daß ein *Zeichen* eines Urbildes einen *Gegenstand* desselben Urbildes vertritt. Das Zeichen und die interne Relation zum Bezeichneten bestimmen das Urbild dieses; wie Grundkoordinaten und Ordinaten die Punkte einer Figur bestimmen.

9. 5. 15.

Eine Frage: Können wir ohne einfache Gegenstände in der LOGIK auskommen?

Offenbar sind Sätze möglich welche keine einfachen Zeichen enthalten, d. h. keine Zeichen, welche unmittelbar eine Bedeutung haben. Und diese sind wirklich *Sätze*, die einen Sinn haben, und die Definitionen ihrer Bestandteile brauchen auch nicht bei ihnen zu stehen.

Es ist doch klar, daß Bestandteile unserer Sätze durch Definitionen zerlegt werden können, und müssen, wenn wir uns der eigentlichen Struktur des Satzes nähern wollen. *Jedenfalls gibt es also einen Prozeß der Analyse*. Und kann nun nicht gefragt werden, ob dieser Prozeß einmal zu einem Ende kommt? Und wenn ja: Was wird das Ende sein??

Wenn es wahr ist, daß jedes definierte Zeichen via seine Definitionen bezeichnet, dann muß wohl die Kette der Definitionen einmal ein Ende haben. [*Vgl.* 3.261.]

Der zerlegte Satz redet von mehr als der unzerlegte.

Zerlegung macht den Satz komplizierter als er war; aber kann und darf ihn nicht komplizierter machen als seine Bedeutung von Haus aus war.

Wenn der Satz so komplex ist wie seine Bedeutung, dann ist er *ganz* zerlegt.

Die Bedeutung unserer Sätze aber ist nicht unendlich kompliziert.

Der Satz ist das Bild der Tatsache. Ich kann von einer Tatsache verschiedene Bilder entwerfen. (Dazu dienen mir die logischen

Even if the sentences which we ordinarily use all contain generalizations, still there must surely occur in them the proto-pictures of the component parts of their special cases. Thus the question remains how we arrive at those.

8.5.15.

The fact that there is no sign for a particular proto-picture does not show that that proto-picture is not present. Portrayal by means of sign language does not take place in such a way that a *sign* of a proto-picture goes proxy for an *object* of that proto-picture. The sign and the internal relation to what is signified determine the proto-picture of the latter; as the fundamental co-ordinates together with the ordinates determine the points of a figure.

9.5.15.

A question: can we manage without simple objects in LOGIC?

Obviously propositions are possible which contain no simple signs, i.e. no signs which have an immediate reference. And these are really *propositions* making sense, nor do the definitions of their component parts have to be attached to them.

But it is clear that components of our propositions can be analysed by means of a definition, and must be, if we want to approximate to the real structure of the proposition. *At any rate, then, there is a process of analysis*. And can it not now be asked whether this process comes to an end? And if so: What will the end be?

If it is true that every defined sign signifies *via* its definitions then presumably the chain of definitions must some time have an end. [*Cf*. 3.261.]

The analysed proposition mentions more than the unanalysed.

Analysis makes the proposition more complicated than it was, but it cannot and must not make it more complicated than its meaning was from the first.

When the proposition is just as complex as its reference, then it is *completely* analysed.

But the reference of our propositions is not infinitely complicated.

The proposition is the picture of the fact. I can devise different pictures of a fact. (The logical operations serve this purpose.) But

Operationen.) Aber das für die *Tatsache* Charakteristische in diesen Bildern wird in allen dasselbe sein und von mir nicht abhängen.

Mit der Zeichenklasse des Satzes "p" ist bereits die Klasse "~p" etc., etc., gegeben. Wie es auch sein muß.

Aber, setzt das nicht schon voraus, daß uns die Klasse aller Sätze gegeben ist? Und wie kommen wir zu *ihr*?

11. 5. 15.

Ist die logische Summe zweier Tautologien eine Tautologie im ersten Sinne? Gibt es wirklich die Dualität: Tautologie—Kontradiktion?

Unser Einfaches IST: das Einfachste, was wir kennen.——Das Einfachste zu dem unsere Analyse vordringen kann—es braucht nur als Urbild, als Variable in unseren Sätzen zu erscheinen——*dies* ist das Einfache, welches wir meinen und suchen.

12. 5. 15.

Der allgemeine Begriff der Abbildung und *der* der Koordinaten.

Angenommen, der Ausdruck "$\sim(\exists x)x = x$" wäre ein Satz, nämlich etwa der: "Es gibt keine Dinge", dann müßte es sehr wunder nehmen, daß wir, um diesen Satz in Symbolen auszudrücken, eine Relation (=) benützen müssen, von der in ihm eigentlich gar nicht die Rede ist.

13. 5. 15.

Eine eigentümliche logische Manipulation, die *Personifizierung* der *Zeit*!

Nur nicht den Knoten zusammenziehen, bevor man sicher ist, daß man das rechte Ende erwischt hat.

Dürfen wir einen Teil des Raumes als Ding betrachten? Dies tun wir offenbar in gewissem Sinne immer, wo wir von den räumlichen Dingen reden.

Es scheint nämlich—zum mindesten so weit ich jetzt sehen kann—mit dem Wegschaffen von Namen durch Definitionen nicht getan zu sein: die komplexen räumlichen Gegenstände, zum Beispiel, scheinen mir in irgend einem Sinn wesentlich Dinge zu sein—ich sehe sie, sozusagen, als Dinge.—Und ihre Bezeichnung vermittelst Namen scheint mehr zu sein als ein bloß sprachlicher Trick. Die räumlichen zusammengesetzten Gegenstände—z. B.—erscheinen—wie es scheint—wirklich als Dinge.

Aber was bedeutet das alles?

what is characteristic of the *fact* will be the same in all of these pictures and will not depend on me.

With the class of signs of the proposition "p" the class "$\sim$p", etc. etc. is already given. As indeed is necessary.

But does not that of itself presuppose that the class of all propositions is given us? And how do we arrive at *it*?

11.5.15.

Is the logical sum of two tautologies a tautology in the first sense? Is there really such a thing as the duality: tautology—contradiction?

The simple thing for us IS: the simplest thing that we are acquainted with.——The simplest thing which our analysis can attain—it need appear only as a prototype, as a variable in our propositions——*that* is the simple thing that we mean and look for.

12.5.15.

The general concepts (*a*) of portrayal and (*b*) of co-ordinates.

Supposing that the expression "$\sim (\exists x) x = x$" were a proposition, namely (say), this one: "There are no things", then it would be matter for great wonder that, in order to express this proposition in symbols, we had to make use of a relation (=) with which it was really not concerned at all.

13.5.15.

A singular logical manipulation, the *personification* of *time*!

Just don't pull the knot tight before being certain that you have got hold of the right end.

Can we regard a part of space as a thing? In a certain sense we obviously always do this when we talk of spatial things.

For it seems—at least so far as I can see at present—that the matter is not settled by getting rid of names by means of definitions: complex spatial objects, for example, seem to me in some sense to be essentially things—I as it were see them as things.—And the designation of them by means of names seems to be more than a mere trick of language. Spatial complex objects—for example—really, so it seems, do appear as things.

But what does all that signify?

Schon, daß wir so ganz instinktiv jene Gegenstände durch Namen bezeichnen.——

14. 5. 15.

Die Sprache ist ein Teil unseres Organismus, und nicht weniger kompliziert als dieser. [*Vgl.* 4.002.]

Das alte Problem von Komplex und Tatsache.

15. 5. 15.

Die Komplex-Theorie drückt sich in Sätzen aus wie dieser: "Wenn ein Satz wahr ist, dann existiert Etwas"; es scheint ein Unterschied zu sein zwischen der Tatsache, welche der Satz ausdrückt: a steht in der Relation R zu b, und dem Komplex: *a in der Relation R zu b*, welcher eben dasjenige ist, welches "existiert", wenn jener Satz wahr ist. Es scheint, als könnten wir dieses Etwas *bezeichnen*, und zwar mit einem eigentlichen "zusammengesetzten Zeichen".—Die Gefühle, die sich in diesen Sätzen ausdrücken, sind ganz natürlich und ungekünstelt; es muß ihnen also eine Wahrheit zu Grunde liegen. Aber welche?

Was liegt an meinem Leben?

Soviel ist klar, daß ein Komplex nur durch seine Beschreibung gegeben sein kann; und diese stimmen oder nicht stimmen wird. [*S.* 3.24.]

Der Satz, in welchem von einem Komplex die Rede ist, wird, wenn dieser nicht existiert, nicht unsinnig sondern einfach falsch sein! [*S.* 3.24.]

16. 5. 15.

Wenn ich den Raum sehe, sehe ich alle seine Punkte?

Etwas "der Logik widersprechendes" in der Sprache darstellen kann man ebensowenig, wie in der Geometrie eine den Gesetzen des Raumes widersprechende Figur durch ihre Koordinaten darstellen, oder etwa die Koordinaten eines Punktes geben, welcher nicht existiert. [3.032.]

Gäbe es Sätze, welche die Existenz von Urbildern besagten, dann wären diese unik und eine Art "logische Sätze", und die Anzahl dieser Sätze würde der Logik eine unmögliche Realität geben. Es gäbe Koordination in der Logik.

18. 5. 15.

Die Möglichkeit aller Gleichnisse, der ganzen Bildhaftigkeit unserer Ausdrucksweise, ruht in der Logik der Abbildung. [4.015.]

At any rate that we quite instinctively designate those objects by means of names.——

14.5.15.

Language is a part of our organism, and no less complicated than it. [*Cf.* 4.002.]

The old problem of complex and fact!

15.5.15.

The theory of the complex is expressed in such propositions as: "If a proposition is true then Something exists"; there seems to be a difference between the fact expressed by the proposition: a stands in the relation R to b, and the complex: *a in the relation* R *to b*, which is just that which "exists" if that proposition is true. It seems as if we could *designate* this Something, and what's more with a real "complex sign".—The feelings expressed in these sentences are quite natural and unartificial, so there must be some truth at the bottom of them. But what truth?

What depends on my life?

So much is clear, that a complex can only be given by means of its description; and this description will hold or not hold. [*See* 3.24.]

The proposition dealing with a complex will not be nonsensical if the complex does not exist, but simply false. [*See* 3.24.]

16.5.15.

When I see space do I see all its points?

It is no more possible to present something "contradicting logic" in language than to present a figure contradicting the laws of space in geometry by means of its co-ordinates, or, say, to give the co-ordinates of a point that does not exist. [3.032.]

If there were propositions asserting the existence of proto-pictures they would be unique and would be a kind of "logical propositions" and the set of these propositions would give logic an impossible reality. There would be co-ordination in logic.

18.5.15.

The possibility of all similes, of the whole pictorial character of our language, is founded in the logic of portrayal. [4.015.]

19. 5. 15.

Wir können sogar einen in Bewegung begriffenen Körper, *und zwar mit seiner Bewegung zusammen*, als Ding auffassen. So bewegt sich der um die Erde sich drehende Mond um die Sonne. Hier scheint es nur klar, daß in dieser Verdinglichung nichts als eine logische Manipulation vorliegt—deren Möglichkeit übrigens höchst bedeutungsvoll sein mag.

Oder betrachten wir Verdinglichungen wie: eine Melodie, ein gesprochener Satz.—

Wenn ich sage "'x' hat Bedeutung", empfinde ich da: "es ist unmöglich, daß "x" etwa dieses Messer oder diesen Brief bedeute"? Durchaus nicht. Im Gegenteil.

20. 5. 15.

Ein Komplex ist eben ein Ding!

21. 5. 15.

Wohl können wir einen Tatbestand räumlich darstellen, welcher den Gesetzen der Physik, aber keinen, der den Gesetzen der Geometrie zuwiderliefe. [3.0321.]

22. 5. 15.

Die mathematische Notation der unendlichen Reihen, wie "$1 + \frac{x}{1!} + \frac{x^2}{2!} + \ldots$" *mit den Pünktchen* ist ein Beispiel jener erweiterten Allgemeinheit. Ein Gesetz ist gegeben und die hingeschriebenen Glieder dienen als Illustration.

So könnte man statt (x)fx schreiben "fx.fy ...".

Räumliche und *zeitliche* Komplexe.

23. 5. 15.

Die Grenzen meiner Sprache bedeuten die Grenzen meiner Welt. [5.6.]

Es gibt wirklich nur eine Weltseele, welche ich vorzüglich *meine* Seele nenne, und als welche allein ich das erfasse, was ich die Seelen anderer nenne.

Die vorige Bemerkung gibt den Schlüssel zur Entscheidung, inwieweit der Solipsismus eine Wahrheit ist. [*S.* 5.62.]

Schon lange war es mir bewußt, daß ich ein Buch schreiben könnte "Was für eine Welt ich vorfand". [*Vgl.* 5.631.]

Haben wir nicht eben das Gefühl von der Einfachen Relation, welches uns immer als Hauptgrund für die Annahme der "einfacher

19.5.15.

We can even conceive a body apprehended as in movement, *and together with its movement*, as a thing. So the moon circling round the earth moves round the sun. Now here it seems clear that this reification is nothing but a logical manipulation—though the possibility of this may be extremely significant.

Or let us consider reifications like: a tune, a spoken sentence.—

When I say "'x' has reference" do I have the feeling: "it is impossible that "x" should stand for, say, this knife or this letter"? Not at all. On the contrary.

20.5.15.

A complex just is a thing!

21.5.15.

We can quite well give a spatial representation of a set of circumstances which contradict the laws of physics, but not of one contradicting the laws of geometry. [3.0321.]

22.5.15.

The mathematical notation for infinite series like

$$\text{“}1 + \frac{x}{1!} + \frac{x^2}{2!} + \ldots\ldots\text{”}$$

together with the dots is an example of that extended generality. A law is given and the terms that are written down serve as an illustration.

In this way instead of (x)fx one might write "fx.fy . . . .".

Spatial and *temporal* complexes.

23.5.15.

The limits of my language mean the limits of my world. [5.6]

There really is only one world soul, which I for preference call *my* soul and as which alone I conceive what I call the souls of others.

The above remark gives the key for deciding the way in which solipsism is a truth. [*See* 5.62.]

I have long been conscious that it would be possible for me to write a book: "The world I found". [*Cf.* 5.631.]

The feeling of the simple relation which always comes before our mind as the main ground for the assumption of "simple objects"—

Gegenstände" vorschwebt, haben wir nicht dieses selbe Gefühl, wenn wir an die Relation zwischen Namen und komplexem Gegenstand denken?

Nehmen wir an, der komplexe Gegenstand sei dies Buch; es heiße "A". Dann zeigt doch das Vorkommen des "A" im Satz das Vorkommen des Buches in der Tatsache. *Es löst sich eben auch bei der Analyse nicht willkürlich auf, so daß etwa seine Auflösung in jedem Satzgefüge eine gänzlich verschiedene wäre.*——[*S.* 3.3442.]

Und so wie das Vorkommen eines Ding-Namens in verschiedenen Sätzen, so zeigt das Vorkommen des Namens zusammengesetzter Gegenstände die Gemeinsamkeit einer Form und eines Inhalts.

Trotzdem scheint nun der *unendlich* komplexe Sachverhalt ein Unding zu sein!

Aber auch das scheint sicher, daß wir die Existenz einfacher Gegenstände nicht aus der Existenz bestimmter einfacher Gegenstände schließen, sondern sie vielmehr als Endresultat einer Analyse—sozusagen durch die Beschreibung—durch einen zu ihnen führenden Prozeß, kennen.

Deswegen, weil eine Redewendung unsinnig ist, kann man sie noch immer gebrauchen—siehe die letzte Bemerkung.

In dem Buch "Die Welt, welche ich vorfand" wäre auch über meinen Leib zu berichten und zu sagen, welche Glieder meinem Willen unterstehen etc. Dies ist nämlich eine Methode, das Subjekt zu isolieren, oder vielmehr zu zeigen, daß es in einem wichtigen Sinne kein Subjekt gibt: von ihm allein nämlich könnte in diesem Buche *nicht* die Rede sein.—[*S.* 5.631.]

24. 5. 15.

Wenn wir auch die einfachen Gegenstände nicht aus der Anschauung kennen; die komplexen Gegenstände *kennen* wir aus der Anschauung, wir wissen aus der Anschauung, daß sie komplex sind.—Und daß sie zuletzt aus einfachen Dingen bestehen müssen?

Wir nehmen zum Beispiel aus unserem Gesichtsfeld einen Teil heraus, wir sehen, daß er noch immer komplex ist, daß ein Teil von ihm noch immer komplex aber schon einfacher ist, u.s.w.——

Ist es denkbar, daß wir—z. B.—*sehen*, daß *alle Punkte einer Fläche gelb sind*, ohne irgend *einen* Punkt dieser Fläche zu sehen? Fast scheint es so.

Die Entstehung der Probleme: die drückende Spannung, die sich einmal in eine Frage zusammenballt, und sich objektiviert.

haven't we got this very same feeling when we think of the relation between name and complex object?

Suppose the complex object is this book. Let it be called "A". Then surely the occurrence of "A" in the proposition shews the occurrence of the book in the fact. *For it is not arbitrarily resolved even when it is analysed, so as, e.g., to make its resolution a completely different one in each propositional formation.*——[*See* 3.3442.]

And like the occurrence of the name of a thing in different propositions, the occurrence of the name of compounded objects shews that there is a form and a content in common.

In spite of this the *infinitely* complex situation seems to be a chimera.

But it also seems certain that we do not infer the existence of simple objects from the existence of particular simple objects, but rather know them—by description, as it were—as the end-product of analysis, by means of a process that leads to them.

For the very reason, that a bit of language is nonsensical, it is still possible to go on using it—see the last remark.

In the book "The world I found" I should also have to report on my body and say which members are subject to my will, etc. For this is a way of isolating the subject, or rather of shewing that in an important sense there is no such thing as the subject; for it would be the one thing that could *not* come into this book. [*See* 5.631.]

24.5.15.

Even though we have no acquaintance with simple objects we *do* know complex objects by acquaintance, we know by acquaintance that they are complex.—And that in the end they must consist of simple things?

We single out a part of our visual field, for example, and we see that it is always complex, that any part of it is still complex but is already simpler, and so on——.

Is it imaginable that—e.g.—we should *see* that *all the points of a surface are yellow*, without seeing any *single* point of this surface? It almost seems to be so.

The way problems arise: the pressure of a tension which then concentrates into a question, and becomes objective.

Wie würden wir, z. B., eine gleichmäßig mit Blau bedeckte Fläche beschreiben?

25. 5. 15.

Erscheint uns das Gesichtsbild eines minimum visibile wirklich als unteilbar? Was Ausdehnung hat, ist teilbar. Gibt es Teile in unserem Gesichtsbild, die *keine* Ausdehnung haben? Etwa die der Fixsterne?——

Der Trieb zum Mystischen kommt von der Unbefriedigtheit unserer Wünsche durch die Wissenschaft. Wir *fühlen*, daß selbst wenn alle *möglichen* wissenschaftlichen Fragen beantwortet sind, *unser Problem noch gar nicht berührt ist.* Freilich bleibt dann eben keine Frage mehr; und eben dies ist die Antwort. [*Vgl.* 6.52.]

Die Tautologie wird von *jedem* Satz bejaht; die Kontradiktion von jedem verneint. (Man könnte ja an jeden Satz, ohne seinen Sinn zu ändern, irgend eine Tautologie mit "und" anhängen und ebenso die Verneinung einer Kontradiktion.)

Und "ohne seinen Sinn zu ändern" heißt: ohne das *Wesentliche* am Zeichen selbst zu ändern. Denn; man kann das *Zeichen* nicht ändern, ohne seinen Sinn zu ändern. [*Vgl.* 4.465.]

"aRa" *muß* Sinn haben, wenn "aRb" Sinn hat.

26. 5. 15.

Wie aber soll ich jetzt das allgemeine Wesen des *Satzes* erklären? Wir können wohl sagen: alles, was der Fall ist (oder nicht ist), kann durch einen Satz abgebildet werden. Aber hier haben wir den Ausdruck "*der Fall sein*"! Er ist ebenso problematisch.

Das Gegenstück zum Satze bilden die Gegenstände.

Die Gegenstände kann ich nur *nennen.* Zeichen vertreten sie. [*S.* 3.221.]

27. 5. 15.

Ich kann nur *von* ihnen sprechen, sie aussprechen kann ich nicht. [*S.* 3.221.]

"Aber könnte es nicht etwas geben, was durch einen *Satz* sich nicht ausdrücken läßt (und auch kein Gegenstand ist)?" Das ließe sich eben dann durch die *Sprache* nicht ausdrücken; und wir können auch nicht darnach *fragen.*

Wie, wenn es etwas außerhalb den *Tatsachen* gibt? Was unsere Sätze nicht auszudrücken vermögen? Aber da haben wir ja z. B. die *Dinge*, *und wir fühlen gar kein Verlangen*, sie in Sätzen auszudrücken.

How should we describe, e.g., a surface uniformly covered with blue?

25.5.15.

Does the visual image of a *minimum visibile* actually appear to us as indivisible? What has extension is divisible. Are there parts in our visual image that have no extension? E.g., the images of the fixed stars?——

The urge towards the mystical comes of the non-satisfaction of our wishes by science. We *feel* that even if all *possible* scientific questions are answered *our problem is still not touched at all*. Of course in that case there are no questions any more; and that is the answer. [*Cf.* 6.52.]

The tautology is asserted, the contradiction denied, by *every* proposition. (For one could append 'and' and some tautology to any proposition without altering its sense; and equally the negation of a contradiction.)

And "without altering its sense" means: without altering the *essential* thing about the sign itself. For: the *sign* cannot be altered without altering its sense. [*Cf.* 4.465.]

"aRa" *must* make sense if "aRb" makes sense.

26.5.15.

But how am I to explain the general nature of the *proposition* now? We can indeed say: everything that is (or is not) the case can be pictured by means of a proposition. But here we have the expression "*to be the case*"! It is just as problematic.

Objects form the counterpart to the proposition.

Objects I can only *name*. Signs go proxy for them. [*See* 3.221.]

27.5.15.

I can only speak *of* them, I cannot express them. [*See* 3.221.]

"But might there not be something which cannot be expressed by a *proposition* (and which is also not an object)?" In that case this could not be expressed by means of *language*; and it is also impossible for us to *ask* about it.

Suppose there is something outside the *facts*? Which our propositions are impotent to express? But here we do have, e.g., *things and we feel no demand at all* to express them in propositions.

Was sich nicht ausdrücken läßt, das drücken wir nicht aus——. Und wie wollen wir *fragen*, ob sich DAS ausdrücken läßt, was sich nicht AUSDRÜCKEN läßt?

Gibt es kein Bereich außerhalb den Tatsachen?

28. 5. 15.

"Zusammengesetztes Zeichen" und "Satz" sind *gleichbedeutend.*

Ist es eine Tautologie zu sagen: die *Sprache* besteht aus *Sätzen?*
Es scheint, *ja.*

29. 5. 15.

Aber ist die *Sprache*, die *einzige* Sprache?
Warum soll es nicht eine Ausdrucksweise geben, mit der ich *über* die Sprache reden kann, so daß diese mir in Koordination mit etwas Anderem erscheinen kann?

Nehmen wir an, die Musik wäre eine solche Ausdrucksweise: Dann ist jedenfalls charakteristisch für die *Wissenschaft*, daß in ihr *keine* musikalischen Themen vorkommen.

Ich selbst schreibe hier nur Sätze hin. Und warum?

Wie ist die Sprache unik?

30. 5. 15.

Die Worte sind wie die Haut auf einem tiefen Wasser.

Es ist klar, daß es auf dasselbe hinauskommt zu fragen, was ist ein Satz, wie zu fragen, was ist eine Tatsache—oder ein Komplex.

Und warum soll man nicht sagen: "Es gibt Komplexe; man kann sie mit Namen benennen oder durch Sätze abbilden"?

Der Name eines Komplexes fungiert im Satz wie der Name eines Gegenstandes, welchen ich nur durch eine *Beschreibung* kenne.—— Als Beschreibung fungiert der ihn abbildende Satz.

Aber wenn es nun einfache Gegenstände gibt, ist es richtig, ihre Zeichen, und jene anderen "Namen" zu nennen?

Oder ist Name sozusagen ein *logischer* Begriff?
"Er kennzeichnet die Gemeinsamkeit einer Form und eines Inhalts".——
Je nach der Verschiedenheit der Struktur des Komplexes bezeichnet sein Name in anderer Art und Weise und unterliegt anderen syntaktischen Gesetzen.

What cannot be expressed we do not express——. And how try to *ask* whether THAT can be expressed which cannot be EXPRESSED?

Is there no domain outside the facts?

28.5.15.

"Complex sign" and "proposition" are *equivalent*.

Is it a tautology to say: *Language* consists of *sentences*?
It seems it *is*.

29.5.15.

But is *language*: the *only* language?
Why should there not be a mode of expression through which I can talk *about* language in such a way that it can appear to me in co-ordination with something else?

Suppose that music were such a mode of expression: then it is at any rate characteristic of *science* that *no* musical themes can occur in it.

I myself only write *sentences* down here. And why?

How is language unique?

30.5.15.

Words are like the film on deep water.

It is clear that it comes to the same thing to ask what a sentence is, and to ask what a fact is—or a complex.

And why should we not say: "There are complexes; one can use names to name them, or propositions to portray them"?

The name of a complex functions in the proposition like the name of an object that I only know by *description*.——The proposition that depicts it functions as a description.

But if there are simple objects, is it correct to call both the signs for them and those other signs "names"?

Or is "name" so to speak a *logical* concept?
"It signalises what is common to a form and a content."——
According to the difference in the structure of the complex its name denotes in a different way and is subject to different syntactical laws.

Der Fehler in dieser Auffassung muß darin liegen, daß sie einerseits komplexe und einfache Gegenstände einander entgegenstellt, andererseits aber sie als verwandt behandelt.

Und doch: *Bestandteile* und *Komplex* scheinen einander verwandt *und* entgegengesetzt zu sein!

(Wie der Plan einer Stadt und die Karte eines Landes, die vor uns in gleicher Größe, und verschiedenen Maßstäben liegen.)

Woher dies Gefühl: "Allem, was ich sehe, dieser Landschaft, dem Fliegen der Samen in der Luft, all diesem kann ich einen Namen zuordnen; ja, was, wenn nicht dieses, sollten wir Namen benennen"?!

Namen kennzeichnen die Gemeinsamkeit *einer* Form und *eines* Inhalts.——Sie kennzeichnen erst *mit* ihrer syntaktischen Verwendung zusammen *eine bestimmte* logische Form. [*Vgl.* 3.327.]

31. 5. 15.

Mit der Weltbeschreibung durch Namen kann man nicht mehr leisten als mit der allgemeinen Weltbeschreibung!!!

Könnte man also ohne Namen auskommen?? Doch wohl nicht.

Die Namen sind notwendig zu einer Aussage, daß *dieses* Ding *jene* Eigenschaft besitzt u.s.f.

Sie verknüpfen die Satzform mit ganz bestimmten Gegenständen.

Und wenn die allgemeine Weltbeschreibung wie eine Schablone der Welt ist, so nageln sie die Namen so an die Welt, daß sie sich überall mit ihr deckt.

1. 6. 15.

Das große Problem, um welches sich alles dreht, was ich schreibe, ist: Ist, a priori, eine Ordnung in der Welt, und wenn ja, worin besteht sie?

Du siehst in die Nebelwolke und kannst dir daher einreden, das Ziel sei schon nahe. Aber der Nebel zerrinnt, und das Ziel ist noch nicht in Sicht!

2. 6. 15.

Ich sagte: "Eine Tautologie wird von *jedem* Satze bejaht"; damit ist aber noch nicht gesagt, warum sie kein *Satz* ist. Ist denn damit schon gesagt, *warum* ein Satz nicht von p *und* von ~p bejaht werden kann?!

Meine Theorie bringt nämlich eigentlich nicht heraus, daß der Satz zwei Pole haben *muß*.

The mistake in this conception must lie in its, on the one hand, contrasting complexes and simple objects, while on the other hand it treats them as akin.

And yet: *Components* and *complex* seem to be akin, *and* to be opposed to one another.

(Like the plan of a town and the map of a country which we have before us, the same size and on different scales.)

What is the source of the feeling "I can correlate a name with all that I see, with this landscape, with the dance of motes in the air, with all this; indeed, what should we call a name if not this"?!

Names signalise what is common to a single form and a single content.——Only *together with* their syntactical use do they signalise *one particular* logical form. [*Cf.* 3.327.]

31.5.15.

One cannot achieve any more by using names in describing the world than by means of the general description of the world!!!

Could one then manage without names? Surely not.

Names are necessary for an assertion that *this* thing possesses *that* property and so on.

They link the propositional form with quite definite objects.

And if the general description of the world is like a stencil of the world, the names pin it to the world so that the world is wholly covered by it.

1.6.15.

The great problem round which everything that I write turns is: Is there an order in the world *a priori*, and if so what does it consist in?

You are looking into fog and for that reason persuade yourself that the goal is already close. But the fog disperses and the goal is not yet in sight.

2.6.15.

I said: "A tautology is asserted by every proposition"; but that is not enough to tell us why it is not a *proposition*. For has it told us *why* a proposition cannot be asserted by p *and* $\sim$ p?

For my theory does not really bring it out that the proposition *must* have two poles.

Ich müßte nämlich jetzt in der Redeweise dieser Theorie einen Ausdruck dafür finden, WIEVIEL *ein Satz sagt*. Und es müßte sich dann eben ergeben, daß Tautologien NICHTS sagen.

Aber wie ist dies Maß Vielsagendheit zu finden?

Es ist jedenfalls vorhanden; und unsere Theorie *muß* es zum Ausdruck bringen können.

3. 6. 15.

Man könnte wohl sagen: *Der* Satz sagt am meisten, aus welchem am meisten folgt.

Könnte man sagen: "aus welchem die meisten, von einander unabhängigen Sätze folgen"?

Aber geht es nicht so: Wenn p aus q folgt, aber nicht q aus p, dann sagt q mehr als p?

Nun aber folgt aus einer Tautologie gar nichts.——Sie aber folgt aus jedem Satz. [*Vgl.* 5.142.]

Analoges gilt von ihrem Gegenteil.

Aber wie! Wäre da die Kontradiktion nicht der vielsagendste Satz? Aus "p. ~p" folgt ja nicht nur "p" sondern auch "~p"! Aus ihnen folgt jeder Satz und sie folgen aus keinem!? Aber ich kann doch aus einer Kontradiktion nichts schließen, eben *weil* sie eine Kontradiktion ist!

Aber wenn die Kontradiktion die Klasse *aller Sätze* ist, so wird die Tautologie das Gemeinsame aller Klassen von Sätzen, welche nichts Gemeinsames haben, und verschwindet gänzlich. [*Vgl.* 5.143.]

"pv~p" wäre also nur scheinbar ein Zeichen. In Wirklichkeit aber die Auflösung des Satzes.

Die Tautologie verschwindet sozusagen innerhalb aller Sätze, die Kontradiktion außerhalb aller Sätze. [*S.* 5.143.]

Bei diesen Betrachtungen scheine ich übrigens immer unbewußt vom Elementarsatz auszugehen.——

Die Kontradiktion ist die äußere Grenze der Sätze; kein Satz bejaht sie. Die Tautologie ist ihr substanzloser Mittelpunkt. (Man kann den Mittelpunkt einer Kreisfläche als deren innere Begrenzung auffassen.) [*Vgl.* 5.143.]

(Das erlösende Wort ist übrigens hier noch nicht gesprochen.)

For what I should now have to do is to find an expression in the language of this theory for HOW MUCH *a proposition says*. And this would have to yield the result that tautologies say NOTHING.

But how can we find the measure of amount-that-is-said?

At any rate it is there; and our theory *must* be able to give it expression.

3.6.15.

One could certainly say: *That* proposition says the most from which the most follows.

Could one say: "From which the most mutually independent propositions follow"?

But doesn't it work like this: If p follows from q but not q from p, then q says more than p?

But now nothing at all follows from a tautology.——It however follows from every proposition. [*Cf.* 5.142.]

The analogous thing holds of its opposite.

But then! Won't contradiction now be the proposition that says the most? From "p.∼p" there follows not merely "p" but also "∼p"! Every proposition follows from them and they follow from none!? But I surely can't infer anything from a contradiction, just *because* it is a contradiction.

But if contradiction is the class of *all propositions*, then tautology becomes what is common to any classes of propositions that have nothing in common and vanishes completely. [*Cf.* 5.143.]

"pv∼p" would then be a sign only in appearance. But in reality the dissolution of the proposition.

The tautology as it were vanishes inside all propositions, the contradiction outside all propositions. [*See* 5.143.]

In these investigations I always seem to be unconsciously taking the elementary proposition as my starting point.——

Contradiction is the outer limit of propositions; no proposition asserts it. Tautology is their substanceless centre. (The middle point of a circle can be conceived as its inner boundary.) [*Cf.* 5.143.]

(The key word still hasn't yet been spoken.)

Es ist hier nämlich sehr leicht, die logische Addition und das logische Produkt miteinander zu verwechseln.

Wir kommen nämlich zu dem scheinbar merkwürdigen Resultat, daß zwei Sätze etwas gemeinsam haben müssen, um von einem Satz bejaht werden zu können.

(Die Gehörigkeit zu *einer* Klasse ist aber auch etwas, was Sätze *gemeinsam* haben können!)

(Hier liegt noch eine entschiedene und entscheidende Unklarheit in meiner Theorie. Daher ein gewisses Gefühl der Unbefriedigung!)

4. 6. 15.

"p.q" hat nur dann Sinn, wenn "pvq" Sinn hat.

5. 6. 15.

"p.q" bejaht "p" und "q". Das heißt aber doch nicht, daß "p.q" der gemeinsame Bestandteil von "p" und "q" ist, sondern im Gegenteil, daß sowohl "p" als auch "q" in "p.q" enthalten sind.

In diesem Sinne hätten p und ~p sogar etwas gemein, zum Beispiel Sätze wie ~pvq und pvq. Das heißt: es gibt allerdings Sätze welche sowohl von "p" als auch von "~p" bejaht werden—z.ß. die obigen—es gibt aber keine, die sowohl p als auch ~p bejahen.

Damit ein Satz wahr sein kann, muß er auch falsch sein können.

Warum sagt die Tautologie nichts? Weil in ihr von vornherein jede Möglichkeit zugegeben wird; weil . . .

Es muß sich *im Satz selbst* zeigen, daß er *etwas* sagt und an der Tautologie, daß sie nichts sagt.

p . ~p ist dasjenige—etwa *das Nichts*—welches p und ~p gemeinsam haben.

In dem *eigentlichen* Zeichen für p liegt wirklich schon das Zeichen "pvq". (Denn es ist dann möglich, dies Zeichen OHNE WEITERES zu bilden.)

6. 6. 15.

(Diese Theorie behandelt die Sätze exklusiv, sozusagen als eine eigene Welt und nicht in Verbindung mit dem, was sie darstellen.)

Die Verbindung der Bild-Theorie mit der Klassen-Theorie[1] wird erst später ganz einleuchtend werden.

Man kann von einer Tautologie nicht sagen, daß sie wahr ist, denn sie ist *wahr gemacht*.

[1] Die Theorie des Satzes als Klasse. (Herausg.)

The thing is that here it is very easy to confuse the logical product and the logical sum.

For we come to the apparently remarkable result that two propositions must have something in common in order to be capable of being asserted by one proposition.

(Belonging to a single class, however, is also something that propositions can have in *common.*)

(Here there is still a definite and decisive lack of clarity in my theory. Hence a certain feeling of dissatisfaction!)

4.6.15.

"p.q" only makes sense if "pvq" makes sense.

5.6.15.

"p.q" asserts "p" and "q" but that surely does not mean that "p.q" is the common component of "p" and "q", but on the contrary that "p" and also "q" are equally contained in "p.q".

In this sense p and ~p would have something in common, for example propositions like ~pvq and pvq. That is: there are indeed propositions which are asserted by "p" as well as by "~p"—e.g. the above ones—but there are none that assert p as well as also asserting ~p.

In order for a proposition to be capable of being true it must also be capable of being false.

Why does tautology say nothing? Because every possibility is admitted in it in advance; because . . . . .

It must shew *in the proposition itself* that it says *something* and in the tautology that it says nothing.

p.~p is that thing—perhaps *that nothing*—that p and ~p have in common.

In the *real* sign for p there is already contained the sign "pvq". (For it is then possible to form this sign WITHOUT FURTHER ADO.)

6.6.15.

(This theory treats of propositions exclusively, so to speak, as a world on their own and not in connexion with what they present.)

The connexion of the picture-theory with the class-theory[1] will only become quite obvious later.

One cannot say of a tautology that it is true, for it is *made so as to be true.*

[1] I.e. the theory of a proposition as a class. (*Edd.*)

Sie ist kein Bild der Wirklichkeit insofern als sie nichts DARSTELLT. Sie ist das, was alle *Bilder*—einander widersprechende—gemeinsam haben.

In der Klassen-Theorie ist noch nicht ersichtlich, warum der Satz seinen Gegensatz *bedarf*. Warum er ein von dem übrigen Teil des logischen Raumes *abgetrennter* Teil ist.

Der Satz sagt, es ist: *so*, und nicht: *so*. Er stellt eine Möglichkeit dar und bildet doch schon *ersichtlich* den Teil eines Ganzen—dessen Züge er trägt—und von welchem er sich abhebt.

pvqv ~p ist auch eine Tautologie.——

Es gibt wohl Sätze, die sowohl p als auch ~p *zulassen*, aber *keinen*, den sowohl p als auch ~p *bejaht*.

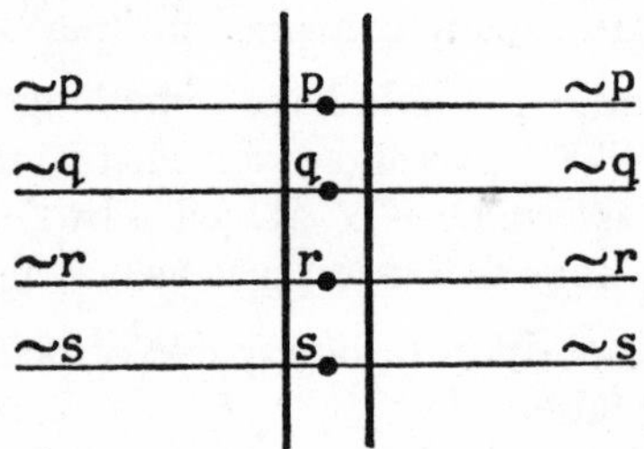

Die Möglichkeit von "pvq", wenn "p" gegeben ist, ist eine Möglichkeit nach einer anderen Dimension als die Unmöglichkeit von "~p".

"pv ~p" ist ein GANZ SPEZIELLER FALL von "pvq".

"p" hat nichts mit "~pvq" gemein.

Dadurch daß ich an "p" das "~" hänge, tritt der Satz in eine andere Satzklasse.

Jeder Satz hat nur ein Negativ; . . . Es gibt nur einen Satz der ganz außerhalb von "p" liegt. [*Vgl.* 5.513.]

Man könnte auch so sagen: Der Satz, welcher p und ~p bejaht, wird von allen Sätzen verneint; der Satz, welcher p oder ~p bejaht, wird von allen Sätzen bejaht.

Mein Fehler muß darin liegen, daß ich dasjenige, was aus dem Wesen der Verneinung u. a. folgt, zu ihrer Definition gebrauchen

It is not a picture of reality, in the sense that it does not PRESENT anything; it is what all—mutually contradictory—*pictures* have in common.

In the class-theory it is not yet evident why the proposition needs its counter-proposition. Why it is a part of logical space which is *separated* from the remaining part of logical space.

The proposition says: *this* is how it is and not: *that.* It presents a possibility and itself *conspicuously* forms one part of a whole,—whose features it bears—and from which it stands out.

pvqv~p is also a tautology.——

There are certainly propositions that *allow* p as well as ~p but *none* that *assert* p as well as ~p.

~p	p	~p
~q	q	~q
~r	r	~r
~s	s	~s

The possibility of "pvq" when "p" is given, is a possibility in a different dimension from the impossibility of "~p".

"pv~p" is A QUITE SPECIAL CASE of "pvq".

"p" has nothing in common with "~pvq".

By my attaching the "~" to "p" the proposition gets into a different class of propositions.

Every proposition has only one negative; . . . There is only one proposition lying quite outside "p". [*Cf.* 5.513.]

It could also be said: The proposition which asserts p and ~p is negated by all propositions; the proposition which asserts p or ~p is asserted by all propositions.

My mistake must lie in my wanting to use what follows from the nature of negation, etc. in its definition.——That "p" and "~p" have

will.——Die Gemeinsamkeit der Grenze von "p" und "~p" kommt in der von mir versuchten Erklärung der Verneinung gar nicht vor.

7. 6. 15.

Wenn man z. B. sagen könnte: alle Sätze, die p nicht bejahen, bejahen ~p, so hätte man damit eine genügende Beschreibung.—Aber so geht es nicht.

Kann man aber nicht sagen "~p" ist dasjenige, was nur solche Sätze gemeinsam haben, welche "p" nicht bejahen?——Und hieraus folgt ja schon die Unmöglichkeit von "p. ~p".
(All dies setzt natürlich schon die Existenz der gesammten *Satzwelt* voraus. Mit Recht?)

Es GENÜGT NICHT, darauf hinzuweisen, daß ~p außerhalb p liegt! Nur dann wird man alle Eigenschaften von "~p" ableiten können, wenn "~p" *wesentlich als das Negativ von p* eingeführt wird!!
Aber wie das tun!?—

Oder verhält es sich so, daß wir den Satz ~p überhaupt nicht "einführen" können, sondern, er tritt uns als vollendete Tatsache entgegen, und wir können nur auf seine einzelnen formellen Eigenschaften hinweisen, wie z. B., daß er nichts mit p gemeinsam hat, daß kein Satz ihn und p enthält etc. etc..?

8. 6. 15.

Jeder "mathematische Satz" ist ein in Zeichen dargestellter Modus ponens. (Und es ist klar, daß man den Modus ponens nicht in einem Satz ausdrücken kann.) [*Vgl.* 6.1264.]

Die Gemeinsamkeit der Grenze von p und ~p drückt sich dadurch aus, daß das Negativ eines Satzes nur mit Hilfe eben dieses bestimmt wird. Wir sagen ja eben: das Negativ eines Satzes ist der Satz, welcher ... und nun folgt die Beziehung von ~p zu p.——

9. 6. 15.

Man könnte natürlich einfach so sagen: Die Verneinung von p ist der Satz, welcher keinen Satz mit p gemeinsam hat.

Der Ausdruck "tertium non datur" ist eigentlich ein Unsinn. (Von einem Dritten ist eben in p v ~p nicht die Rede!)

Sollten wir das nicht auf unsere Erklärung des Negativs eines Satzes anwenden können?

Können wir nicht sagen: Unter allen Sätzen, welche nur von p abhängig sind, gibt es nur solche welche p bejahen und solche, welche es verneinen.

a common boundary is no part of the explanation of negation that I am trying for.

7.6.15.

If, e.g., it could be said: All propositions that do not assert p assert ~p, then that would give us an adequate description.—But that doesn't work.

But can't we say that "~p" is what is common only to such propositions as do not assert "p"?——And from this there already follows the impossibility of "p.~p".

(All this, of course, already presupposes the existence of the whole *world of propositions*. Rightly?)

IT IS NOT ENOUGH to point to ~p's lying outside p. It will only be possible to derive all the properties of "~p" if "~p" is introduced *essentially as the negative of p*.

But how to do that?—

Or is it like this: We cannot "introduce" the proposition ~p at all, but we encounter it as a *fait accompli* and we can only point to its individual formal properties, as, e.g., that it has nothing in common with p, that no proposition contains it and p, etc. etc.?

8.6.15.

Every mathematical proposition is a symbolic representation of a *modus ponens*. (And it is clear that the *modus ponens* cannot be expressed in a proposition.) [*Cf.* 6.1264.]

p and ~p have a common boundary: this is expressed by the fact that the negative of a proposition is only determined by means of the proposition itself. For we say: The negative of a proposition is a proposition which . . . and now follows the relation of ~p to p.——

9.6.15.

It will, of course, be possible simply to say: The negation of p is the proposition which has no proposition in common with p.

The expression "tertium non datur" is really a piece of nonsense. (For no third thing is in question in pv~p.)

Should we not be able to use this for our definition of the negative of a proposition?

Can't we say: Among all the propositions that are dependent on p alone, there are only such as assert p and such as deny it?

Ich kann also sagen, das Negativ von p ist die Klasse aller Sätze, welche nur von "p" abhängig sind und "*p*" *nicht bejahen.*

10. 6. 15.

"*p.qv∼q*" *ist von* "*q*" NICHT *abhängig*!!

Ganze Sätze, verschwinden!

Schon das, daß "p.qv∼q" von "q" unabhängig ist, obwohl es das Schriftzeichen "q" offenbar enthält, zeigt uns, wie Zeichen von der Form ηv∼η scheinbar, aber doch nur *scheinbar* existieren können.

Dies kommt natürlich daher, daß diese Zusammenstellung "pv ∼p' zwar äußerlich möglich ist, aber nicht den Bedingungen genügt unter welchen ein solcher Komplex *etwas sagt*, also ein Satz ist.

"p.qv∼q" sagt dasselbe wie
"p.rv∼r"
was immer q und r besagen mag: Alle Tautologien besagen dasselbe. (Nämlich nichts.) [*Vgl.* 5.43.]

Aus der letzten Erklärung der Verneinung folgt, daß alle von p allein abhängigen Sätze, welche p nicht bejahen—und nur solche—p verneinen. Also sind "pv∼p" und "p.∼p" keine Sätze, denn das erste Zeichen bejaht weder noch verneint es p, und das zweite müßte beide bejahen.

Da ich nun aber doch pv∼p und p.∼p hinschreiben kann, zumal in Verbindung mit anderen Sätzen, so muß klar gestellt werden, welche Rolle diese Scheinsätze nun, besonders in jenen Verbindungen, spielen. Denn sie sind natürlich nicht als ein völlig bedeutungsloses Anhängsel—wie etwa ein bedeutungsloser Name—zu behandeln. Sie gehören vielmehr mit in den Symbolismus—wie die "0" in der Arithmetik. [*Vgl.* 4.4611.]

Da ist es klar, daß p v ∼p die Rolle eines wahren Satzes spielt, der aber *zero* sagt.

Wir sind also wieder bei der Quantität des Sagens.

11. 6. 15.

Aus allen Sätzen folgt das Gegenteil von "p. ∼p", heißt das soviel, daß "p. ∼p" nichts sagt?—Nach meiner früheren Regel müßte die Kontradiktion ja mehr sagen als alle anderen Sätze.

Kontradiktion |————0————| Tautologie

Satz

Wenn ein vielsagender Satz auch falsch ist, so sollte eben das

So I can say that the negative of p is the class of all propositions which are dependent on "p" alone and *do not assert "p"*.

10.6.15.

"p.qv~q" is NOT *dependent on "q"*!

Whole propositions, to disappear!

The very fact that "p.qv~q" is independent of "q", although it obviously contains the written sign "q", shews us how signs of the form ηv~η can apparently, but still only *apparently*, exist.

This naturally arises from the fact that this arrangement "pv~p" is indeed externally possible, but does not satisfy the conditions for such a complex to *say something* and so be a proposition.

"p.qv~q" says the same as
"p.rv~r"
—whatever q and r may say—: All tautologies say the same thing. (Namely nothing.) [*Cf.* 5.43.]

From the last explanation of negation it follows that all propositions which are dependent on p alone and which do not assert p—and only these—negate p. So "pv~p" and "p . ~p" are not propositions, for the first sign neither asserts nor denies p and the second would have to affirm both.

But since I can after all write down pv~p and p.~p, particularly in connexion with other sentences, it must be clearly set forth what role these pseudo-propositions have, especially in such connexions. For they are not, of course, to be treated as a completely meaningless appendix—like e.g. a meaningless name. Rather do they belong in the symbolism—like "o" in arithmetic. [*Cf.* 4.4611.]

Here it is clear that pv~p has the role of a true proposition, which however says *nought*.

So we have again arrived at the quantity of what is said.

11.6.15.

The opposite of "p.~p" follows from all propositions; is that as much as to say that "p.~p" says nothing?—By my earlier rule the contradiction would have to say more than all other propositions.

Contradiction |———————o———————| Tautology

Proposition

If a proposition saying a great deal is false, it ought to be interesting

interessant sein, daß er falsch ist. Es ist befremdend, daß das Negativ eines vielsagenden Satzes gänzlich nichtssagend sein soll.

Wir sagten: Wenn p aus q folgt aber nicht q aus p, so sagt q mehr als p. Wenn nun aber aus p folgt, daß q falsch ist, nicht aber aus q, daß p falsch ist, was dann?

Aus p folgt ~q, aus q nicht ~p.——?

12. 6. 15.

Man könnte eigentlich bei jedem Satz fragen: Was hat es zu bedeuten, wenn er wahr ist, was hat es zu bedeuten, wenn er falsch ist?

Nun ist p. ~p seiner Annahme nach immer nur falsch, und dies hat also nichts zu bedeuten; und wieviel es bedeutet, wenn er wahr ist, kann man ja gar nicht fragen.

13. 6. 15.

Wenn "p. ~p" wahr sein KÖNNTE, so würde es allerdings *sehr* viel besagen. Aber *die Annahme*, daß es wahr ist, kommt eben bei ihm nicht in Betracht, da es seiner Annahme nach immer falsch ist.

Eigentümlich: Die Wörter "Wahr" und "Falsch" beziehen sich auf die Beziehung des Satzes zur Welt; daß diese Wörter in ihm selbst zur Darstellung verwendet werden können!

Wir sagten: Wenn ein Satz nur von p abhängig ist, und wenn er p bejaht, dann verneint er es nicht, und umgekehrt: *Ist dies das Bild jener gegenseitigen Ausschließung von p und ~p?* Der Tatsache, daß ~p *das* ist, was *außerhalb* p liegt?

Es scheint doch so! Der Satz "~p" ist in demselben Sinne das, was außerhalb "p" liegt.——(Vergiß auch nicht, daß das Bild sehr komplizierte Koordinaten zur Welt haben kann.)

Man könnte übrigens einfach sagen: "p. ~p" sagt im eigentlichen Sinne des Wortes nichts. Weil im vornherein keine Möglichkeit gelassen ist, die er *richtig* darstellen kann.

Wenn, beiläufig gesprochen, "p folgt aus q" heißt, wenn q wahr ist, so muß p wahr sein, dann kann man überhaupt nicht sagen, daß irgend etwas aus "p. ~p" folgt, da es die Hypothese, daß "p. ~p" wahr sei, nicht gibt!!

14. 6. 15.

Wir sind uns also darüber klar geworden, daß Namen für die verschiedensten Formen stehen, und stehen dürfen, und daß nun erst die syntaktische Anwendung die darzustellende Form charakterisiert.

Was ist nun die syntaktische Anwendung von Namen einfacher Gegenstände?

Was ist mein Grundgedanke, wenn ich von den einfachen Gegenständen rede? Genügen nicht am Ende die 'zusammengesetzten Gegen-

that it is false. It is astonishing that the negative of a proposition that says a great deal should say absolutely nothing.

We said: If p follows from q but not q from p, q says more than p. But now, if it follows from p that q is false, but not from q that p is false, what then?

From p there follows ~q, from q not ~p.——?

12.6.15.

In connexion with any proposition it could really be asked: what does it come to for it to be true? What does it come to for it to be false?

Now the 'assumption' in p.~p is never anything but false, and so *this* does not come to anything; and as for what it would amount to if it were true. of course, that can't be asked at all.

13.6.15.

If "p.~p" COULD be true it would indeed say a *very* great deal. But the *assumption* that it is true does not come into consideration in connexion with it, as the 'assumption' in it is always false.

Singular, since the words "true" and "false" refer to the relation of the proposition to the world, that these words can be used in the proposition itself for purposes of representation!

We have said: if a proposition depends only on p and it asserts p then it does not negate it, and vice versa: *Is this the picture of that mutual exclusion of p and ~p?* Of the fact that ~p is *what* lies *outside* p?

It seems so! The proposition "~p" is in the same sense what lies outside "p".——(Do not forget either that the picture may have very complicated co-ordinates to the world.)

One might simply say: "p.~p" says nothing in the proper sense of the word. For in advance there is no possibility left which it can *correctly* present.

Incidentally, if "p follows from q" means: If q is true then p must be true, then it cannot be said at all that anything follows from "p.~p", since there is no such thing as the hypothesis that "p.~p" is true.

14.6.15.

We have become clear, then, that names may and do stand for the most various forms, and that it is only the syntactical application that signalises the form that is to be presented.

Now what is the syntactical application of names of simple objects?

What is my fundamental thought when I talk about simple objects? Do not 'complex objects' in the end satisfy just the demands which I

stände' gerade den Anforderungen, die ich scheinbar an jene stelle? Gebe ich diesem Buch einen Namen "N" und rede nun von N, ist nicht das Verhältnis von N zu jenem 'zusammengesetzten Gegenstand', zu jenen Formen und Inhalten *wesentlich* dasselbe, welches ich mir zwischen Namen und einfachem Gegenstand dachte?

Denn wohlgemerkt: wenn auch der Name "N" bei weiterer Analyse verschwindet, so deutet er doch *Ein Gemeinsames* an.

Wie steht es aber mit der Bedeutung der Namen außerhalb des Satzzusammenhanges?

Man könnte aber die Frage auch so vorbringen: Es scheint, daß die Idee des EINFACHEN in der des Komplexen und in der Idee der Analyse bereits enthalten liegt, so zwar, daß wir ganz absehend von irgendwelchen Beispielen einfacher Gegenstände oder von Sätzen, in welchen von solchen die Rede ist, zu dieser Idee kommen und die Existenz der einfachen Gegenstände als eine logische Notwendigkeit—a priori—einsehen.

Es hat also den Anschein, daß sich die Existenz der einfachen Gegenstände zu der der komplexen so verhält, wie der Sinn von ~p zum Sinn von p: Der *einfache* Gegenstand sei im komplexen *präjudiziert*.

15. 6. 15.

(Dies ist JA nicht zu verwechseln mit der *Tatsache*, daß der *Bestandteil* im Komplex präjudiziert ist.)

(Eine der schwersten Aufgaben des Philosophen ist es zu finden, wo ihn der Schuh druckt.)

Es ist ganz klar, daß ich tatsächlich dieser Uhr, wie sie hier vor mir liegt und geht, einen Namen zuordnen kann, und daß dieser Name außerhalb jedes Satzes Bedeutung haben wird in demselben Sinne des Wortes, wie ich es überhaupt jemals gemeint habe, und ich empfinde, daß jener Name in einem Satze allen Anforderungen an den 'Namen des einfachen Gegenstandes' entsprechen wird'.

16. 6. 15.

Wir wollen jetzt einmal sehen, ob diese Uhr tatsächlich allen Bedingungen entspricht, um ein 'einfacher Gegenstand' zu sein!——

Die Frage ist eigentlich die: Muß ich, um die syntaktische Behandlungsweise eines Namens zu kennen, die Zusammensetzung seiner Bedeutung kennen? Wenn ja, so drückt sich die ganze Zusammensetzung auch schon in unanalysierten Sätzen aus. . . .——

(Man versucht oft, zu große Gedankenklüfte zu überspringen und fällt dann mitten hinein.)

apparently make on the simple ones? If I give this book a name "N" and now talk about N, is not the relation of N to that 'complex object', to those forms and contents, *essentially* the same as I imagined only between name and simple object?

For N.B.: even if the name "N" vanishes on further analysis, still it indicates a *single common* thing.

But what about the reference of names out of the context of the proposition?

The question might however also be presented like this: It seems that the idea of the SIMPLE is already to be found contained in that of the complex and in the idea of analysis, and in such a way that we come to this idea quite apart from any examples of simple objects, or of propositions which mention them, and we realize the existence of the simple object—*a priori*—as a logical necessity.

So it looks as if the existence of the simple objects were related to that of the complex ones as the sense of $\sim p$ is to the sense of p: the *simple* object is *prejudged* in the complex.

15.6.15.

(This is NOT to be confused with the *fact* that its *component* is prejudged in the complex.)

(One of the most difficult of the philosopher's tasks is to find out where the shoe pinches.)

It is quite clear that I can in fact correlate a name with this watch just as it lies here ticking in front of me, and that this name will have reference outside any proposition in the very sense I have always given that word, and I feel that that name in a proposition will correspond to all the requirements of the 'names of simple objects'.

16.6.15.

Now we just want to see whether this watch in fact corresponds to all the conditions for being a 'simple object'.——

The question is really this: In order to know the syntactical treatment of a name, must I know the composition of its reference? If so, then the whole composition is already expressed even in the unanalysed proposition. . . .

(One often tries to jump over too wide chasms of thought and then falls in.)

Das, was uns a priori gegeben scheint, ist der Begriff: *Dieses*.—Identisch mit dem Begriff des *Gegenstands*.

Auch Relationen und Eigenschaften etc. sind *Gegenstände*.

Meine Schwierigkeit besteht doch darin: In allen mir vorkommenden Sätzen kommen Namen vor, welche aber bei weiterer Analyse wieder verschwinden müssen. Ich weiß, daß eine solche weitere Analyse möglich ist, bin aber nicht im Stande, sie vollständig durchzuführen. Trotzdem nun weiß ich allem Anscheine nach, daß, wenn die Analyse vollständig durchgeführt wäre, ihr Resultat ein Satz sein müßte, der wieder Namen, Relationen etc. enthielte. Kurz: es scheint, als wüßte ich auf diese Weise nur eine Form, von welcher ich kein einziges Beispiel kenne.

Ich sehe: die Analyse kann weitergeführt werden und kann mir nun sozusagen nicht vorstellen, daß sie zu etwas Anderem führt als zu den mir bekannten Satzgattungen.

Wenn ich sage, diese Uhr ist glänzend und das, was ich mit diese Uhr meine, ändert seine Zusammensetzung im geringsten, so ändert sich damit nicht nur der Sinn des Satzes dem Inhalt nach, sondern die *Aussage über diese Uhr* ändert sofort *auch* ihren Sinn. Die ganze Form des Satzes ändert sich.

Das heißt, die syntaktische Verwendung der Namen charakterisiert vollständig die Form der zusammengesetzten Gegenstände, welche sie bezeichnen.

Jeder Satz, der einen Sinn hat, hat einen KOMPLETTEN Sinn, und er ist ein Bild der Wirklichkeit, so daß, was in ihm noch nicht gesagt ist, einfach nicht zu seinem Sinn gehören kann.

Wenn der Satz "diese Uhr glänzt" einen Sinn hat, so muß es erklärbar sein, WIE DIESER Satz DIESEN Sinn hat.

Wenn ein Satz uns etwas sagt, so muß er, wie er da steht, ein Bild der Wirklichkeit sein und zwar ein vollständiges.——Es wird natürlich auch etwas geben, was er *nicht* sagt—aber *was* er sagt, sagt er vollständig, und es muß sich SCHARF begrenzen lassen.

Ein Satz mag also zwar ein unvollständiges Bild einer gewissen Tatsache sein, aber er ist IMMER *ein vollständiges Bild*. [*Vgl*. 5.156.]

Daraus schiene es nun, als ob in gewissem Sinne alle Namen *echte Namen* wären. Oder wie ich auch sagen könnte, als ob alle Gegenstände in gewissem Sinne einfache Gegenstände wären.

What seems to be given us *a priori* is the concept: *This*.—Identical with the concept of the *object*.

Relations and properties, etc. are *objects* too.

My difficulty surely consists in this: In all the propositions that occur to me there occur names, which, however, must disappear on further analysis. I know that such a further analysis is possible, but am unable to carry it out completely. In spite of this I certainly seem to know that if the analysis were completely carried out, its result would have to be a proposition which once more contained names, relations, etc. In brief it looks as if in this way I knew a form without being acquainted with any single example of it.

I see that the analysis can be carried farther, and can, so to speak, not imagine its leading to anything different from the species of propositions that I am familiar with.

When I say this watch is shiny, and what I mean by this watch alters its composition in the smallest particular, then this means not merely that the sense of the sentence alters in its content, but also *what I am saying about this watch* straightway alters its sense. The whole form of the proposition alters.

That is to say, the syntactical employment of the names completely characterizes the form of the complex objects which they denote.

Every proposition that has a sense has a COMPLETE sense, and it is a picture of reality in such a way that what is not yet said in it simply cannot belong to its sense.

If the proposition "this watch is shiny" has a sense, it must be explicable HOW THIS proposition has THIS sense.

If a proposition tells us something, then it must be a picture of reality just as it is, and a complete picture at that.——There will, of course, also be something that it does *not* say—but what it does say it says completely and it must be susceptible of SHARP definition.

So a proposition may indeed be an incomplete picture of a certain fact, but it is ALWAYS *a complete picture*. [*Cf.* 5.156.]

From this it would now seem as if in a certain sense all names were *genuine names*. Or, as I might also say, as if all objects were in a certain sense simple objects.

17. 6. 15.

Nehmen wir an, jeder räumliche Gegenstand bestehe aus unendlich vielen Punkten, dann ist es klar, daß ich diese nicht alle namentlich anführen kann, wenn ich von jenem Gegenstand spreche. Hier wäre also ein Fall, wo ich zur vollständigen Analyse im alten Sinne gar nicht kommen *kann*; und vielleicht ist gerade dieser der gewöhnliche Fall.

Das ist doch klar, daß die Sätze, die die Menschheit ausschließlich benützt, daß diese, so wie sie stehen, einen Sinn haben werden und nicht erst auf eine zukünftige Analyse warten, um einen Sinn zu erhalten.

Nun scheint es aber doch eine legitime Frage: sind—z. B.—räumliche Gegenstände aus einfachen Teilen zusammengesetzt, kommt man bei ihrer Zerlegung auf Teile, die nicht mehr zerlegbar sind, oder ist dies nicht der Fall?

——Was für eine Art Frage ist aber dies?——

Ist es, A PRIORI, *klar*, *daß wir bei der Zerlegung auf einfache Bestandteile kommen müßten—liegt dies etwa schon im Begriff der Zerlegung*—, oder ist eine Zerlegbarkeit ad infinitum möglich?——Oder am Ende gar ein Drittes?

Jene Frage ist eine logische, und die Zusammengesetztheit der räumlichen Gegenstände ist eine logische, denn zu sagen, daß ein Ding ein Teil eines anderen sei, ist immer eine Tautologie.

Wie aber, wenn ich etwa sagen wollte, daß EIN Bestandteil einer Tatsache eine bestimmte Eigenschaft habe? Dann müßte ich sie namentlich anführen und eine logische Summe verwenden.

Gegen eine unendliche Zerlegbarkeit scheint auch nichts zu sprechen.

Und immer wieder drängt es sich uns auf, daß es etwas Einfaches, Unzerlegbares gibt, ein Element des Seins, kurz ein Ding.

Es geht zwar nicht gegen unser Gefühl, daß *wir* SÄTZE nicht soweit zerlegen können, um die Elemente namentlich anzuführen, aber wir fühlen, daß die WELT aus Elementen bestehen muß. Und es scheint, als sei das identisch mit dem Satz, die Welt müße eben sein, was sie ist, sie müße bestimmt sein. Oder mit anderen Worten, was schwankt, sind unsere Bestimmungen, nicht die Welt. Es scheint, als hieße die Dinge leugnen soviel als zu sagen: Die Welt könne sozusagen unbestimmt sein in dem Sinne etwa, in welchem unser Wissen unsicher und unbestimmt ist.

Die Welt hat eine feste Struktur.

17.6.15.

Let us assume that every spatial object consists of infinitely many points, then it is clear that I cannot mention all these by name when I speak of that object. Here then would be a case in which I *cannot* arrive at the complete analysis in the old sense at all; and perhaps just this is the usual case.

But this is surely clear: the propositions which are the only ones that humanity uses will have a sense just as they are and do not wait upon a future analysis in order to acquire a sense.

Now, however, it seems to be a legitimate question: Are—e.g.—spatial objects composed of simple parts; in analysing them, does one arrive at parts that cannot be further analysed, or is this not the case?

——But what kind of question is this?——

Is it, A PRIORI, *clear that in analysing we must arrive at simple components—is this, e.g., involved in the concept of analysis—*, or is analysis *ad infinitum* possible?—Or is there in the end even a third possibility?

This question is a logical one and the complexity of spatial objects is a logical complexity, for to say that one thing is part of another is always a tautology.

But suppose, for example, that I wanted to say that ONE component of a fact had a particular property? Then I should have to mention it by name and use a logical sum.

And nothing seems to speak against infinite divisibility.

And it keeps on forcing itself upon us that there is some simple indivisible, an element of being, in brief a thing.

It does not go against our feeling, that *we* cannot analyse PROPOSITIONS so far as to mention the elements by name; no, we feel that the WORLD must consist of elements. And it appears as if that were identical with the proposition that the world must be what it is, it must be definite. Or in other words, what vacillates is our determinations, not the world. It looks as if to deny things were as much as to say that the world can, as it were, be indefinite in some such sense as that in which our knowledge is uncertain and indefinite.

The world has a fixed structure.

Ob nicht die Darstellung durch unzerlegbare Namen *nur ein System* ist?

Alles, was ich will, ist ja nur vollständige Zerlegtheit *meines Sinnes*!! Mit anderen Worten, der Satz muß vollkommen artikuliert sein. Alles, was sein Sinn mit einem andern Sinn gemeinsam hat, muß im Satz separat enthalten sein. Kommen Verallgemeinerungen vor, so müssen die Formen der besonderen Fälle ersichtlich sein.——Und es ist klar, daß diese Forderung berechtigt ist, sonst kann der Satz überhaupt kein Bild von *irgend etwas* sein. [*Vgl.* 3.251.]

Denn wenn im Satze Möglichkeiten *offen gelassen werden*, so muß *eben das bestimmt* sein: *was* offen gelassen wird. Die Verallgemeinerungen der Form—z. B.—müssen bestimmt sein. Was ich nicht weiß, das weiß ich nicht, aber der Satz muß mir zeigen, WAS ich weiß. Und ist dann nicht dies *Bestimmte*, zu dem ich kommen *muß*, gerade einfach in dem Sinn, der mir immer vorgeschwebt hat? Es ist sozusagen das Harte.

"Zusammengesetzte Gegenstände gibt es nicht", heißt dann also für uns: Im Satz muß klar sein, wie der Gegenstand zusammengesetzt ist, soweit wir überhaupt von seiner Zusammengesetztheit reden können.—Der Sinn des Satzes muß im Satze in seine *einfachen* Bestandteile zerlegt erscheinen—. Und diese Teile sind dann wirklich unzerlegbar, denn weiter zerlegte wären eben nicht DIESE. Mit anderen Worten, der Satz läßt sich eben dann nicht mehr durch einen ersetzen, welcher mehr Bestandteile hat, sondern jeder, der mehr Bestandteile hat, hat auch nicht *diesen* Sinn.

Immer, wenn der Sinn des Satzes vollkommen in ihm selbst ausgedrückt ist, ist der Satz in seine einfachen Bestandteile zerlegt—eine weitere Zerlegung ist unmöglich, und eine scheinbare überflüssig—und diese sind Gegenstände im ursprünglichen Sinne.

18. 6. 15.

Ist die Zusammengesetztheit eines Gegenstandes für den Sinn eines Satzes bestimmend, dann muß sie soweit im Satze abgebildet sein, als sie seinen Sinn bestimmt. Und soweit die Zusammensetzung für *diesen* Sinn *nicht* bestimmend ist, soweit sind die Gegenstände dieses Satzes *einfach*. SIE *können* nicht weiter zerlegt werden.———

Die Forderung der einfachen Dinge *ist* die Forderung der Bestimmtheit des Sinnes. [*Vgl.* 3.23.]

——Denn rede ich etwa von dieser Uhr und meine damit etwas Komplexes, und es kommt auf die Zusammensetzung nicht an, so wird

Is the representation by means of unanalysable names *only one system*?

All I want is only for *my meaning* to be completely analysed!

In other words the proposition must be completely articulated. Everything that its sense has in common with another sense must be contained separately in the proposition. If generalizations occur, then the forms of the particular cases must be manifest——and it is clear that this demand is justified, otherwise the proposition cannot be a picture at all, of *anything*. [*Cf.* 3.251.]

For if possibilities *are left open* in the proposition, *just this* must be *definite*: *what* is left open. The generalizations of the form—e.g.—must be definite. What I do not know I do not know, but the proposition must shew me WHAT I know. And in that case, is not this *definite* thing at which I *must* arrive precisely simple in that sense that I have always had in mind? It is, so to speak, what is hard.

In that case, then, what we mean by "complex objects do not exist" is: It must be clear in the proposition how the object is composed, so far as it is possible for us to speak of its complexity at all.—The sense of the proposition must appear in the proposition as divided into its *simple* components—. And these parts are then actually indivisible, for further divided they just would not be THESE. In other words, the proposition can then no longer be *replaced* by one that has more components, but any that has more components also does not have *this* sense.

When the sense of the proposition is completely expressed in the proposition itself, the proposition is always divided into its simple components—no further division is possible and an apparent one is superfluous—and these are objects in the original sense.

18.6.15.

If the complexity of an object is definitive of the sense of the proposition, then it must be portrayed in the proposition to the extent that it does determine the sense. And to the extent that its composition is *not* definitive of *this* sense, to this extent the objects of this proposition are *simple*. THEY *cannot* be further divided.————

The demand for simple things *is* the demand for definiteness of sense. [*Cf.* 3.23.]

——For if I am talking about, e.g., this watch, and mean something complex by that and nothing depends upon the way it is compounded,

im Satz eine Verallgemeinerung auftreten, und ihre Grundformen werden, *soweit sie überhaupt gegeben sind*, vollkommen bestimmt sein.

Wenn es einen endlichen Sinn gibt, und einen Satz, der diesen vollständig ausdrückt, dann gibt es auch Namen für einfache Gegenstände.

Das ist die richtige Designiation.

Wenn nun aber ein einfacher Name einen unendlich komplexen Gegenstand bezeichnet? Wir sagen zum Beispiel etwas von einem Fleck unseres Gesichtsbilds aus, etwa, daß er rechts von einer Linie liege, und wir nehmen an, daß jeder Fleck unseres Gesichtsbilds unendlich komplex ist. Sagen wir dann von einem Punkt in jenem Fleck, daß er rechts von der Linie liege, dann folgt dieser Satz aus dem früheren, und wenn unendlich viele Punkte in dem Fleck liegen, *dann folgen unendlich viele Sätze verschiedenen Inhalts* LOGISCH *aus jenem ersten*! Und dies zeigt schon, daß er tatsächlich selbst unendlich komplex war. Nämlich nicht das Satzzeichen allein, wohl aber *mit seiner syntaktischen Verwendung.*

Nun ist es aber natürlich *sehr* leicht möglich, daß in Wirklichkeit *nicht* unendlich viele verschiedene Sätze aus einem solchen Satz folgen, weil unser Gesichsbild vielleicht—oder wahrscheinlich—nicht aus unendlich vielen Teilen besteht—sondern jener kontinuierliche Gesichtsraum erst eine nachträgliche Konstruktion ist——; und dann folgt eben nur eine endliche Zahl Sätze aus dem bewußten, und er selbst ist in jedem Sinne *endlich.*

Aber beeinträchtigt nun diese *mögliche* unendliche Zusammengesetztheit des Sinnes dessen Bestimmtheit?

Man könnte die Bestimmtheit auch so fordern!: Wenn ein Satz Sinn haben soll, so muß vorerst die syntaktische Verwendung jedes seiner Teile festgelegt sein.—Man kann z. B. nicht *erst nachträglich draufkommen*, daß ein Satz aus ihm folgt. Sondern z. B. welche Sätze aus einem Satz folgen, muß vollkommen feststehen, ehe dieser Satz einen Sinn haben kann!

Es scheint mir durchaus möglich, daß Flächen in unserem Gesichtsbild einfache Gegenstände sind, indem wir nämlich keinen einzigen Punkt dieser Fläche separat wahrnehmen; Gesichtsbilder von Sternen scheinen es sogar sicher zu sein. Wenn ich nämlich z. B. sage, diese Uhr liegt nicht in der Lade, so braucht daraus durchaus nicht LOGISCH FOLGEN, daß ein Rad, welches in der Uhr ist, nicht in der Lade liegt, denn *ich wußte* vielleicht *gar nicht*, daß das Rad in der Uhr

then a generalization will make its appearance in the proposition and the fundamental forms of the generalization will be completely determinate *so far as they are given at all.*

If there is a final sense and a proposition expressing it completely, then there are also names for simple objects.

That is the correct designation.

But suppose that a simple name denotes an infinitely complex object? For example, perhaps we assert of a patch in our visual field that it is to the right of a line, and we assume that every patch in our visual field is infinitely complex. Then if we say that a point in that patch is to the right of the line, this proposition follows from the previous one, and if there are infinitely many points in the patch *then infinitely many propositions of different content follow* LOGICALLY *from that first one.* And this of itself shews that the proposition itself was as a matter of fact infinitely complex. That is, not the propositional sign by itself, but it *together with its syntactical application.*

Now it seems, of course, *perfectly* possible that in reality infinitely many different propositions do *not* follow from such a proposition, because our visual field perhaps—or probably—does not consist of infinitely many parts—but continuous visual space is only a subsequent construction——; and in that case only a finite number of propositions follow from the one known and it itself is *finite* in every sense.

But now, does not this *possible* infinite complexity of the sense impair its definiteness?

We might demand definiteness in this way too!: if a proposition is to make sense then the syntactical employment of each of its parts must be settled in advance.—It is, e.g., not possible *only subsequently to come upon* the fact that a proposition follows from it. But, e.g., what propositions follow from a proposition must be completely settled before that proposition can have a sense!

It seems to me perfectly possible that patches in our visual field are simple objects, in that we do not perceive any single point of a patch separately; the visual appearances of stars even seem certainly to be so. What I mean is: if, e.g., I say that this watch is not in the drawer, there is absolutely no need for it to FOLLOW LOGICALLY that a wheel which is in the watch is not in the drawer, for perhaps *I had not the least knowledge* that the wheel was in the watch, and hence

war, habe daher auch nicht mit "diese Uhr" einen Komplex meinen können, in welchem das Rad vorkommt. Und es ist gewiß, daß ich—beiläufig gesprochen—nicht alle Teile meines *theoretischen* Gesichtsbildes sehe. Wer weiß, *ob* ich unendlich viele Punkte sehe!

Nehmen wir nun an, wir sähen einen kreisförmigen Fleck: ist die Kreisform seine *Eigenschaft*? Gewiß nicht. Sie scheint eine strukturelle "Eigenschaft" zu sein. Und wenn ich bemerke, daß ein Fleck kreisrund ist, bemerke ich da nicht eine unendlich komplexe strukturelle Eigenschaft? Oder ich bemerke nur, daß der Fleck eine endliche Ausdehnung hat, und auch das schon scheint eine unendlich komplexe Struktur *vorauszusetzen*.

Nicht: ein Satz folgt aus einem anderen, sondern die Wahrheit des einen folgt aus der Wahrheit des anderen. (Darum *folgt* aus "Alle Menschen sind sterblich", "Wenn Sokrates ein Mensch ist, so ist er sterblich".)

Es kann aber wohl ein Satz von unendlich vielen Punkten handeln ohne in einem gewissen Sinne unendlich komplex zu sein.

19. 6. 15.

Wenn wir sehen, daß unser Gesichtsbild komplex ist, so sehen wir aber auch, daß es aus *einfacheren* Teilen besteht.

Wir können, ohne eine bestimmte Anwendung im Auge zu haben von Funktionen der und jener Art reden.

Es schwebt uns nämlich kein Beispiel vor, wenn wir Fx und alle anderen variablen Formzeichen benutzen.

Kurz: Wenn wir die Urbilder nur bei Namen anwenden würden, so wäre die Möglichkeit, daß wir die Existenz der Urbilder aus der Existenz ihrer einzelnen Fälle erkennen würden. Nun aber wenden wir *Variable* an, das heißt, wir reden sozusagen von den Urbildern allein, ganz abgesehen von irgend welchen einzelnen Fällen.

Wir bilden das Ding, die Relation, die Eigenschaft vermittelst Variablen ab und zeigen so, daß wir diese Ideen nicht aus gewissen uns vorkommenden Fällen ableiten, sondern sie irgendwie a priori besitzen.

Es fragt sich nämlich: Wenn die einzelnen Formen mir sozusagen in der Erfahrung gegeben sind, dann darf ich doch in der Logik von ihnen nicht Gebrauch machen, dann darf ich eigentlich kein x und kein ϕy schreiben. Aber das kann ich doch gar nicht vermeiden.

could not have meant by "this watch" the complex in which the wheel occurs. And it is certain—moreover—that I do not see all the parts of my *theoretical* visual field. Who knows *whether* I see infinitely many points?

Let us suppose that we were to see a circular patch: is the circular form its *property*? Certainly not. It seems to be a structural "property". And if I notice that a spot is round, am I not noticing an infinitely complicated structural property? Or I notice only that the spot has finite extension, and this of itself seems to *presuppose* an infinitely complex structure.

Not: One proposition follows from another, but the truth of the one follows from the truth of the other. (That is why it *follows* from "All men are mortal" that "If Socrates is a man, then he is mortal.")

A proposition can, however, quite well treat of infinitely many points without being infinitely complex in a particular sense.

19.6.15.

When we see that our visual field is complex we also see that it consists of *simpler* parts.

We can talk of functions of this and that kind without having any particular application in view.

For we don't have any examples before our minds when we use Fx and all the other variable form-signs.

In short: if we were to apply the prototypes only in connexion with names, there would be the possibility that we should know the existence of the prototypes from the existence of their special cases. But as it is we use *variables*, that is to say we talk, so to speak, of the prototypes by themselves, quite apart from any individual cases.

We portray the thing, the relation, the property, by means of variables and so shew that we do not derive these ideas from particular cases that occur to us, but possess them somehow *a priori*.

For the question arises: If the individual forms are, so to speak, given me in experience, then I surely can't make use of them in logic; in that case I cannot write down an x or a ϕy. But this I can surely not avoid at all.

Beiläufig gefragt: handelt die Logik von gewissen Gattungen von Funktionen und dergleichen? Und wenn nicht, was bedeuten dann Fx, ϕz *u.s.w.* in der Logik?

Dies müßen dann Zeichen allgemeinerer Bedeutung sein!

Das Aufstellen einer Art logischen Inventars, wie ich mir das früher vorstellte, scheint es doch wohl nicht zu geben.

Die Bestandteile des Satzes müssen einfach sein = Der Satz muß vollkommen artikuliert sein. [*Vgl.* 3.251.]

Nun SCHEINT dies aber den Tatsachen zu widersprechen?——

In der Logik nämlich wollen wir scheinbar Idealbilder artikulierter Sätze vorführen. Aber wie ist das möglich?

Oder können wir einen Satz wie "die Uhr liegt auf dem Tisch" ohne weiteres nach den Regeln der Logik behandeln? Nein. Da sagen wir z. B., daß die Zeitangabe in dem Satze verschwiegen ist, daß er nur scheinbar . . . etc. etc.

Also ehe wir ihn behandeln können, müssen wir ihn, wie es scheint, auf eine gewisse Art und Weise umgestalten.

Aber dies ist vielleicht nicht maßgebend, denn könnten wir nicht ebensogut unsere gewohnte *logische* Schreibweise dem speziellen Satz anpassen?

20. 6. 15.

Ja, darum handelt es sich: Könnten wir mit Recht die Logik, wie sie etwa in den "Principia Mathematica" steht, ohne weiteres auf die *gebräuchlichen Sätze* anwenden?

Natürlich dürfen wir nicht außeracht lassen, was in unseren Sätzen durch Endungen, Vorsilben, Umlaute etc. etc. *ausgedrückt* ist.

Aber wir wenden ja die Mathematik, und zwar mit bestem Erfolge, auf die gewöhnlichen Sätze, nämlich auf die der Physik, an !!

Aber wie merkwürdig: in den bekannten Lehrsätzen der mathematischen Physik erscheinen weder Dinge noch Funktionen noch Relationen noch sonst logische Gegenstandsformen!! Statt der Dinge haben wir da Zahlen, und die Funktionen und Relationen sind durchweg rein mathematisch!!

Aber es ist doch Tatsache, daß diese Sätze auf die solide Wirklichkeit angewandt werden.

An incidental question: Does logic deal with certain classes of functions and the like? And if not, what then is the import of Fx, ϕz, *and so on* in logic?

Then these must be signs of more general import!

There doesn't after all seem to be any setting up of a kind of logical inventory as I formerly imagined it.

The component parts of the proposition must be simple = The proposition must be completely articulated. [*Cf.* 3.251.]

But now does this SEEM to contradict the facts?——

For in logic we are apparently trying to produce ideal pictures of articulated propositions. But how is that possible?

Or can we deal with a proposition like "The watch is on the table" without further ado according to the rules of logic? No, here we say, for example, that no date is given in the proposition, that the proposition is only apparently . . . etc. etc.

So before we can deal with it we must, so it seems, transform it in a particular way.

But perhaps this is not conclusive, for could we not just as well apply our usual *logical* notation to the special proposition?

20.6.15.

Yes, this is the point: Can we justly apply logic just as it stands, say in *Principia Mathematica*, straightaway to *ordinary propositions*?

Of course we cannot disregard what is *expressed* in our propositions by means of endings, prefixes, vowel changes, etc. etc.

But we do apply mathematics, and with the greatest success, to ordinary propositions, namely to those of physics.

But how remarkable: in the familiar theorems of mathematical physics there appear neither things nor functions nor relations nor any other logical forms of object! Instead of things what we have here is numbers, and the functions and relations are purely mathematical throughout!

But it is surely a fact that these propositions are applied to solid reality.

Die Variablen in jenen Lehrsätzen stehen durchaus nicht—wie man häufig sagt—für Längen, Gewichte, Zeiträume etc., sondern sie stehen einfach für Zahlen und weiter nichts.

Wenn ich nun aber die Zahlen anwenden will, dann komme ich zu den Relationen, den Dingen etc. etc. Ich sage z. B.: diese Länge ist 5 Meter und spreche da von Relationen und Dingen, und zwar in dem *ganz gewöhnlichen* Sinne.

Wir kommen hier zur Frage nach der Bedeutung der Variablen in den physikalischen Sätzen. Diese sind ja keine Tautologien.

Der physikalische Satz ohne Angabe seiner Anwendung ist offenbar sinnlos. Was hätte es für einen Sinn zu sagen: "k=m.p"?
Also handelt der vervollständigte physikalische Satz doch von den Dingen, Relationen u.s.w. (Was eigentlich zu erwarten war.)

Es liegt nun alles darin, daß ich die Zahlen auf die gewöhnlichen Dinge etc. anwende, was wieder nicht mehr sagt, als daß in unseren ganz gewöhnlichen Sätzen Zahlen vorkommen.

Die Schwierigkeit ist eigentlich die: daß, wenn wir auch einen *ganz bestimmten* Sinn ausdrücken wollen, die Möglichkeit besteht, daß wir dieses Ziel verfehlen. Es scheint also sozusagen, daß wir keine Garantie haben, daß unser Satz wirklich ein Bild der Wirklichkeit ist.

Die Zerlegung der Körper in *materielle Punkte*, wie wir sie in der Physik haben, ist weiter nichts als die Analyse in *einfache Bestandteile*.

Aber sollte es möglich sein, daß die von uns gewöhnlich gebrauchten Sätze gleichsam nur einen unvollkommenen Sinn haben (ganz abgesehen von ihrer Wahr- oder Falschheit) und die physikalischen Sätze sich sozusagen dem Stadium nähern, wo ein Satz wirklich einen vollkommenen Sinn hat??

Wenn ich sage "das Buch liegt auf dem Tisch", hat dies wirklich einen vollkommen klaren Sinn? (Eine HÖCHST bedeutungsvolle Frage!)
Der Sinn muß doch klar sein, denn *etwas* meinen wir doch mit dem Satz, und soviel als wir *sicher* meinen, muß doch klar sein.

Wenn der Satz "das Buch liegt auf dem Tisch" einen klaren Sinn hat, dann muß ich, was immer auch *der Fall ist*, sagen können, ob der Satz wahr oder falsch ist. Es könnten aber sehr wohl *Fälle* eintreten, in welchen ich nicht ohne weiteres sagen könnte, ob das Buch noch "auf dem Tisch liegend" zu nennen ist. Also?

The variables in those theorems do not—as is often said—stand for lengths, weights, time intervals, etc. at all, they simply stand for numbers and for nothing else.

When, however, I want to apply numbers, I come to relations, things, etc. etc. I say, e.g.: This length is 5 yards and here I am talking of relations and things, and in the *completely ordinary* sense at that.

Here we come to the question about the reference of variables in the propositions of physics. For these are not tautologies.

A proposition of physics is obviously senseless if its application is not given. What sort of sense would it make to say: "k=m.p"?

So the complete physical proposition does after all deal with things, relations and so on. (Which was really to be expected.)

Now everything turns on the fact that I apply numbers to ordinary things, etc., which in fact says no more than that numbers occur in our quite ordinary sentences.

The difficulty is really this: even when we want to express a *completely definite* sense there is the possibility of failure. So it seems that we have, so to speak, no guarantee that our proposition is really a picture of reality.

The division of the body into *material points*, as we have it in physics, is nothing more than analysis into *simple components*.

But could it be possible that the sentences in ordinary use have, as it were, only an incomplete sense (quite apart from their truth or falsehood), and that the propositions in physics, as it were, approach the stage where a proposition really has a complete sense?

When I say, "The book is lying on the table", does this really have a completely clear sense? (An EXTREMELY important question.)

But the sense must be clear, for after all we mean *something* by the proposition, and as much as we *certainly* mean must surely be clear.

If the proposition "The book is on the table" has a clear sense, then I must, whatever *is the case*, be able to say whether the proposition is true or false. There could, however, very well occur *cases* in which I should not be able to say straight off whether the book is still to be called "lying on the table". Then—?

Ist also etwa der Fall der, daß ich zwar genau weiß, was ich sagen will, aber dann im Ausdruck Fehler mache?

Oder kann diese Unsicherheit AUCH noch in den Satz eingeschlossen werden?

Aber es kann auch sein, daß der Satz "das Buch liegt auf dem Tisch" meinen Sinn zwar vollkommen darstellt, daß ich aber die Worte, z. B. "darauf-liegen", hier in einer *speziellen* Bedeutung gebrauche, und es anderswo eine andere Bedeutung hat. Ich meine mit dem Verbum etwa die ganz spezielle Relation, die das Buch jetzt wirklich zu dem Tisch hat.

Sind also im Grunde die Sätze der Physik und die Sätze des gewöhnlichen Lebens gleich scharf, und besteht der Unterschied nur in der konsequenteren Anwendung der Zeichen in der Sprache der Wissenschaft??

Kann man davon reden oder nicht, daß ein Satz einen mehr oder weniger scharfen Sinn hat??

Es scheint klar, daß das, was wir MEINEN, immer "*scharf*" sein muß. Unser Ausdruck dessen, was wir meinen, kann wieder nur richtig oder falsch sein. Und nun können noch die Worte konsequent oder inkonsequent angewendet sein. Eine andere Möglichkeit scheint es nicht zu geben.

Wenn ich z. B. sage "der Tisch ist einen Meter lang", so ist es höchst fraglich, was ich damit meine. Aber ich meine wohl "der Abstand DIESER zwei Punkte ist ein Meter, und die Punkte gehören zum Tisch".

Wir sagten, die Mathematik würde ja schon mit Erfolg auf gewöhnliche Sätze angewandt, aber die Sätze der Physik handeln durchwegs von anderen Gegenständen als denen unserer gewöhnlichen Sprache! Müssen unsere Sätze *so* präpariert werden, um mathematisch behandelt werden zu können? Offenbar ja! Wenn Quantitäten in Frage kommen, so würde z. B. ein Ausdruck wie "die Länge dieses Tisches" nicht genügen. Diese Länge müßte definiert werden, etwa als Abstand zweier Flächen etc. etc.

Ja, die mathematischen Wissenschaften unterscheiden sich von den nicht mathematischen dadurch, daß jene von Dingen handeln, von welchen die gewöhnliche Sprache nicht spricht, während diese von den allgemein bekannten Dingen redet.——

21. 6. 15.

Unsere Schwierigkeit war doch die, daß wir immer von einfachen Gegenständen sprachen und nicht einen einzigen anzuführen wußten.

Then is the case here one of my knowing exactly what I want to say, but then making mistakes in expressing it?

Or can this uncertainty TOO be included in the proposition?

But it may also be that the proposition "The book is lying on the table" represents my sense completely, but that I am using the words, e.g., "lying on", with a *special* reference here, and that elsewhere they have another reference. What I mean by the verb is perhaps a quite special relation which the book now actually has to the table.

Then are the propositions of physics and the propositions of ordinary life at bottom equally sharp, and does the difference consist only in the more consistent application of signs in the language of science?

Is it or is it not possible to talk of a proposition's having a more or less sharp sense?

It seems clear that what we MEAN must always be "*sharp*".
Our expression of what we mean can in its turn only be right or wrong. And further the words can be applied consistently or inconsistently. There does not seem to be any other possibility.

When I say, e.g., that the table is a yard long, it is extremely questionable what I mean by this. But I presumably mean that the distance between THESE two points is a yard, and that the points belong to the table.

We said that mathematics has already been applied with success to ordinary propositions, but in propositions of physics it treats of completely different objects from those of our ordinary language. Must our propositions undergo *such* preparation, to make them capable of being dealt with mathematically? Evidently they must. When quantities come in question, then an expression like, e.g., "the length of this table" would not be adequate. This length would have to be defined, say, as the distance between two surfaces, etc. etc.

Mathematical sciences are distinguished from non-mathematical ones by treating of things of which ordinary language does not speak, whereas the latter talk about things that are generally familiar.——

21.6.15.

Our difficulty was that we kept on speaking of simple objects and were unable to mention a single one.

Wenn der Punkt im Raume nicht existiert, dann existieren auch seine Koordinaten nicht, und wenn die Koordinaten existieren, dann existiert auch der Punkt.—So ist es in der Logik.

Das einfache Zeichen ist *wesentlich einfach*.
Es fungiert als einfacher Gegenstand. (Was heißt das?)
Seine Zusammensetzung wird vollkommen *gleichgültig*. Sie verschwindet uns aus den Augen.

Es scheint immer so, als ob es komplexe Gegenstände gäbe, die als einfache fungieren und dann auch *wirklich* einfache, wie die materiellen Punkte der Physik, etc.

Daß ein Name einen komplexen Gegenstand bezeichnet, sieht man aus einer Unbestimmtheit in den Sätzen, in welchen er vorkommt, die eben von der Allgemeinheit solcher Sätze herrührt. Wir *wissen*, durch diesen Satz ist noch nicht alles bestimmt. Die Allgemeinheitsbezeichnung *enthält* ja ein Urbild. [*Vgl.* 3.24.]

Alle unsichtbaren Massen etc. etc. müssen unter die Allgemeinheitsbezeichnung kommen.

Wie ist das, wenn sich Sätze der Wahrheit nähern?

Aber die Logik, wie sie etwa in den "Principia Mathematica" steht, läßt sich ganz gut auf unsere gewöhnlichen Sätze anwenden. Z. B. aus "Alle Menschen sind sterblich" und "Sokrates ist ein Mensch" folgt nach dieser Logik "Sokrates ist sterblich", was offenbar richtig ist, obwohl ich, ebenso offenbar, nicht weiß, welche Struktur das Ding Sokrates oder die Eigenschaft der Sterblichkeit hat. Diese fungieren eben hier als einfache Gegenstände.

Offenbar garantiert schon der Umstand, der es möglich macht, daß gewisse Formen durch eine Definition in einen Namen projiziert werden, dafür, daß dieser Name dann auch wie ein wirklicher behandelt werden kann.

Es is ja dem Klarsehenden offenbar, daß ein Satz wie "Diese Uhr liegt auf dem Tisch" eine Menge Unbestimmtheit enthält, trotzdem seine Form äußerlich vollkommen klar und einfach erscheint. Wir *sehen* also, daß diese Einfachheit nur konstruiert ist.

22. 6. 15.

Es ist also auch *dem* UNBEFANGENEN *Geist* klar, daß der Sinn des Satzes "die Uhr liegt auf dem Tisch" komplizierter ist als der Satz selbst.

If a point in space does not exist, then its co-ordinates do not exist either, and if the co-ordinates exist then the point exists too.—That's how it is in logic.

The simple sign is *essentially simple.*

It functions as a simple object. (What does that mean?)

Its composition becomes completely *indifferent.* It disappears from view.

It always looks as if there were complex objects functioning as simples, and then also *really* simple ones, like the material points of physics, etc.

It can be seen that a name stands for a complex object from an indefiniteness in the proposition in which it occurs. This comes of the generality of such propositions. We *know* that not everything is yet determined by this proposition. For the generality notation *contains* a proto-picture. [*Cf.* 3.24.]

All invisible masses, etc. etc. must come under the generality notation.

What is it for propositions to approximate to the truth?

But logic as it stands, e.g., in *Principia Mathematica* can quite well be applied to our ordinary propositions, e.g., from "All men are mortal" and "Socrates is a man" there follows according to this logic "Socrates is mortal" which is obviously correct although I equally obviously do not know what structure is possessed by the thing Socrates or the property of mortality. Here they just function as simple objects.

Obviously the circumstance that makes it possible for certain forms to be projected by means of a definition into a name, guarantees of itself that this name can then also be treated as a real one.

To anyone that sees clearly, it is obvious that a proposition like "This watch is lying on the table" contains a lot of indefiniteness, in spite of its form's being completely clear and simple in outward appearance. So we see that this simplicity is only constructed.

22.6.15.

It is then also clear to *the UNPREJUDICED mind* that the sense of the proposition "The watch is lying on the table" is more complicated than the proposition itself.

Die Abmachungen unserer Sprache sind außerordentlich kompliziert. Es wird enorm viel zu jedem Satz dazugedacht, was nicht gesagt wird. (Diese Abmachungen sind ganz wie die "Conventions" Whiteheads. Sie sind wohl Definitionen mit *einer gewissen Allgemeinheit der Form*.) [*Vgl.* 4.002.]

Ich will nur die Vagheit der gewöhnlichen Sätze rechtfertigen, denn sie *läßt* sich rechtfertigen.

Es ist klar: *Ich weiß*, was ich mit dem vagen Satz *meine*. Nun versteht es aber ein Anderer nicht und sagt "ja aber wenn du das meinst, hättest du—das und das—dazu setzen müssen"; und nun wird es noch Einer nicht verstehen und den Satz noch ausführlicher verlangen. Ich werde dann antworten: Ja, DAS versteht sich *doch von* SELBST.

Sage ich jemandem "die Uhr liegt auf dem Tisch", und nun sagt er "ja aber wenn die Uhr so und so läge, würdest du da auch noch sagen, 'sie liegt auf dem Tisch' ". Und ich würde unsicher. Das zeigt, daß ich nicht wußte, was ich mit dem "liegen" *im Allgemeinen* meinte. Wenn man mich so in die Enge triebe, um mir zu zeigen, daß ich nicht wisse, was ich meine, würde ich sagen: "*Ich weiß*, was ich meine; ich meine eben DAS" und würde dabei etwa auf den betreffenden Komplex mit dem Finger zeigen. Und in diesem Komplex habe ich nun tatsächlich die zwei Gegenstände in einer Relation.——Das heißt aber *wirklich* nur: Die Tatsache läßt sich IRGENDWIE auch durch diese Form abbilden.

Wenn ich dies nun tue und die Gegenstände mit *Namen* bezeichne, werden sie dadurch einfach?

Aber doch ist dieser Satz ein Bild jenes Komplexes.

Dieser Gegenstand ist für *mich einfach*!

Nenne ich z. B. irgend einen Stab "A", eine Kugel "B", so kann ich von A sagen, es lehnt an der Wand, aber nicht von B. Hier macht sich die interne Natur von A und B bemerkbar.

Wenn ein Name einen Gegenstand bezeichnet, so steht er damit in einer Beziehung zu ihm, die ganz von der logischen Art des Gegenstandes bedingt ist und diese wieder charakterisiert.

Und das ist klar, daß der Gegenstand eine bestimmte logische Art haben muß, er ist so zusammengesetzt oder so einfach als er eben ist.

"Die Uhr *sitzt* auf dem Tisch" ist sinnlos!

The conventions of our language are extraordinarily complicated. There is enormously much added in thought to each proposition and not said. (These conventions are exactly like Whitehead's 'Conventions'. They are definitions with *a certain generality of form.*) [*Cf.* 4.002.]

I only want to justify the vagueness of ordinary sentences, for it *can* be justified.

It is clear that *I know* what I *mean* by the vague proposition. But now someone else doesn't understand and says: "Yes, but if you mean that then you should have added such and such"; and now someone else again will not understand it and will demand that the proposition should be given in more detail still. I shall then reply: Now THAT can *surely* be taken for granted.

I tell someone "The watch is lying on the table" and now he says: "Yes, but if the watch were in such-and-such a position would you still say it was lying on the table?" And I should become uncertain. This shews that I did not know what I meant by "lying" *in general.* If someone were to drive me into a corner in this way in order to shew that I did not know what I meant, I should say: "*I know* what I mean; I mean just THIS", pointing to the appropriate complex with my finger. And in this complex I do actually have the two objects in a relation.——But all that this *really* means is: The fact can SOMEHOW be portrayed by means of this form too.

Now when I do this and designate the objects by means of *names*, does that make them simple?

All the same, however, this proposition is a picture of that complex.

This object is *simple* for *me*!

If, e.g., I call some rod "A", and a ball "B", I can say that A is leaning against the wall, but not B. Here the internal nature of A and B comes into view.

A name designating an object thereby stands in a relation to it which is wholly determined by the logical kind of the object and which signalises that logical kind.

And it is clear that the object must be of a particular logical kind, it just is as complex, or as simple, as it is.

"The watch *is sitting* on the table" is senseless!

Nur der zusammengesetzte Teil des Satzes kann wahr oder falsch sein.

Der Name faßt seine ganze komplexe Bedeutung in Eins zusammen.

---

15. 4. 16.

Nur was wir selbst konstruieren, können wir voraussehen! [*S.* 5.556.]

Aber wo bleibt da der Begriff des einfachen Gegenstandes?

Dieser Begriff kommt hier überhaupt noch nicht in Betracht.

Wir mußen die enfachen Funktionen darum konstruieren können, weil wir jedem Zeichen eine Bedeutung geben können müssen.

Denn das einzige Zeichen, welches für seine Bedeutung bürgt, ist Funktion und Argument.

16. 4. 16.

Jeder einfache Satz läßt sich auf die Form ϕx bringen.

Darum darf man aus dieser Form alle einfachen Sätze zusammenstellen.

Angenommen, mir wären *alle* einfachen Sätze gegeben: Dann läßt sich einfach fragen: welche Sätze kann ich aus ihnen bilden. Und das sind *alle* Sätze, und *so* sind sie *begrenzt*. [4.51.]

(p): p = aRx.xRy . . . zRb
(p): p=aRx.

17. 4. 16.

Die obige Definition kann in ihrer Allgemeinheit nur eine Schriftzeichenregel sein, die mit dem Sinne der Zeichen nichts zu tun hat.

Aber kann es eine solche Regel geben?

Nur dann ist die Definition möglich, wenn sie selbst kein Satz ist.

Dann kann ein Satz nicht von allen Sätzen handeln, wohl aber eine Definition.

23. 4. 16.

Die obige Definition handelt aber gar nicht von allen Sätzen, denn sie enthält wesentlich wirkliche Variable. Sie ist ganz analog einer Operation, als deren Basis auch ihr eigenes Resultat genommen werden kann.

26. 4. 16.

So und nur so ist das Fortschreiten von einer Type zur anderen möglich. [*Vgl.* 5.252]

Und man kann sagen, alle Typen stehen in Hierarchien.

Only the complex part of the proposition can be true or false.

The name compresses its whole complex reference into one.

15.4.16.

We can only foresee what we ourselves construct. [*See* 5.556.]

But then where is the concept of a simple object still to be found?

This concept does not so far come in here at all.

We must be able to construct the simple functions because we must be able to give each sign a meaning.

For the only sign which guarantees its meaning is function and argument.

16.4.16.

Every simple proposition can be brought into the form ϕx.

That is why we may compose all simple propositions from this form.

Suppose that *all* simple propositions were given me: then it can simply be asked what propositions I can construct from them. And these are *all* propositions and this is *how* they are *bounded*. [4.51.]

(p): p = aRx.xRy . . . zRb
(p): p=aRx

17.4.16.

The above definition can in its general form only be a rule for a written notation which has nothing to do with the sense of the signs.

But can there be such a rule?

The definition is only possible if it is itself not a proposition.

In that case a proposition cannot treat of all propositions, while a definition can.

23.4.16.

The above definition, however, just does not deal with all propositions, for it essentially contains real variables. It is quite analogous to an operation whose own result can be taken as its base.

26.4.16.

In this way, and in this way alone, is it possible to proceed from one type to another. [*Cf.* 5.252.]

And we can say that all types stand in hierarchies.

Und die Hierarchie ist nur möglich durch den Aufbau durch die Operation.

Die empirische Realität ist begrenzt durch die Zahl der Gegenstände. Die Grenze zeigt sich wieder in der Gesamtheit der einfachen Sätze. [*S*. 5.5561.]

Die Hierarchien sind und müssen unabhängig sein von der Realität. [*S*. 5.5561.]
Die Bedeutungen ihrer Glieder werden erst durch Zuordnung der Gegenstände zu den Namen bestimmt.

27. 4. 16.

Sagen wir, ich wollte eine Funktion von 3 unter einander unauswechselbaren Argumenten darstellen.

$$\phi(x): \phi(\quad), x$$

Soll nun aber in der Logik von unvertauschbaren Argumenten die Rede sein? Wenn ja, so setzt dies doch etwas über die Beschaffenheit der Realität voraus.

6. 5. 16.

Der ganzen Weltanschauung der Modernen liegt diese Täuschung zu Grunde, daß die sogenannten Naturgesetze die Erklärungen der Naturerscheinungen seien. [6.371.]

So bleiben sie bei den "Naturgesetzen" als bei etwas *Unantastbarem* stehen, wie die Älteren bei Gott und dem Schicksal. [*S*. 6.372.]

Und sie haben ja beide recht und unrecht. Die Alten sind allerdings insofern klarer, als sie einen klaren Abschluß anerkannten, während es bei dem neuen System scheinen soll, als sei *alles* begründet. [*S*. 6.372.]

11. 5. 16.

$|p \qquad |(a, a)$

Es gibt eben auch Operationen mit zwei Basen. Und die "|"-Operation ist von dieser Art.

$|(\xi, \eta)$ . . . ist ein beliebiges Glied der Reihe der Operationsresultate.

$(\exists x).\phi x$

Ist denn $(\exists x)$ etc. wirklich eine Operation?

Was wäre aber ihre Basis?

11. 6. 16.

Was weiß ich über Gott und den Zweck des Lebens?
Ich weiß, daß diese Welt ist.

And the hierarchy is only possible by being built up by means of operations.

Empirical reality is bounded by the number of objects.

The boundary turns up again in the totality of simple propositions. [*See* 5.5561.]

The hierarchies are and must be independent of reality. [*See* 5.5561.]

The meanings of their terms are only determined by the correlation of objects and names.

27.4.16.

Say I wanted to represent a function of three non-interchangeable arguments.

$\phi(x)$: $\phi(\ )$, x

But should there be any mention of non-interchangeable arguments in logic? If so, this surely presupposes something about the character of reality.

6.5.16.

At bottom the whole *Weltanschauung* of the moderns involves the illusion that the so-called laws of nature are explanations of natural phenomena. [6.371.]

In this way they stop short at the laws of nature as at something *impregnable* as men of former times did at God and fate. [*See* 6.372.]

And both are right and wrong. The older ones are indeed clearer in the sense that they acknowledge a clear terminus, while with the new system it is supposed to look as if *everything* had a foundation. [*See* 6.372.]

11.5.16.

$|p$ $|(a, a)$

There are also operations with two bases. And the "|"-operation is of this kind.

$|(\xi, \eta)$ . . . is an arbitrary term of the series of results of an operation.

$(\exists x) . \phi x$

Is $(\exists x)$ etc. really an operation?

But what would be its base?

11.6.16.

What do I know about God and the purpose of life?

I know that this world exists.

Daß ich in ihr stehe wie mein Auge in seinem Gesichtsfeld.

Daß etwas an ihr problematisch ist, was wir ihren Sinn nennen.

Daß dieser Sinn nicht in ihr liegt sondern außer ihr. [*Vgl.* 6.41.]

Daß das Leben die Welt ist. [*Vgl.* 5.621.]

Daß mein Wille die Welt durchdringt.

Daß mein Wille gut oder böse ist.

Daß also Gut und Böse mit dem Sinn der Welt irgendwie zusammenhängt.

Den Sinn des Lebens, d. i. den Sinn der Welt, können wir Gott nennen.

Und das Gleichnis von Gott als einem Vater daran knüpfen.

Das Gebet ist der Gedanke an den Sinn des Lebens.

Ich kann die Geschehnisse der Welt nicht nach meinem Willen lenken, sondern bin vollkommen machtlos.

Nur so kann ich mich unabhängig von der Welt machen—und sie also doch in gewissem Sinne beherrschen—indem ich auf einen Einfluß auf die Geschehnisse verzichte.

5. 7. 16.

Die Welt ist unabhängig von meinem Willen. [6.373.]

Auch wenn alles, was wir wünschen, geschähe, so wäre das doch nur sozusagen eine Gnade des Schicksals, denn es ist kein logischer Zusammenhang zwischen Willen und Welt, der dies verbürgte, und den angenommenen physikalischen könnten wir doch nicht wieder wollen. [6.374.]

Wenn das gute oder böse Wollen eine Wirkung auf die Welt hat, so kann es sie nur auf die Grenzen der Welt haben, nicht auf die Tatsachen, auf das, was durch die Sprache nicht abgebildet, sondern nur in der Sprache gezeigt werden kann. [*Vgl.* 6.43.]

Kurz, die Welt muß dann dadurch überhaupt eine andere werden. [*S.* 6.43.]

Sie muß sozusagen als Ganzes zunehmen oder abnehmen. Wie durch Dazukommen oder Wegfallen eines Sinnes. [*Vgl.* 6.43.]

Wie auch beim Tod die Welt sich nicht ändert, sondern aufhört zu sein. [6.431.]

6. 7. 16.

Und insofern hat wohl auch Dostojewski recht, wenn er sagt, daß der, welcher glücklich ist, den Zweck des Daseins erfüllt.

Oder man könnte auch so sagen, der erfüllt den Zweck des Daseins, der keinen Zweck außer dem Leben mehr braucht. Das heißt nämlich, der befriedigt ist.

That I am placed in it like my eye in its visual field.

That something about it is problematic, which we call its meaning.

That this meaning does not lie in it but outside it. [*Cf.* 6.41.]

That life is the world. [*Cf.* 5.621.]

That my will penetrates the world.

That my will is good or evil.

Therefore that good and evil are somehow connected with the meaning of the world.

The meaning of life, i.e. the meaning of the world, we can call God.

And connect with this the comparison of God to a father.

To pray is to think about the meaning of life.

I cannot bend the happenings of the world to my will: I am completely powerless.

I can only make myself independent of the world—and so in a certain sense master it—by renouncing any influence on happenings.

5.7.16.

The world is independent of my will. [6.373.]

Even if everything that we want were to happen, this would still only be, so to speak, a grace of fate, for what would guarantee it is not any logical connexion between will and world, and we could not in turn will the supposed physical connexion. [6.374.]

If good or evil willing affects the world it can only affect the boundaries of the world, not the facts, what cannot be portrayed by language but can only be shewn in language. [*Cf.* 6.43.]

In short, it must make the world a wholly different one. [*See* 6.43.]

The world must, so to speak, wax or wane as a whole. As if by accession or loss of meaning. [*Cf.* 6.43.]

As in death, too, the world does not change but stops existing. [6.431.]

6.7.16.

And in this sense Dostoievsky is right when he says that the man who is happy is fulfilling the purpose of existence.

Or again we could say that the man is fulfilling the purpose of existence who no longer needs to have any purpose except to live. That is to say, who is content.

Die Lösung des Problems des Lebens merkt man am Verschwinden dieses Problems. [*S.* 6.521.]

Kann man aber so leben, daß das Leben aufhört, problematisch zu sein? Daß man im Ewigen *lebt* und nicht in der Zeit?

7. 7. 16.

Ist nicht dies der Grund, warum Menschen, denen der Sinn des Lebens nach langen Zweifeln klar wurde, warum diese dann nicht sagen konnten, worin dieser Sinn bestand. [*S.* 6.521.]

Wenn ich mir eine "*Art* von Gegenständen" denken kann, ohne zu wissen, ob es solche Gegenstände gibt, so muß ich mir ihr Urbild konstruiert haben.

Beruht hierauf nicht die Methode der Mechanik?

8. 7. 16.

An einen Gott glauben heißt, die Frage nach dem Sinn des Lebens verstehen.

An einen Gott glauben heißt sehen, daß es mit den Tatsachen der Welt noch nicht abgetan ist.

An Gott glauben heißt sehen, daß das Leben einen Sinn hat.

Die Welt ist mir *gegeben*, d. h. mein Wille tritt an die Welt ganz von außen als an etwas Fertiges heran.

(Was mein Wille ist, das weiß ich noch nicht.)

Daher haben wir das Gefühl, daß wir von einem fremden Willen abhängig sind.

Wie dem auch sei, jedenfalls *sind* wir in einem gewissen Sinne abhängig und das, wovon wir abhängig sind, können wir Gott nennen.

Gott wäre in diesem Sinne einfach das Schicksal oder, was dasselbe ist: die—von unserem Willen unabhängige—Welt.

Vom Schicksal kann ich mich unabhängig machen.

Es gibt zwei Gottheiten: die Welt und mein unabhängiges Ich.

Ich bin entweder glücklich oder unglücklich, das ist alles. Man kann sagen: gut oder böse gibt es nicht.

Wer glücklich ist, der darf keine Furcht haben. Auch nicht vor dem Tode.

Nur wer nicht in der Zeit, sondern in der Gegenwart lebt, ist glücklich.

The solution of the problem of life is to be seen in the disappearance of this problem. [*See* 6.521.]

But is it possible for one so to live that life stops being problematic? That one is *living* in eternity and not in time?

7.7.16.

Isn't this the reason why men to whom the meaning of life had become clear after long doubting could not say what this meaning consisted in? [*See* 6.521.]

If I can imagine a "*kind* of object" without knowing whether there are such objects, then I must have constructed their proto-picture for myself.

Isn't the method of mechanics based on this?

8.7.16.

To believe in a God means to understand the question about the meaning of life.

To believe in a God means to see that the facts of the world are not the end of the matter.

To believe in God means to see that life has a meaning.

The world is *given* me, i.e. my will enters into the world completely from outside as into something that is already there.

(As for what my will is, I don't know yet.)

That is why we have the feeling of being dependent on an alien will.

However this may be, at any rate we *are* in a certain sense dependent, and what we are dependent on we can call God.

In this sense God would simply be fate, or, what is the same thing: The world—which is independent of our will.

I can make myself independent of fate.

There are two godheads: the world and my independent I.

I am either happy or unhappy, that is all. It can be said: good or evil do not exist.

A man who is happy must have no fear. Not even in face of death.

Only a man who lives not in time but in the present is happy.

Für das Leben in der Gegenwart gibt es keinen Tod.

Der Tod ist kein Ereignis des Lebens. Er ist keine Tatsache der Welt. [*Vgl.* 6.4311.]

Wenn man unter Ewigkeit nicht unendliche Zeitdauer, sondern Unzeitlichkeit versteht, dann kann man sagen, daß der ewig lebt, der in der Gegenwart lebt. [*S.* 6.4311.]

Um glücklich zu leben, muß ich in Übereinstimmung sein mit der Welt. Und dies *heißt* ja "glücklich sein".

Ich bin dann sozusagen in Übereinstimmung mit jenem fremden Willen, von dem ich abhängig erscheine. Das heißt: 'ich tue den Willen Gottes'.

Die Furcht vor dem Tode ist das beste Zeichen eines falschen, d. h. schlechten Lebens.

Wenn mein Gewissen mich aus dem Gleichgewicht bringt, so bin ich nicht in Übereinstimmung mit Etwas. Aber was ist dies? Ist es *die Welt*?

Gewiß ist es richtig zu sagen: Das Gewissen ist die Stimme Gottes.

Zum Beispiel: es macht mich unglücklich zu denken, daß ich den und den beleidigt habe. Ist das mein Gewissen?

Kann man sagen: "Handle nach deinem Gewissen, es sei beschaffen wie es mag"?

Lebe glücklich!

9. 7. 16.

Wenn man nicht die allgemeinste Satzform angeben könnte, dann müßte ein Moment kommen, wo wir plötzlich eine neue Erfahrung machen, sozusagen eine logische.
Dies ist natürlich unmöglich.

Nicht vergessen, daß (∃x)fx nicht heißt: es gibt ein x so daß fx, sondern: es gibt einen wahren Satz "fx".

Der Satz fa spricht von bestimmten Gegenständen, der allgemeine Satz von *allen* Gegenständen.

11. 7. 16.

Der bestimmte Gegenstand ist eine sehr merkwürdige Erscheinung.

Statt "alle Gegenstände" könnte man sagen: alle *bestimmten Gegenstände*.

For life in the present there is no death.

Death is not an event in life. It is not a fact of the world. [*Cf.* 6.4311.]

If by eternity is understood not infinite temporal duration but non-temporality, then it can be said that a man lives eternally if he lives in the present. [*See* 6.4311.]

In order to live happily I must be in agreement with the world. And that is what "being happy" *means*.

I am then, so to speak, in agreement with that alien will on which I appear dependent. That is to say: 'I am doing the will of God'.

Fear in face of death is the best sign of a false, i.e. a bad, life.

When my conscience upsets my equilibrium, then I am not in agreement with Something. But what is this? Is it *the world*?

Certainly it is correct to say: Conscience is the voice of God.

For example: it makes me unhappy to think that I have offended such and such a man. Is that my conscience?

Can one say: "Act according to your conscience whatever it may be"?

Live happy!

9.7.16.

If the most general form of proposition could not be given, then there would have to come a moment where we suddenly had a new experience, so to speak a logical one.

That is, of course, impossible.

Do not forget that (∃x)fx does not mean: There is an x such that fx, but: There is a true proposition "fx".

The proposition fa speaks of particular objects, the general proposition of *all* objects.

11.7.16.

The particular object is a very remarkable phenomenon.

Instead of "all objects" we might say: All *particular objects*.

Wenn alle bestimmten Gegenstände gegeben sind, sind "alle Gegenstände" gegeben.

Kurz, mit den bestimmten Gegenständen sind alle Gegenstände gegeben. [*Vgl.* 5.524.]

Wenn es Gegenstände gibt, gibt es damit auch "alle Gegenstände". [*Vgl.* 5.524.]

Darum muß sich auch die Einheit der Elementarsätze und der allgemeinen Sätze herstellen lassen.

Wenn nämlich die Elementarsätze gegeben sind, so sind damit auch *alle* Elementarsätze gegeben und damit der allgemeine Satz.—Und ist damit nicht schon die Einheit hergestellt? [*Vgl.* 5.524.]

13. 7. 16.

Immer wieder fühlt man, daß auch im Elementarsatz von allen Gegenständen die Rede ist.

$(\exists x)\phi x . x = a$

Wenn zwei Operationen gegeben sind, die sich nicht auf *eine* reduzieren lassen, so muß sich zum mindesten eine allgemeine Form ihrer Kombination aufstellen lassen.

$\phi x \;,\; \psi y | \chi z \;,\; (\exists x). \;,\; (x).$

Da sich offenbar leicht erklären läßt, wie mit diesen Operationen sich Sätze bilden lassen und wie Sätze nicht zu bilden sind, so muß sich dies auch *irgendwie* exakt ausdrücken lassen.

14. 7. 16.

Und dieser Ausdruck muß auch schon in der allgemeinen Form des Operationszeichens gegeben sein.

Ja muß dies nicht der einzige legitime Ausdruck der Anwendung der Operation sein? Offenbar ja!

Denn wenn die Operationsform überhaupt ausgedrückt werden kann, dann muß sie es so, daß sie nur richtig angewendet werden *kann*.

Der Mensch kann sich nicht ohne weiteres glücklich machen.

Wer in der Gegenwart lebt, lebt ohne Furcht und Hoffnung.

21. 7. 16.

Was für eine Bewandtnis hat es eigentlich mit dem menschlichen Willen? Ich will "Willen" vor allem den Träger von Gut und Böse nennen.

Stellen wir uns einen Menschen vor, der keines seiner Glieder gebrauchen und daher im gewöhnlichen Sinne seinen *Willen* nicht betätigen könnte. Er könnte aber denken und *wünschen* und einem

If all particular objects are given, "all objects" are given.
In short with the particular objects all objects are given. [*Cf.* 5.524.]

If there are objects, then that gives us "all objects" too. [*Cf.* 5.524.]

That is why it must be possible to construct the unity of the elementary propositions and of the general propositions.

For if the elementary propositions are given, that gives us *all* elementary propositions, too, and that gives us the general proposition. —And with that has not the unity been constructed? [*Cf.* 5.524.]

13.7.16.

One keeps on feeling that even in the elementary proposition mention is made of all objects.

$(\exists x)\phi x . x = a$

If two operations are given which cannot be reduced to *one*, then it must at least be possible to set up a general form of their combination.

ϕx, $\psi y | \chi z$, $(\exists x)$. , (x).

As obviously it can easily be explained how propositions can be formed by means of these operations and how propositions are not to be formed, this must also be capable *somehow* of exact expression.

14.7.16.

And this expression must already be given in the general form of the sign of an operation.

And mustn't this be the only legitimate expression of the application of an operation? Obviously it must!

For if the form of operation can be expressed at all, then it must be expressed in such a way that it *can* only be applied correctly.

Man cannot make himself happy without more ado.

Whoever lives in the present lives without fear and hope.

21.7.16.

What really is the situation of the human will? I will call "will" first and foremost the bearer of good and evil.

Let us imagine a man who could use none of his limbs and hence could, in the ordinary sense, not exercise his *will*. He could, however, think and *want* and communicate his thoughts to someone else. Could

Anderen seine Gedanken mitteilen. Könnte also auch durch den Anderen Böses oder Gutes tun. Dann ist klar, daß die Ethik auch für ihn Geltung hätte, und er im *ethischen Sinne* Träger eines *Willens* ist.

Ist nun ein prinzipieller Unterschied zwischen diesem Willen und *dem*, der den menschlichen Körper in Bewegung setzt?

Oder liegt hier der Fehler darin, daß auch schon das *Wünschen* (resp. Denken) eine Handlung des Willens ist? (Und in diesem Sinne wäre allerdings der Mensch *ohne* Willen nicht lebendig.)

Ist aber ein Wesen denkbar, das nur vorstellen (etwa sehen), aber gar nicht wollen könnte? In irgend einem Sinne scheint dies unmöglich. Wäre es aber möglich, dann könnte es auch eine Welt geben ohne Ethik.

24. 7. 16.

Die Welt und das Leben sind Eins. [5.621.]

Das physiologische Leben ist natürlich nicht "das Leben". Und auch nicht das psychologische. Das Leben ist die Welt.

Die Ethik handelt nicht von der Welt. Die Ethik muß eine Bedingung der Welt sein, wie die Logik.

Ethik und Aesthetik sind Eins. [*S.* 6.421.]

29. 7. 16.

Denn daß der Wunsch mit seiner Erfüllung in keinem logischen Zusammenhang steht, ist eine logische Tatsache. Und daß die Welt des Glücklichen eine *andere* ist als die Welt des Unglücklichen, ist auch klar. [*Vgl.* 6.43.]

Ist sehen eine Tätigkeit?

Kann man gut wollen, böse wollen und nicht wollen?

Oder ist nur der glücklich, der *nicht* will?

"Seinen Nächsten lieben", das hieße wollen!

Kann man aber wünschen und doch nicht unglücklich sein, wenn der Wunsch nicht in Erfüllung geht? (Und diese Möglichkeit besteht ja immer.)

Ist es, nach den allgemeinen Begriffen, gut, seinem Nächsten *nichts* zu wünschen, weder Gutes noch Schlechtes?

Und doch scheint in einem gewissen Sinne das Nichtwünschen das einzig Gute zu sein.

therefore do good or evil through the other man. Then it is clear that ethics would have validity for him, too, and that he in the *ethical sense* is the bearer of a *will*.

Now is there any difference in principle between this will and that which sets the human body in motion?

Or is the mistake here this: even *wanting* (thinking) is an activity of the will? (And in this sense, indeed, a man *without* will would not be alive.)

But can we conceive a being that isn't capable of Will at all, but only of Idea (of seeing for example)? In some sense this seems impossible. But if it were possible then there could also be a world without ethics.

24.7.16.

The World and Life are one. [5.621.]

Physiological life is of course not "Life". And neither is psychological life. Life is the world.

Ethics does not treat of the world. Ethics must be a condition of the world, like logic.

Ethics and aesthetics are one. [*See* 6.421.]

29.7.16.

For it is a fact of logic that wanting does not stand in any logical connexion with its own fulfilment. And it is also clear that the world of the happy is a *different* world from the world of the unhappy. [*Cf.* 6.43.]

Is seeing an activity?

Is it possible to will good, to will evil, and not to will?

Or is only he happy who does *not* will?

"To love one's neighbour" would mean to will!

But can one want and yet not be unhappy if the want does not attain fulfilment? (And this possibility always exists.)

Is it, according to common conceptions, good to want *nothing* for one's neighbour, neither good nor evil?

And yet in a certain sense it seems that not wanting is the only good.

Hier mache ich noch grobe Fehler! Kein Zweifel!

Allgemein wird angenommen, daß es böse ist, dem Anderen Unglück zu wünschen. Kann das richtig sein? Kann es schlechter sein, als dem Anderen Glück zu wünschen?

Es scheint da sozusagen darauf anzukommen, *wie* man wünscht.

Man scheint nicht mehr sagen zu können als: Lebe glücklich!

Die Welt des Glücklichen ist eine andere als die des Unglücklichen. [*S.* 6.43.]

Die Welt des Glücklichen ist *eine glückliche Welt*.

Kann es also eine Welt geben, die weder glücklich noch unglücklich ist?

30. 7. 16.

Der erste Gedanke bei der Aufstellung eines allgemeinen ethischen Gesetzes von der Form "Du sollst . . ." ist: "Und was dann, wenn ich es nicht tue?"

Es ist aber klar, daß die Ethik nichts mit Strafe und Lohn zu tun hat. Also muß diese Frage nach den Folgen einer Handlung belanglos sein. Zum mindesten dürfen diese Folgen nicht Ereignisse sein. Denn etwas muß doch an jener Fragestellung richtig sein. Es muß zwar eine *Art* von ethischem Lohn und ethischer Strafe geben, aber diese müssen in der Handlung selbst liegen.

Und das ist auch klar, daß der Lohn etwas Angenehmes, die Strafe etwas Unangenehmes sein muß.

[6.422.]

Immer wieder komme ich darauf zurück, daß einfach das glückliche Leben gut, das unglückliche schlecht ist. Und wenn ich mich *jetzt* frage: aber *warum* soll ich gerade glücklich leben, so erscheint mir das von selbst als eine tautologische Fragestellung; es scheint, daß sich das glückliche Leben von selbst rechtfertigt, daß es das einzig richtige Leben *ist*.

Alles dies ist eigentlich in gewissem Sinne tief geheimnisvoll! *Es ist klar*, daß sich die Ethik nicht aussprechen *läßt*! [*Vgl.* 6.421.]

Man könnte aber so sagen: Das glückliche Leben scheint in irgend einem Sinne *harmonischer* zu sein als das unglückliche. In welchem aber??

Was ist das objektive Merkmal des glücklichen, harmonischen Lebens? Da ist es wieder klar, daß es kein solches Merkmal, das sich *beschreiben* ließe, geben kann.

Dies Merkmal kann kein physisches, sondern nur ein metaphysisches, ein transcendentes sein.

Here I am still making crude mistakes! No doubt of that!

It is generally assumed that it is evil to want someone else to be unfortunate. Can this be correct? Can it be worse than to want him to be fortunate?

Here everything seems to turn, so to speak, on *how* one wants.

It seems one can't say anything more than: Live happily!

The world of the happy is a different world from that of the unhappy. [*See* 6.43.]

The world of the happy is *a happy world.*

Then can there be a world that is neither happy nor unhappy?

30.7.16.

When a general ethical law of the form "Thou shalt . . ." is set up, the first thought is: Suppose I do not do it?

But it is clear that ethics has nothing to do with punishment and reward. So this question about the consequences of an action must be unimportant. At least these consequences cannot be events. For there must be something right about that question after all. There must be a *kind* of ethical reward and of ethical punishment but these must be involved in the action itself.

And it is also clear that the reward must be something pleasant, the punishment something unpleasant.

[6.422.]

I keep on coming back to this! simply the happy life is good, the unhappy bad. And if I *now* ask myself: But why should I live *happily*, then this of itself seems to me to be a tautological question; the happy life seems to be justified, of itself, it seems that it *is* the only right life.

But this is really in some sense deeply mysterious! *It is clear* that ethics *cannot* be expressed! [*Cf.* 6.421.]

But we could say: The happy life seems to be in some sense more *harmonious* than the unhappy. But in what sense??

What is the objective mark of the happy, harmonious life? Here it is again clear that there cannot be any such mark, that can be *described.*

This mark cannot be a physical one but only a metaphysical one, a transcendental one.

Die Ethik ist transcendent. [*S.* 6.421.]

1. 8. 16.

Wie sich alles verhält, ist Gott.

Gott ist, wie sich alles verhält.

Nur aus dem Bewußtsein der *Einzigkeit meines Lebens* entspringt Religion—Wissenschaft—und Kunst.

2. 8. 16.

Und dieses Bewußtsein ist das Leben selber.

Kann es eine Ethik geben, wenn es außer mir kein Lebewesen gibt?

Wenn die Ethik etwas Grundlegendes sein soll: ja!

Wenn ich recht habe, so genügt es nicht zum ethischen Urteil, daß eine Welt gegeben sei.

Die Welt ist dann an sich weder gut noch böse.

Denn es muß für die Existenz der Ethik gleich bleiben, ob es auf der Welt lebende Materie gibt oder nicht. Und es ist klar, daß eine Welt, in der nur tote Materie ist, an sich weder gut noch böse ist, also kann auch die Welt der Lebewesen an sich weder gut noch böse sein.

Gut und Böse tritt erst durch das *Subjekt* ein. Und das Subjekt gehört nicht zur Welt, sondern ist eine Grenze der Welt. [*Vgl.* 5.632.]

Man könnte (Schopenhauerisch) sagen: Die Welt der Vorstellung ist weder gut noch böse, sondern das wollende Subjekt.

Die völlige Unklarheit aller dieser Sätze ist mir bewußt.

Nach dem Früheren müßte also das wollende Subjekt glücklich oder unglücklich sein, und Glück und Unglück können nicht zur Welt gehören.

Wie das Subjekt kein Teil der Welt ist, sondern eine Voraussetzung ihrer Existenz, so sind gut und böse, Prädikate des Subjekts, nicht Eigenschaften in der Welt.

Ganz verschleiert ist hier das Wesen des Subjekts.

Ja, meine Arbeit hat sich ausgedehnt von den Grundlagen der Logik zum Wesen der Welt.

Ethics is transcendental. [*See* 6.421.]

1.8.16.

How things stand, is God.

God is, how things stand.

Only from the consciousness of the *uniqueness of my life* arises religion—science—and art.

2.8.16.

And this consciousness is life itself.

Can there be any ethics if there is no living being but myself?

If ethics is supposed to be something fundamental, there can.

If I am right, then it is not sufficient for the ethical judgment that a world is given.

Then the world in itself is neither good nor evil.

For it must be all one, as far as concerns the existence of ethics, whether there is living matter in the world or not. And it is clear that a world in which there is only dead matter is in itself neither good nor evil, so even the world of living things can in itself be neither good nor evil.

Good and evil only enter through the *subject*. And the subject is not part of the world, but a boundary of the world. [*Cf.* 5.632.]

It would be possible to say (à la Schopenhauer): It is not the world of Idea that is either good or evil; but the willing subject.

I am conscious of the complete unclarity of all these sentences.

Going by the above, then, the willing subject would have to be happy or unhappy, and happiness and unhappiness could not be part of the world.

As the subject is not a part of the world but a presupposition of its existence, so good and evil which are predicates of the subject, are not properties in the world.

Here the nature of the subject is completely veiled.

My work has extended from the foundations of logic to the nature of the world.

4. 8. 16.

Ist nicht am Ende das vorstellende Subjekt bloßer Aberglaube?

Wo in der Welt ist ein metaphysisches Subjekt zu merken? [*S.* 5.633.]

Du sagst, es verhält sich hier ganz wie bei Auge und Gesichtsfeld. Aber das Auge siehst du wirklich *nicht*. [*S.* 5.633.]

Und ich glaube, daß nichts am Gesichtsfeld darauf schließen läßt, daß es von einem Auge gesehen wird. [*Vgl.* 5.633.]

5. 8. 16.

Das vorstellende Subjekt ist wohl leerer Wahn. Das wollende Subjekt aber gibt es. [*Vgl.* 5.631.]

Wäre der Wille nicht, so gäbe es auch nicht jenes Zentrum der Welt, das wir das Ich nennen, und das der Träger der Ethik ist.

Gut und böse ist wesentlich nur das Ich, nicht die Welt.

Das Ich, das Ich ist das tief Geheimnisvolle!

7. 8. 16.

Das Ich ist kein Gegenstand.

11. 8. 16.

Jedem Gegenstand stehe ich objektiv gegenüber. Dem Ich nicht.

Es gibt also wirklich eine Art und Weise, wie in der Philosophie *in einem nicht psychologischen Sinne* vom Ich die Rede sein kann und muß. [*Vgl.* 5.641.]

12. 8. 16.

Das Ich tritt in die Philosophie dadurch ein, daß die Welt *meine* Welt ist. [*S.* 5.641.]

Das Gesichtsfeld hat nämlich nicht etwa eine solche Form:

[5.6331.]

Das hängt damit zusammen, daß kein Teil unserer Erfahrung a priori ist. [*S.* 5.634.]

Alles, was wir sehen, könnte auch anders sein.

Alles, was wir überhaupt beschreiben können, könnte auch anders sein.

[*S.* 5.634.]

4.8.16.

Isn't the thinking subject in the last resort mere superstition?

Where in the world is a metaphysical subject to be found? [*See* 5.633.]

You say that it is just as it is for the eye and the visual field. But you do *not* actually see the eye. [*See* 5.633.]

And I think that nothing in the visual field would enable one to infer that it is seen from an eye. [*Cf.* 5.633.]

5.8.16.

The thinking subject is surely mere illusion. But the willing subject exists. [*Cf.* 5.631.]

If the will did not exist, neither would there be that centre of the world, which we call the I, and which is the bearer of ethics.

What is good and evil is essentially the I, not the world.

The I, the I is what is deeply mysterious!

7.8.16.

The I is not an object.

11.8.16.

I objectively confront every object. But not the I.

So there really is a way in which there can and must be mention of the I in a *non-psychological sense* in philosophy. [*Cf.* 5.641.]

12.8.16.

The I makes its appearance in philosophy through the world's being *my* world. [*See* 5.641.]

The visual field has not, e.g., a form like this:

[5.6331.]

This is connected with the fact that none of our experience is *a priori*. [*See* 5.634.]

All that we see could also be otherwise.

All that we can describe at all could also be otherwise. [*See* 5.634.]

13. 8. 16.

Angenommen, der Mensch könnte seinen Willen nicht betätigen, müßte aber alle Not dieser Welt leiden, was könnte ihn dann glücklich machen?

Wie kann der Mensch überhaupt glücklich sein, da er doch die Not dieser Welt nicht abwehren kann?

Eben durch das Leben der Erkenntnis.

Das gute Gewissen ist das Glück, welches das Leben der Erkenntnis gewährt.

Das Leben der Erkenntnis ist das Leben, welches glücklich ist, der Not der Welt zum Trotz.

Nur das Leben ist glücklich, welches auf die Annehmlichkeiten der Welt verzichten kann.

Ihm sind die Annehmlichkeiten der Welt nur so viele Gnaden des Schicksals.

16. 8. 16.

Daß ein Punkt nicht zugleich rot und grün sein kann, muß dem ersten Anschein nach keine *logische* Unmöglichkeit sein. Aber schon die physikalische Ausdrucksweise reduziert sie zu einer kinetischen Unmöglichkeit. Man sieht, zwischen Rot und Grün besteht eine Verschiedenheit der Struktur.

Und nun ordnet sie die Physik gar noch in eine Reihe. Und nun sieht man, wie hier die wahre Struktur der Gegenstände ans Licht gebracht wird.

Daß ein Teilchen nicht zu gleicher Zeit an zwei Orten sein kann, das sieht schon vielmehr aus wie eine *logische* Unmöglichkeit.

Fragen wir z. B. warum, so taucht sofort der Gedanke auf: Nun, wir würden eben Teilchen, die sich an zwei Orten befänden, verschiedene nennen, und das scheint alles wieder aus der Struktur des Raumes und der Teilchen zu folgen.

[*Vgl.* 6.3751.]

17. 8. 16.

Operation ist der Übergang von einem Glied zum folgenden einer Formen-Reihe.

Operation und Formen-Reihe sind Äquivalente.

29. 8. 16.

Die Frage ist, ob die gewöhnliche, kleine Anzahl von Grundoperationen genügt, um alle möglichen Operationen herzustellen.

Es scheint, daß dies so sein muß.

13.8.16.

Suppose that man could not exercise his will, but had to suffer all the misery of this world, then what could make him happy?

How can man be happy at all, since he cannot ward off the misery of this world?

Through the life of knowledge.

The good conscience is the happiness that the life of knowledge preserves.

The life of knowledge is the life that is happy in spite of the misery of the world.

The only life that is happy is the life that can renounce the amenities of the world.

To it the amenities of the world are so many graces of fate.

16.8.16.

A point cannot be red and green at the same time: at first sight there seems no need for this to be a logical impossibility. But the very language of physics reduces it to a kinetic impossibility. We see that there is a difference of structure between red and green.

And then physics arranges them in a series. And then we see how here the true structure of the objects is brought to light.

The fact that a particle cannot be in two places at the same time does look more like a logical impossibility.

If we ask why, for example, then straight away comes the thought: Well, we should call particles that were in two places different, and this in its turn all seems to follow from the structure of space and of particles.

[*Cf.* 6.3751.]

17.8.16.

An operation is the transition from one term to the next one in a series of forms.

The operation and the series of forms are equivalents.

29.8.16.

The question is whether the usual small number of fundamental operations is adequate for the construction of all possible operations.

It looks as if it must be so.

Man kann auch fragen, ob man von jedem Ausdruck auf jeden verwandten mit jenen Grundoperationen übergehen kann.

2. 9. 16.

Hier sieht man, daß der Solipsismus streng durchgeführt mit dem reinen Realismus zusammenfällt.

Das Ich des Solipsismus schrumpft zum ausdehnungslosen Punkt zusammen, und es bleibt die ihm koordinierte Realität bestehen. [5.64.]

Was geht mich die Geschichte an? Meine Welt ist die erste und einzige!

Ich will berichten, wie *ich* die Welt vorfand.

Was andere mir auf der Welt über die Welt sagten, ist ein ganz kleiner und nebensächlicher Teil meiner Welt-Erfahrung.

Ich habe die Welt zu beurteilen, die Dinge zu messen.

Das philosophische Ich ist nicht der Mensch, nicht der menschliche Körper oder die menschliche Seele mit den psychologischen Eigenschaften, sondern das metaphysische Subjekt, die Grenze (nicht ein Teil) der Welt. Der menschliche Körper aber, *mein* Körper insbesondere, ist ein Teil der Welt unter anderen Teilen der Welt, unter Tieren, Pflanzen, Steinen etc. etc. [*Vgl.* 5.641.]

Wer das einsieht, wird seinem Körper oder dem menschlichen Körper nicht eine bevorzugte Stelle in der Welt einräumen wollen.

Er wird Menschen und Tiere ganz naiv als ähnliche und zusammengehörige Dinge betrachten.

11. 9. 16.

Die Art und Weise, wie die Sprache bezeichnet, spiegelt sich in ihrem Gebrauche wieder.

Daß die Farben keine Eigenschaften sind, zeigt die Analyse der Physik, zeigen die internen Relationen, in welchen die Physik die Farben zeigt.

Wende dies auch auf Klänge an.

12. 9. 16.

Jetzt wird klar, warum ich dachte, Denken und Sprechen wäre dasselbe. Das Denken nämlich ist eine Art Sprache. Denn der Gedanke ist natürlich *auch* ein logisches Bild des Satzes und somit ebenfalls eine Art Satz.

We can also ask whether those fundamental operations enable us to pass from any expression to any related ones.

2.9.16.

Here we can see that solipsism coincides with pure realism, if it is strictly thought out.

The I of solipsism shrinks to an extensionless point and what remains is the reality co-ordinate with it.

[5.64.]

What has history to do with me? Mine is the first and only world!

I want to report how *I* found the world.

What others in the world have told me about the world is a very small and incidental part of my experience of the world.

I have to judge the world, to measure things.

The philosophical I is not the human being, not the human body or the human soul with the psychological properties, but the metaphysical subject, the boundary (not a part) of the world. The human body, however, my body in particular, is a part of the world among others, among beasts, plants, stones etc., etc. [*Cf.* 5.641.]

Whoever realizes this will not want to procure a pre-eminent place for his own body or for the human body.

He will regard humans and beasts quite naïvely as objects which are similar and which belong together.

11.9.16.

The way in which language signifies is mirrored in its use.

That the colours are not properties is shewn by the analysis of physics, by the internal relations in which physics displays the colours.

Apply this to sounds too.

12.9.16.

Now it is becoming clear why I thought that thinking and language were the same. For thinking is a kind of language. For a thought too is, of course, a logical picture of the proposition, and therefore it just is a kind of proposition.

19. 9. 16.

Die Menschheit hat immer nach einer Wissenschaft gesucht, in welcher simplex sigillum veri ist. [*Vgl.* 5.4541.]

Es kann nicht eine ordentliche oder eine unordentliche Welt geben, so daß man sagen könnte, unsere Welt ist ordentlich. Sondern in jeder möglichen Welt ist eine, wenn auch komplizierte Ordnung geradeso, wie es im Raum auch nicht unordentliche und ordentliche Punktverteilungen gibt, sondern jede Punktverteilung ist ordentlich.
(Diese Bemerkung ist nur Material für einen Gedanken.)

Die Kunst ist ein Ausdruck.

Das gute Kunstwerk ist der vollendete Ausdruck.

7. 10. 16.

Das Kunstwerk ist der Gegenstand sub specie aeternitatis gesehen; und das gute Leben ist die Welt sub specie aeternitatis gesehen. Dies ist der Zusammenhang zwischen Kunst und Ethik.

Die gewöhnliche Betrachtungsweise sieht die Gegenstände gleichsam aus ihrer Mitte, die Betrachtung sub specie aeternitatis von außerhalb.

So daß sie die ganze Welt als Hintergrund haben.

Ist es etwa das, daß sie den Gegenstand *mit* Raum und Zeit sieht statt *in* Raum und Zeit?

Jedes Ding bedingt die ganze logische Welt, sozusagen den ganzen logischen Raum.

(Es drängt sich der Gedanke auf): Das Ding sub specie aeternitatis gesehen ist das Ding mit dem ganzen logischen Raum gesehen.

8. 10. 16.

Als Ding unter Dingen ist jedes Ding gleich unbedeutend, als Welt jedes gleichbedeutend.

Habe ich den Ofen kontempliert, und es wird mir nun gesagt: jetzt kennst du aber nur den Ofen, so scheint mein Resultat allerdings kleinlich. Denn das stellt es so dar, als hätte ich den Ofen unter den vielen, vielen Dingen der Welt studiert. Habe ich aber den Ofen kontempliert, so war *er* meine Welt, und alles Andere dagegen blaß.
(Manches Gute im Großen, im Einzelnen aber schlecht.)

Man kann eben die bloße gegenwärtige Vorstellung sowohl auffassen, als das nichtige momentane Bild in der ganzen zeitlichen Welt, als auch als die wahre Welt unter Schatten.

19.9.16.

Mankind has always looked for a science in which *simplex sigillum veri* holds. [*Cf.* 5.4541.]

There cannot be an orderly or a disorderly world, so that one could say that our world is orderly. In every possible world there is an order even if it is a complicated one, just as in space too there are not orderly and disorderly distributions of points, but every distribution of points is orderly.

(This remark is only material for a thought.)

Art is a kind of expression.

Good art is complete expression.

7.10.16.

The work of art is the object seen *sub specie aeternitatis*; and the good life is the world seen *sub specie aeternitatis*. This is the connexion between art and ethics.

The usual way of looking at things sees objects as it were from the midst of them, the view *sub specie aeternitatis* from outside.

In such a way that they have the whole world as background.

Is this it perhaps—in this view the object is seen *together with* space and time instead of *in* space and time?

Each thing modifies the whole logical world, the whole of logical space, so to speak.

(The thought forces itself upon one): The thing seen *sub specie aeternitatis* is the thing seen together with the whole logical space.

8.10.16.

As a thing among things, each thing is equally insignificant; as a world each one equally significant.

If I have been contemplating the stove, and then am told: but now all you know is the stove, my result does indeed seem trivial. For this represents the matter as if I had studied the stove as one among the many things in the world. But if I was contemplating the stove *it* was my world, and everything else colourless by contrast with it.

(Something good about the whole, but bad in details.)

For it is equally possible to take the bare present image as the worthless momentary picture in the whole temporal world, and as the true world among shadows.

9. 10. 16.

Nun ist aber endlich der Zusammenhang der Ethik mit der Welt klarzumachen.

12. 10. 16.

Ein Stein, der Körper eines Tieres, der Körper eines Menschen, mein Körper, stehen alle auf gleicher Stufe.

Darum ist, was geschieht, ob es von einem Stein oder von meinem Körper geschieht, weder gut noch schlecht.

"Die Zeit ist einsinnig", muß ein Unsinn sein.

Die Einsinnigkeit ist eine logische Eigenschaft der Zeit.

Denn wenn man jemanden fräge, wie er sich die Einsinnigkeit vorstellt, so würde er sagen: die Zeit wäre nicht einsinnig, wenn sich ein Ereignis wiederholen könnte.

Daß sich aber ein Ereignis nicht wiederholen kann, liegt, geradeso wie, daß ein Körper nicht zu gleicher Zeit an zwei Orten sein kann, im logischen Wesen des Ereignisses.

Es ist wahr: der Mensch *ist* der Mikrokosmos:
Ich bin meine Welt. [*Vgl.* 5.63.]

15. 10. 16.

Was man sich nicht denken kann, darüber kann man auch nicht reden. [*Vgl.* 5.61.]

"Bedeutung" bekommen die Dinge erst durch ihr Verhältnis zu meinem Willen.

Denn "Jedes Ding ist, was es ist, und kein ander Ding".

Eine Auffassung: Wie ich aus meiner Physiognomie auf meinen Geist (Charakter, Willen) schließen kann, so aus der Physiognomie jedes Dinges auf *seinen* Geist (Willen).

Kann ich aber aus meiner Physiognomie auf meinen Geist *schließen*?
Ist dieses Verhältnis nicht rein empirisch?

Drückt mein Körper wirklich etwas aus?
Ist er selbst der interne Ausdruck von etwas?

Ist etwa das böse Gesicht an sich böse oder bloß, weil es empirisch mit böser Laune verbunden ist?

Aber es ist klar, daß der Kausalnexus gar kein Nexus ist. [*Vgl.* 5.136.]

9.10.16.

But now at last the connexion of ethics with the world has to be made clear.

12.10.16.

A stone, the body of a beast, the body of a man, my body, all stand on the same level.

That is why what happens, whether it comes from a stone or from my body is neither good nor bad.

"Time has only one direction" must be a piece of nonsense.

Having only one direction is a logical property of time.

For if one were to ask someone how he imagines having only one direction he would say: Time would not be confined to one direction if an event could be repeated.

But the impossibility of an event's being repeated, like that of a body's being in two places at once, is involved in the logical nature of the event.

It is true: Man *is* the microcosm:
I am my world. [*Cf.* 5.63.]

15.10.16.

What cannot be imagined cannot even be talked about. [*Cf.* 5.61.]

Things acquire "significance" only through their relation to my will.

For "Everything is what it is and not another thing".

One conception: As I can infer my spirit (character, will) from my physiognomy, so I can infer the spirit (will) of each thing from *its* physiognomy.

But can I *infer* my spirit from my physiognomy?

Isn't this relationship purely empirical?

Does my body really express anything?
Is it itself an internal expression of something?

Is, e.g., an angry face angry in itself or merely because it is empirically connected with bad temper?

But it is clear that the causal nexus is not a nexus at all. [*Cf.* 5.136.]

Ist es denn wahr, daß sich mein Charakter nach der psychophysischen Auffassung nur im Bau *meines* Körpers oder meines Gehirns und nicht ebenso im Bau der ganzen übrigen Welt ausdrückt?

Hier liegt ein springender Punkt.

Dieser Parallelismus besteht also eigentlich zwischen meinem Geist, i.e. dem Geist, und der Welt.

Bedenke nur, daß der Geist der Schlange, des Löwen, *dein* Geist ist. Denn nur von dir her kennst du überhaupt den Geist.

Es ist nun freilich die Frage, warum habe ich der Schlange gerade diesen Geist gegeben.

Und die Antwort hierauf kann nur im psychophysischen Parallelismus liegen: Wenn ich so aussähe wie die Schlange und das täte, was sie tut, so wäre ich so und so.

Das Gleiche beim Elefanten, bei der Fliege, bei der Wespe.

Es fragt sich aber, ob nicht eben auch hier wieder (und gewiß ist es so) mein Körper mit dem der Wespe und der Schlange auf einer Stufe steht, so daß ich weder von dem der Wespe auf meinen, noch von meinem auf den der Wespe geschlossen habe.

Ist das die Lösung des Rätsels, warum die Menschen immer glaubten, *ein* Geist sei der ganzen Welt gemein?

Und dann wäre er freilich auch den unbelebten Dingen gemeinsam.

Der Weg, den ich gegangen bin, ist der: Der Idealismus scheidet aus der Welt als unik die Menschen aus, der Solipsismus scheidet mich allein aus, und endlich sehe ich, daß auch ich zur übrigen Welt gehöre, auf der einen Seite bleibt also *nichts* übrig, auf der anderen als unik *die Welt*. So führt der Idealismus streng durchdacht zum Realismus. [*Vgl.* 5.64.]

17. 10. 16.

Und in diesem Sinne kann ich auch von einem der ganzen Welt gemeinsamen Willen sprechen.

Aber dieser Wille ist in einem höheren Sinne *mein* Wille.

Wie meine Vorstellung die Welt ist, so ist mein Wille der Weltwille.

20. 10. 16.

Es ist klar, daß mein Gesichtsraum der Länge nach anders beschaffen ist, als der Breite nach.

Now is it true (following the psycho-physical conception) that my character is expressed only in the build of *my* body or brain and not equally in the build of the whole of the rest of the world?

This contains a salient point.

This parallelism, then, really exists between my spirit, i.e. spirit, and the world.

Only remember that the spirit of the snake, of the lion, is *your* spirit. For it is only from yourself that you are acquainted with spirit at all.

Now of course the question is why I have given a snake just this spirit.

And the answer to this can only lie in the psycho-physical parallelism: If I were to look like the snake and to do what it does then I should be such-and-such.

The same with the elephant, with the fly, with the wasp.

But the question arises whether even here, my body is not on the same level with that of the wasp and of the snake (and surely it is so), so that I have neither inferred from that of the wasp to mine nor from mine to that of the wasp.

Is this the solution of the puzzle why men have always believed that there was *one* spirit common to the whole world?

And in that case it would, of course, also be common to lifeless things too.

This is the way I have travelled: Idealism singles men out from the world as unique, solipsism singles me alone out, and at last I see that I too belong with the rest of the world, and so on the one side *nothing* is left over, and on the other side, as unique, *the world*. In this way idealism leads to realism if it is strictly thought out. [*Cf.* 5.64.]

17.10.16.

And in this sense I can also speak of a will that is common to the whole world.

But this will is in a higher sense *my* will.

As my idea is the world, in the same way my will is the world-will.

20.10.16.

It is clear that my visual space is constituted differently in length from breadth.

Es verhält sich nicht so, daß ich mich einfach überall bemerke, wo ich etwas sehe, sondern ich befinde mich auch immer in einem bestimmten Punkt meines Gesichtsraumes, mein Gesichtsraum hat also quasi eine Form.

Trotzdem aber ist es wahr, daß ich das Subjekt nicht sehe.

Es ist wahr, daß das erkennende Subjekt nicht in der Welt ist, daß es kein erkennendes Subjekt gibt. [*Vgl.* 5.631.]

Ich kann mir jedenfalls vorstellen, daß ich den Willensakt ausführe, um meinen Arm zu heben, aber mein Arm sich nicht bewegt. (Eine Sehne sei etwa gerissen.) Ja, aber, wird man sagen, die Sehne bewegt sich doch, und dies zeigt eben, daß sich mein Willensakt auf die Sehne und nicht auf den Arm bezogen hat. Aber gehen wir weiter und nehmen an, auch die Sehne bewegte sich nicht und so fort. Wir würden dann dazu kommen, daß sich der Willensakt überhaupt nicht auf einen Körper bezieht, daß es also im gewöhnlichen Sinne des Wortes keinen Willensakt gibt.

Das künstlerische Wunder ist, daß es die Welt gibt. Daß es das gibt, was es gibt.

Ist das das Wesen der künstlerischen Betrachtungsweise, daß sie die Welt mit glücklichem Auge betrachtet?

Ernst ist das Leben, heiter ist die Kunst.[1]

21. 10. 16.

Denn etwas ist wohl an der Auffassung, als sei das Schöne der Zweck der Kunst.

Und das Schöne ist eben das, was glücklich macht.

29. 10. 16.

Könnte man nicht sagen: die Allgemeinheit ist der Zusammensetzung ebensowenig koordiniert wie Tatsache dem Ding?

Beide Arten von Operationszeichen müssen oder können im Satz nebeneinander vorkommen.

4. 11. 16.

Ist der Wille eine Stellungnahme zur Welt?

Der Wille scheint sich immer auf eine Vorstellung beziehen zu müssen. Wir können uns z. B. nicht vorstellen, daß wir einen Willensakt ausgeführt hätten, ohne gespürt zu haben, daß wir ihn ausgeführt haben.

[1] Schiller, *Wallensteins Lager, Prolog.* (Herausg.)

The situation is not simply that I everywhere notice where I see anything, but I also always find myself at a particular point of my visual space, so my visual space has as it were a shape.

In spite of this, however, it is true that I do not see the subject.

It is true that the knowing subject is not in the world, that there is no knowing subject. [*Cf.* 5.631.]

At any rate I can imagine carrying out the act of will for raising my arm, but that my arm does not move. (E.g., a sinew is torn.) True, but, it will be said, the sinew surely moves and that just shews that the act of will related to the sinew and not to the arm. But let us go farther and suppose that even the sinew did not move, and so on. We should then arrive at the position that the act of will does not relate to a body at all, and so that in the ordinary sense of the word there is no such thing as the act of the will.

Aesthetically, the miracle is that the world exists. That there is what there is.

Is it the essence of the artistic way of looking at things, that it looks at the world with a happy eye?

Life is grave, art is gay.[1]

21.10.16.

For there is certainly something in the conception that the end of art is the beautiful.

And the beautiful *is* what makes happy.

29.10.16.

Could it not be said that generality is no more co-ordinated with the complex than is fact with thing?

Both kinds of operation sign must or can occur in the proposition side by side.

4.11.16.

Is the will an attitude towards the world?

The will seems always to have to relate to an idea. We cannot imagine, e.g., having carried out an act of will without having detected that we have carried it out.

[1] Schiller, Prologue to *Wallensteins Lager*. [*Edd.*]

Es könnte sonst etwa die Frage entstehen, ob er schon *ganz* ausgeführt sei.

Es ist sozusagen klar, daß wir für den Willen einen Halt in der Wel brauchen.

Der Wille ist eine Stellungnahme des Subjekts zur Welt.

Das Subjekt ist das wollende Subjekt.

Haben die Gefühle, die mich von dem Vorgang eines Willensakts überzeugen, irgend eine besondere Eigenschaft, die sie von anderen Vorstellungen unterscheidet?

Es scheint nein!

Dann wäre es aber denkbar, daß ich etwa darauf käme, daß z. B. dieser Sessel direkt meinem Willen folgt.

Ist das möglich?

Bei dem Zeichnen des Vierecks 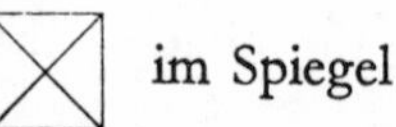 im Spiegel bemerkt man, daß man es nur ausführen kann, wenn man vom Gesichtsbild ganz absieht und nur das Muskelgefühl zu Hilfe nimmt. Also handelt es sich hier doch um zwei ganz verschiedene Willensakte. Der eine bezieht sich auf den Gesichtsteil der Welt, der andere auf den Teil des Muskelgefühls.

Haben wir mehr als erfahrungsmäßige Evidenz, daß es sich in beiden Fällen um die Bewegung desselben Körperteils handelt?

Verhält es sich also so, daß ich meine Handlungen mit meinem Willen nur begleite?

Aber wie kann ich dann voraussagen—und das kann ich doch in einem gewissen Sinne—daß ich in 5 Minuten meinen Arm heben werde? Daß ich dies wollen werde?

Es ist klar: Es ist unmöglich zu wollen, ohne nicht schon den Willensakt auszuführen.

Der Willensakt ist nicht die Ursache der Handlung, sondern die Handlung selbst.

Man kann nicht wollen, ohne zu tun.

Wenn der Wille ein Objekt in der Welt haben muß, so kann es auch die beabsichtigte Handlung sein.

Und der Wille muß ein Objekt haben.

Otherwise there might arise such a question as whether it had yet been *completely* carried out.

It is clear, so to speak, that we need a foothold for the will in the world.

The will is an attitude of the subject to the world.

The subject is the willing subject.

Have the feelings by which I ascertain that an act of the will takes place any particular characteristic which distinguishes them from other ideas?

It seems not!

In that case, however, I might conceivably get the idea that, e.g., this chair was directly obeying my will.

Is that possible?

In drawing the square  in the mirror one notices that one is only able to manage it if one prescinds completely from the visual datum and relies only on muscular feeling. So here after all there are two quite different acts of the will in question. The one relates to the visual part of the world, the other to the muscular-feeling part.

Have we anything more than empirical evidence that the movement of the same part of the body is in question in both cases?

Then is the situation that I merely accompany my actions with my will?

But in that case how can I predict—as in some sense I surely can—that I shall raise my arm in five minutes' time? That I shall will this?

This is clear: it is impossible to will without already performing the act of the will.

The act of the will is not the cause of the action but is the action itself.

One cannot will without acting.

If the will has to have an object in the world, the object can be the intended action itself.

And the will does have to have an object.

Sonst hätten wir gar keinen Halt und könnten nicht wissen, was wir wollten.

Und könnten nicht Verschiedenes wollen.

Geschieht denn nicht die gewollte Bewegung des Körpers gerade so wie jedes Ungewollte in der Welt, nur daß sie vom Willen begleitet ist?

Aber sie ist nicht nur vom *Wunsch* begleitet! Sondern vom Willen.

Wir fühlen uns sozusagen für die Bewegung verantwortlich.

Mein Wille greift irgendwo in der Welt an, und an andern greift er wieder nicht an.

Wünschen ist nicht tun. Aber, Wollen ist tun.

(Mein Wunsch bezieht sich z. B. auf die Bewegung des Sessels, mein Willen auf ein Muskelgefühl.)

Daß ich einen Vorgang will, besteht darin, daß ich den Vorgang mache, nicht darin, daß ich etwas Anders tue, was den Vorgang verursacht.

Wenn ich etwas bewege, so bewege ich mich.

Wenn ich einen Vorgang mache, so gehe ich vor.

Aber: Ich kann nicht alles wollen.—

Aber was heißt das: "Ich kann *das* nicht wollen."
Kann ich denn versuchen, etwas zu wollen?

Es scheint nämlich durch die Betrachtung des Wollens, als stünde ein Teil der Welt mir näher als ein anderer (was unerträglich wäre).

Aber freilich ist es ja unleugbar, daß ich in einem populären Sinne gewisses tue und anderes nicht tue.

So stünde also der Wille der Welt nicht äquivalent gegenüber, was unmöglich sein muß.

Der Wunsch geht dem Ereignis voran, der Wille begleitet es.

Angenommen, ein Vorgang würde meinen Wunsch begleiten. Hätte ich den Vorgang gewollt?

Schiene dies Begleiten nicht zufällig im Gegensatz zu dem gezwungenen des Willens?

Otherwise we should have no foothold and could not know what we willed.

And could not will different things.

Does not the willed movement of the body happen just like any unwilled movement in the world, but that it is accompanied by the will?

Yet it is not accompanied just by a *wish*! But by will.

We feel, so to speak, responsible for the movement.

My will fastens on to the world somewhere, and does not fasten on to other things.

Wishing is not acting. But willing is acting.

(My wish relates, e.g., to the movement of the chair, my will to a muscular feeling.)

The fact that I will an action consists in my performing the action, not in my doing something else which causes the action.

When I move something I move.

When I perform an action I am in action.

But: I cannot will everything.—

But what does it mean to say: "I cannot will *this*"?
Can I try to will something?

For the consideration of willing makes it look as if one part of the world were closer to me than another (which would be intolerable).

But, of course, it is undeniable that in a popular sense there are things that I do, and other things not done by me.

In this way then the will would not confront the world as its equivalent, which must be impossible.

The wish precedes the event, the will accompanies it.

Suppose that a process were to accompany my wish. Should I have willed the process?

Would not this accompanying appear accidental in contrast to the compelled accompanying of the will?

9. 11. 16.

Ist der Glaube eine Erfahrung?
Ist der Gedanke eine Erfahrung?

Alle Erfahrung ist Welt und braucht nicht das Subjekt.

Der Willensakt ist keine Erfahrung.

19. 11. 16.

Was für ein Grund ist da zur Annahme eines wollenden Subjekts?

Genügt nicht wieder *meine Welt* zur Individualisierung?

21. 11. 16.

Daß es möglich ist, die allgemeine Satzform aufzustellen, sagt nichts anderes als: Jede mögliche Satzform muß sich *voraussehen* LASSEN.

Und *das* heißt: Wir können nie zu einer Satzform kommen, von der wir sagen könnten: Ja daß es so etwas gibt, das hat sich nicht voraussehen lassen.
Denn das würde heißen, daß wir eine neue Erfahrung gemacht hätten, die erst diese Satzform ermöglicht hat.

Also: Die allgemeine Satzform muß sich aufstellen lassen, weil die möglichen Satzformen a priori sein müssen. Weil die möglichen Satzformen a priori sind, darum gibt es die allgemeine Satzform.

Dabei ist es vollkommen gleichgültig, ob die gegebenen Grundoperationen, durch die alle Sätze entstehen sollen, dieselben über die logischen Stufen hinausführen, oder ob sie innerhalb der Stufen bleiben.

Einen Satz, den wir jemals werden bilden können, hätten wir auch jetzt gleich bilden können.

Wir brauchen jetzt die Klärung des Begriffes der atomistischen Funktion und des Begriffes "und so weiter".

Der Begriff "und so weiter", in Zeichen ". . .", ist einer der allerwichtigsten und, wie alle anderen, unendlich fundamental.

Durch ihn allein nämlich sind wir berechtigt, die Logik, resp. Mathematik, "so weiter" aus den Grundgesetzen und Urzeichen aufzubauen.

Das "und so weiter" tritt sofort im Uranfang der alten Logik ein, wenn gesagt wird, daß wir nun nach der Angabe der Urzeichen ein Zeichen nach dem anderen "so weiter" entwickeln können.

9.11.16.

Is belief a kind of experience?

Is thought a kind of experience?

All experience is world and does not need the subject.

The act of will is not an experience.

19.11.16.

What kind of reason is there for the assumption of a willing subject?

Is not *my world* adequate for individuation?

21.11.16.

The fact that it is possible to erect the general form of proposition means nothing but: every possible form of proposition must be FORESEEABLE.

And *that* means: We can never come upon a form of proposition of which we could say: it could not have been foreseen that there was such a thing as this.

For that would mean that we had had a new experience, and that it took that to make this form of proposition possible.

Thus it must be possible to erect the general form of proposition, because the possible forms of proposition must be *a priori*. Because the possible forms of proposition are *a priori*, the general form of proposition exists.

In this connexion it does not matter at all whether the given fundamental operations, through which all propositions are supposed to arise, change the logical level of the propositions, or whether they remain on the same logical level.

If a sentence were ever going to be constructable it would already be constructable.

We now need a clarification of the concept of the atomic function and the concept "and so on".

The concept "and so on", symbolized by " . . . . " is one of the most important of all and like all the others infinitely fundamental.

For it alone justifies us in constructing logic and mathematics "so on" from the fundamental laws and primitive signs.

The "and so on" makes its appearance right away at the very beginning of the old logic when it is said that after the primitive signs have been given we can develop one sign after another "so on".

Ohne diesen Begriff würden wir bei den Urzeichen einfach stehen bleiben und könnten nicht "*weiter*".

Der Begriff "und so weiter" ist äquivalent mit dem Begriffe der Operation. [*Vgl.* 5. 2523.]

Nach dem Operationszeichen folgt das Zeichen "...", welches bedeutet, daß das Resultat der Operation wieder zur Basis derselben Operation genommen werden kann, "und so weiter".

22. 11. 16.

Der Begriff der Operation ist ganz allgemein derjenige, nach welchem nach einer Regel Zeichen gebildet werden können.

23. 11. 16.

Worauf stützt sich die Möglichkeit der Operation?

Auf den allgemeinen Begriff der strukturellen Ähnlichkeit.

Wie ich z. B. die Elementarsätze auffasse, muß ihnen etwas gemeinsam sein; sonst könnte ich überhaupt nicht kollektiv von ihnen allen als den "Elementarsätzen" sprechen.

Dann müssen sie aber auch als Resultate von Operationen auseinander entwickelt werden können.

Denn wenn zwei Elementarsätzen wirklich etwas gemeinsam ist, was einem Elementarsatz und einem zusammengesetzten nicht gemeinsam ist, so muß sich dies Gemeinsame irgendwie allgemein zum Ausdruck bringen lassen.

24. 11. 16.

Wenn das allgemeine Kennzeichen der Operation bekannt sein wird, dann wird auch klar sein, aus welchen Elementar-Bestandteilen eine *Operation* immer besteht.

Wenn die allgemeine Form der Operation gefunden ist, so haben wir auch die allgemeine Form des Auftretens des Begriffs "und so weiter".

26. 11. 16.

Alle Operationen sind aus den Grundoperationen zusammengesetzt.

28. 11. 16.

Entweder eine Tatsache ist in einer anderen enthalten, oder sie ist unabhängig von ihr.

2. 12. 16.

Die Ähnlichkeit der Allgemeinheitsbezeichnung mit dem Argument zeigt sich, wenn wir statt ϕa schreiben $(ax)\phi x$. [*Vgl.* 5.523.]

Without this concept we should be stuck at the primitive signs and could not go "*on*".

The concept "and so on" and the concept of the operation are equivalent. [*Cf.* 5.2523.]

After the operation sign there follows the sign " . . . . " which signifies that the result of the operation can in its turn be taken as the base of the operation; "and so on".

22.11.16.

The concept of the operation is quite generally that according to which signs can be constructed according to a rule.

23.11.16.

What does the possibility of the operation depend on?

On the general concept of structural similarity.

As I conceive, e.g., the elementary propositions, there must be something common to them; otherwise I could not speak of them all collectively as the "elementary propositions" at all.

In that case, however, they must also be capable of being developed from one another as the results of operations.

For if there really is something common to two elementary propositions which is not common to an elementary proposition and a complex one, then this common thing must be capable of being given general expression in some way.

24.11.16.

When the general characteristic of an operation is known it will also be clear of what elementary component parts an *operation* always consists.

When the general form of operations is found we have also found the general form of the occurrence of the concept "and so on".

26.11.16.

All operations are composed of the fundamental operations.

28.11.16.

Either a fact is contained in another one, or it is independent of it.

2.12.16.

The similarity of the generality notation and the argument appears if we write $(ax)\phi x$ instead of ϕa. [*Cf.* 5.523.]

Man könnte die Argumente auch so einführen, daß sie nur auf einer Seite des Gleichheitszeichens auftreten. Also immer analog "$(\exists x).\phi x.x = a$" statt "ϕa".

Die richtige Methode in der Philosophie wäre eigentlich die, nichts zu sagen, als was sich sagen läßt, also Naturwissenschaftliches, also etwas, was mit Philosophie nichts zu tun hat, und dann immer, wenn ein anderer etwas Metaphysisches sagen wollte, ihm nachweisen, daß er gewissen Zeichen in seinen Sätzen keine Bedeutung gegeben hat. [*S.* 6.53.]

Diese Methode wäre für den anderen unbefriedigend (er hätte nicht das Gefühl, daß wir ihn Philosophie lehrten), aber sie wäre die einzig richtige. [*S.* 6.53.]

7. 1. 17.

In dem Sinne, in welchem es eine Hierarchie der Sätze gibt, gibt es natürlich auch eine Hierarchie der Wahrheiten und der Verneinungen etc.

In dem Sinne aber, in welchem es im allgemeinsten Sinne Sätze gibt, gibt es nur eine Wahrheit und eine Verneinung.

Dieser Sinn wird aus jenem gewonnen, indem der Satz im allgemeinen aufgefaßt wird als das Resultat der *einen* Operation, welche alle Sätze aus der untersten Stufe erzeugt etc.

Die unterste Stufe und die Operation kann die ganze Hierarchie vertreten.

8. 1. 17.

Es ist klar, daß das logische Produkt zweier Elementarsätze nie eine Tautologie sein kann. [*Vgl.* 6.3751.]

Ist das logische Produkt zweier Sätze eine Kontradiktion, und die Sätze scheinen Elementarsätze zu sein, so sieht man, daß in diesem Falle der Schein trügt. (Z. B.: A ist rot und A ist grün.)

10. 1. 17.

Wenn der Selbstmord erlaubt ist, dann ist alles erlaubt.

Wenn etwas nicht erlaubt ist, dann ist der Selbstmord nicht erlaubt

Dies wirft ein Licht auf das Wesen der Ethik. Denn der Selbstmord ist sozusagen die elementare Sünde.

Und wenn man ihn untersucht, so ist es, wie wenn man den Quecksilberdampf untersucht, um das Wesen der Dämpfe zu erfassen.

Oder ist nicht auch der Selbstmord an sich weder gut noch böse!

We could introduce the arguments also in such a way that they only occurred on one side of the sign of identity, i.e. always on the analogy of "(Ex).ϕx.x = a" instead of "ϕa".

The correct method in philosophy would really be to say nothing except what can be said, i.e. what belongs to natural science, i.e. something that has nothing to do with philosophy, and then whenever someone else tried to say something metaphysical to shew him that he had not given any reference to certain signs in his sentences. [*See* 6.53.]

This method would be unsatisfying for the other person (he would not have the feeling that we were teaching him philosophy) but it would be the only correct one. [*See* 6.53.]

7.1.17.

In the sense in which there is a hierarchy of propositions there is, of course, also a hierarchy of truths and of negations, etc.

But in the sense in which there are, in the most general sense, such things as propositions, there is only one truth and one negation.

The latter sense is obtained from the former by conceiving the proposition in general as the result of the single operation which produces all propositions from the first level. Etc.

The lowest level and the operation can stand for the whole hierarchy.

8.1.17.

It is clear that the logical product of two elementary propositions can never be a tautology. [*Cf.* 6.3751.]

If the logical product of two propositions is a contradiction, and the propositions appear to be elementary propositions, we can see that in this case the appearance is deceptive. (E.g.: A is red and A is green.)

10.1.17.

If suicide is allowed then everything is allowed.

If anything is not allowed then suicide is not allowed.

This throws a light on the nature of ethics, for suicide is, so to speak, the elementary sin.

And when one investigates it it is like investigating mercury vapour in order to comprehend the nature of vapours.

Or is even suicide in itself neither good nor evil?

APPENDIX I

NOTES ON LOGIC

by
Ludwig Wittgenstein
1913

Summary

ONE reason for thinking the old notation wrong is that it is very unlikely that from every proposition p an infinite number of other propositions not-not-p, not-not-not-not-p, etc., should follow. [*Cf.* 5.43.]

If only those signs which contain proper names were complex then propositions containing nothing but apparent variables would be simple. Then what about their denials?

The verb of a proposition cannot be "is true" or "is false", but whatever is true or false must already contain the verb. [*See* 4.063.]

Deductions only proceed according to the laws of deduction but these laws cannot justify the deduction.

One reason for supposing that not all propositions which have more than one argument are relational propositions is that if they were, the relations of judgment and inference would have to hold between an arbitrary number of things.

Every proposition which seems to be about a complex can be analysed into a proposition about its constituents and about the proposition which describes the complex perfectly; i.e., that proposition which is equivalent to saying the complex exists. [*Cf.* 2.0201.]

The idea that propositions are names of complexes suggests that whatever is not a proper name is a sign for a relation. Because spatial complexes[1] consist of Things and Relations only and the idea of a complex is taken from space.

In a proposition convert all its indefinables into variables; there then remains a class of propositions which is not all propositions but a type [*Cf.* 3.315.]

There are thus two ways in which signs are similar. The names "Socrates" and "Plato" are similar: they are both names. But whatever they have in common must not be introduced before "Socrates" and "Plato" are introduced. The same applies to a subject-predicate form etc.. Therefore, thing, proposition, subject-predicate form, etc., are not indefinables, i.e., types are not indefinables.

[1] Russell for instance imagines every fact as a spatial complex.

When we say A judges that etc., then we have to mention a whole proposition which A judges. It will not do either to mention only its constituents, or its constituents and form, but not in the proper order. This shows that a proposition itself must occur in the statement that it is judged; however, for instance, "not-p" may be explained, the question what is negated must have a meaning.

To understand a proposition p it is not enough to know that p implies '"p" is true', but we must also know that ~p implies "p is false". This shows the bi-polarity of the proposition.

To every molecular function a WF[1] scheme corresponds. Therefore we may use the WF scheme itself instead of the function. Now what the WF scheme does is, it correlates the letters W and F with each proposition. These two letters are the poles of atomic propositions. Then the scheme correlates another W and F to these poles. In this notation all that matters is the correlation of the outside poles to the poles of the atomic propositions. Therefore not-not-p is the same symbol as p. And therefore we shall never get two symbols for the same molecular function.

The meaning of a proposition is the fact which actually corresponds to it.

As the ab functions of atomic propositions are bi-polar propositions again we can perform *ab* operations on them. We shall, by doing so, correlate two new outside poles via the old outside poles to the poles of the atomic propositions.

The symbolising fact in a-p-b is that, SAY[2] *a* is on the left of *p* and *b* on the right of *p*; then the correlation of new poles is to be transitive, so that for instance if a new pole *a* in whatever way i.e. via whatever poles is correlated to the inside *a*, the symbol is not changed thereby. It is therefore possible to construct all possible *ab* functions by performing one *ab* operation repeatedly, and we can therefore talk of all *ab* functions as of all those functions which can be obtained by performing this *ab* operation repeatedly.

Naming is like pointing. A function is like a line dividing points of a plane into right and left ones; then "p or not-p" has no meaning because it does not divide the plane.

But though a particular proposition "p or not-p" has no meaning, a general proposition "for all p's, p or not-p" has a meaning because this

[1] W–F = Wahr-Falsch—i.e. True-False.

[2] This is quite arbitrary but, if we once have fixed on which order the poles have to stand we must of course stick to our convention. If for instance "apb" says p then bpa says *nothing*. (It does not say ~p). But a—apb—b is the same symbol as apb (here the ab-function vanishes automatically) for here the new poles are related to the same side of p as the old ones. The question is always: how are the new poles correlated to p compared with the way the old poles are correlated to p.

does not contain the nonsensical function "p or not-p" but the function "p or not-q" just as "for all x's xRx" contains the function "xRy".

A proposition is a standard to which facts behave,[1] with names it is otherwise; it is thus bi-polarity and sense comes in; just as one arrow behaves[2] to another arrow by being in the same sense or the opposite, so a fact behaves to a proposition.

The form of a proposition has meaning in the following way. Consider a symbol "xRy". To symbols of this form correspond couples of things whose names are respectively "x" and "y". The things *xy* stand to one another in all sorts of relations, amongst others some stand in the relation R, and some not; just as I single out a particular thing by a particular name I single out all behaviours of the points x and y with respect to the relation R. I say that if an x stands in the relation R to a y the sign "xRy" is to be called true to the fact and otherwise false. This is a definition of sense.

In my theory p has the same meaning as not-p but opposite sense. The meaning is the fact. The proper theory of judgment must make it impossible to judge nonsense. [*Cf.* 4.0621 and 5.5422.]

It is not strictly true to say that we understand a proposition p if we know that p is equivalent to "p is true" for this would be the case if accidentally both were true or false. What is wanted is the formal equivalence with respect to the forms of the proposition, *i.e.*, all the general indefinables involved. *The sense of* an *ab* function of a proposition is a function of *its* sense. There are only unasserted propositions. Assertion is merely psychological. In *not-p*, *p* is exactly the same as if it stands alone; this point is absolutely fundamental. Among the facts which make "p or q" true there are also facts which make "p and q" true; if propositions have only meaning, we ought, in such a case, to say that these two propositions are identical, but in fact, their sense is different for we have introduced sense by talking of all p's and all q's. Consequently the molecular propositions will only be used in cases where their *ab* function stands under a generality sign or enters into another function such as "I believe that, etc.", because then the sense enters. [*Cf.* 5.2341.]

In "a judges p" p cannot be replaced by a proper name. This appears if we substitute "a judges that p is true and not p is false". The proposition "a judges p" consists of the proper name a, the proposition p with its 2 poles, and *a* being related to both of these poles in a certain way. This is obviously not a relation in the ordinary sense.

The *ab* notation makes it clear that *not* and *or* are dependent on one another and we can therefore not use them as simultaneous indefinables.

[1] I.e. *sich verhalten*, are related. *Edd.*
[2] I.e. *sich verhält*, is related. *Edd.*

Same objections in the case of apparent variables to old indefinables, as in the case of molecular functions. The application of the *ab* notation to apparent variable propositions becomes clear if we consider that, for instance, the proposition "for all x, ϕx" is to be true when ϕx is true for all x's and false when ϕx is false for some x's. We see that *some* and *all* occur simultaneously in the proper apparent variable notation.

The notation is:

for (x)ϕx: a-(x)-aϕxb-(∃x)-b and
for (∃x)ϕx: a-(∃x)-aϕxb-(x)-b

Old definitions now become tautologous.

In "aRb" it is not the complex that symbolises but the fact that the symbol "a" stands in a certain relation to the symbol "b". Thus facts are symbolised by facts, or more correctly: that a certain thing is the case in the symbol says that a certain thing is the case in the world. [*Cf.* 3.1432.]

Judgment, question and command are all on the same level. What interests logic in them is only the unasserted proposition. Facts cannot be named.

A proposition cannot occur in itself. This is the fundamental truth of the theory of types. [*Cf:* 3.332.]

Every proposition that says something indefinable about one thing is a subject-predicate proposition, and so on.

Therefore we can recognize a subject-predicate proposition if we know it contains only one name and one form, etc. This gives the construction of types. Hence the type of a proposition can be recognized by its symbol alone.

What is essential in a correct apparent-variable notation is this:—(1) it must mention a type of propositions; (2) it must show which components of a proposition of this type are constants.

[Components are forms and constituents.]

Take (ϕ).ϕ!x. Then if we describe the *kind* of symbols, for which "ϕ!" stands and which, by the above, is enough to determine the type, then automatically "(ϕ).ϕ!x" cannot be fitted by this description, because it *CONTAINS* "ϕ!x" and the description is to describe *ALL* that symbolises in symbols of the ϕ! kind. If the description is *thus* complete vicious circles can just as little occur as for instance (ϕ).(x)ϕ (where (x)ϕ is a subject-predicate proposition).

First MS

Indefinables are of two sorts: names, and forms. Propositions cannot consist of names alone; they cannot be classes of names. A name can not only occur in two different propositions, but can occur in the same way in both.

Propositions [which are symbols having reference to facts] are themselves facts: that this inkpot is on this table may express that I sit in this chair. [*Cf.* 2.141 and 3.14.]

It can never express the common characteristic of two objects that we designate them by the same name but by two different ways of designation, for, since names are arbitrary, we might also choose different names, and where then would be the common element in the designations? Nevertheless one is always tempted, in a difficulty, to take refuge in different ways of designation. [*Cf.* 3.322.]

Frege said "propositions are names"; Russell said "propositions correspond to complexes". Both are false; and especially false is the statement "propositions are names of complexes". [*Cf.* 3.143.]

It is easy to suppose that only such symbols are complex as contain names of objects, and that accordingly "$(\exists x,\phi) . \phi x$" or "$(\exists x,y) . xRy$" must be simple. It is then natural to call the first of these the name of a form, the second the name of a relation. But in that case what is the meaning of (e.g.) "$\sim(\exists x,y)xRy$? Can we put "not" before a name?

The reason why "$\sim$Socrates" means nothing is that "$\sim x$" does not express a property of x.

There are positive and negative facts: if the proposition "this rose is not red" is true, then what it signifies is negative. But the occurrence of the word "not" does not indicate this unless we know that the signification of the proposition "this rose is red" (when it is true) is positive. It is only from both, the negation and the negated proposition, that we can conclude to a characteristic of the significance of the whole proposition. (We are not here speaking of negations of *general* propositions i.e. of such as contain apparent variables. Negative facts only justify the negations of atomic propositions.)

Positive and *negative* facts there are, but not *true* and *false* facts.

If we overlook the fact that propositions have a *sense* which is independent of their truth or falsehood, it easily seems as if true and false were two equally justified relations between the sign and what is signified. (We might then say e.g. that "q" *signifies* in the true way what "not-q" *signifies* in the false way.) But are not true and false in fact equally justified? Could we not express ourselves by means of false propositions just as well as hitherto with true ones, so long as we know that they are meant falsely? No! For a proposition is then true when it is as we assert in this proposition; and accordingly if by "q" we mean "not-q", and it is as we mean to assert, then in the new interpretation "q" is actually true and *not* false. But it is important that we *can* mean the same by "q" as by "not-q", for it shows that neither to the symbol "not" nor to the manner of its combination with "q" does a

characteristic of the denotation of "*q*" correspond. [*Cf.* 4.061, 4.062, 4.0621.]

Second MS

We must be able to understand propositions which we have never heard before. But every proposition is a new symbol. Hence we must have *general* indefinable symbols; these are unavoidable if propositions are not all indefinable. [*Cf.* 4.02, 4.021, 4.027.]

Whatever corresponds in reality to compound propositions must not be more than what corresponds to their several atomic propositions.

Not only must logic not deal with [particular] things, but just as little with relations and predicates.

There are no propositions containing real variables.

What corresponds in reality to a proposition depends upon whether it is true or false. But we must be able to understand a proposition without knowing if it is true or false.

What we know when we understand a proposition is this: We know what is the case if the proposition is true, and what is the case if it is false. But we do not know (necessarily) whether it is true or false. [*Cf.* 4.024.]

Propositions are not names.

We can never distinguish one logical type from another by attributing a property to members of the one which we deny to members of the other.

Symbols are not what they seem to be. In "aRb", "R" looks like a substantive, but is not one. What symbolizes in "*a*R*b*" is that R occurs between *a* and *b*. Hence "R" is *not* the indefinable in "*a*R*b*". Similarly in "ϕx", "ϕ" looks like a substantive but is not one; in "$\sim$p", "$\sim$" looks like "ϕ" but is not like it. This is the first thing that indicates that there *may* not be logical constants. A reason against them is the generality of logic: logic cannot treat a special set of things. [*Cf.* 3.1423.]

Molecular propositions contain nothing beyond what is contained in their atoms; they add no material information above that contained in their atoms.

All that is essential about molecular functions is their T-F schema (i.e. the statement of the cases when they are true and the cases when they are false).

Alternative indefinability shows that the indefinables have not been reached.

Every proposition is essentially true-false: to understand it, we must know both what must be the case if it is true, and what must be the case if it is false. Thus a proposition has two *poles*, corresponding to the

case of its truth and the case of its falsehood. We call this the *sense* of a proposition.

In regard to notation, it is important to note that not every feature of a symbol symbolizes. In two molecular functions which have the same T-F schema, what symbolizes must be the same. In "not-not-*p*", "not-*p*" does not occur; for "not-not-*p*" is the same as "*p*", and therefore, if "not-*p*" occurred in "not-not-*p*", it would occur in "*p*".

Logical indefinables cannot be predicates or relations, because propositions, owing to sense, cannot have predicates or relations. Nor are "not" and "or", like judgment, *analogous* to predicates or relations, because they do not introduce anything new.

Propositions are always complex even if they contain no names.

A proposition must be understood when *all* its indefinables are understood. The indefinables in "aRb" are introduced as follows:

"*a*" is indefinable;

"*b*" is indefinable;

Whatever "x" and "y" may mean, "xRy" says something indefinable about their meaning. [*Cf.* 4.024.]

A complex symbol must never be introduced as a single indefinable. [Thus e.g. no proposition is indefinable.] For if one of its parts occurs also in another connection, it must there be re-introduced. And would it then mean the same?

The ways by which we introduce our indefinables must permit us to construct all propositions that have sense from these indefinables *alone*. It is easy to introduce "all" and "some" in a way that will make the construction of (say) "(x,y).xRy" possible from "all" and "xRy" *as introduced before*.

Third MS

An analogy for the theory of truth: Consider a black patch on white paper; then we can describe the form of the patch by mentioning, for each point of the surface, whether it is white or black. To the fact that a point is black corresponds a positive fact, to the fact that a point is white (not black) corresponds a negative fact. If I designate a point of the surface (one of Frege's "truth-values"), this is as if I set up an assumption to be decided upon. But in order to be able to say of a point that it is black or that it is white, I must first know when a point is to be called black and when it is to be called white. In order to be able to say that "p" is true (or false), I must first have determined under what circumstances I call a proposition true, and thereby I determine the *sense* of a proposition. The point in which the analogy fails is this: I can indicate a point of the paper which is white and black,[1] but to a

[1] *Sic* in Russell's MS.; but comparison with the *Tractatus* shows that "without knowing" has fallen out after 'paper'. *Edd.*

proposition without sense nothing corresponds, for it does not designate a thing (truth-value), whose properties might be called "false" or "true"; the verb of a proposition is not "is true" or "is false", as Frege believes, but what is true must already contain the verb. [*Cf.* 5.132.]

The comparison of language and reality is like that of retinal image and visual image: to the blind spot nothing in the visual image seems to correspond, and thereby the boundaries of the blind spot determine the visual image – as true negations of atomic propositions determine reality.

Logical inferences can, it is true, be made in accordance with Frege's or Russell's laws of deduction, but this cannot justify the inference; and therefore they are not primitive propositions of logic. If *p* follows from *q*, it can also be inferred from *q*, and the "manner of deduction" is indifferent.

Those symbols which are called propositions in which "variables occur" are in reality not propositions at all, but only schemes of propositions, which only become propositions when we replace the variables by constants. There is no proposition which is expressed by "x=x", for "x" has no signification; but there is a proposition "(x).x=x" and propositions such as "Socrates=Socrates" etc.

In books on logic, no variables ought to occur, but only the general propositions which justify the use of variables. It follows that the so-called definitions of logic are not definitions, but only schemes of definitions, and instead of these we ought to put general propositions; and similarly the so-called primitive ideas (*Urzeichen*) of logic are not primitive ideas, but the schemes of them. The mistaken idea that there are things called facts or complexes and relations easily leads to the opinion that there must be a relation of questioning to the facts, and then the question arises whether a relation can hold between an arbitrary number of things, since a fact can follow from arbitrary cases. It is a fact that the proposition which e.g. expresses that *q* follows from *p* and $p \supset q$ is this: $p.p \supset q. \supset_{p.q}. q$.

At a pinch, one is tempted to interpret "not-*p*" as "everything else, only not *p*". That from a single fact *p* an infinity of others, not-not-p etc., follow, is hardly credible. Man possesses an innate capacity for constructing symbols with which *some* sense can be expressed, without having the slightest idea what each word signifies. The best example of this is mathematics, for man has until lately used the symbols for numbers without knowing what they signify or that they signify nothing. [*Cf.* 5.43.]

Russell's "complexes" were to have the useful property of being compounded, and were to combine with this the agreeable property that they could be treated like "simples". But this alone made them un-

serviceable as logical types, since there would have been significance in asserting, of a simple, that it was complex. But a *property* cannot be a logical type.

Every statement about apparent complexes can be resolved into the logical sum of a statement about the constituents and a statement about the proposition which describes the complex completely. How, in each case, the resolution is to be made, is an important question, but its answer is not unconditionally necessary for the construction of logic. [*Cf.* 2.0201.]

That "or" and "not" etc. are not relations in the same sense as "right" and "left" etc., is obvious to the plain man. The possibility of cross-definitions in the old logical indefinables shows, of itself, that these are not the right indefinables, and, even more conclusively, that they do not denote relations. [*Cf.* 5.42.]

If we change a constituent *a* of a proposition $\phi(a)$ into a variable, then there is a class

$$\hat{p}\{(\exists x).\phi(x) = p\}$$

This class in general still depends upon what, by an *arbitrary convention*, we mean by "$\phi(x)$". But if we change into variables all those symbols whose significance was arbitrarily determined, there is still such a class. But this is not dependent upon any convention, but only upon the nature of the symbol "$\phi(x)$". It corresponds to a logical type. [*Cf.* 3.315.]

Types can never be distinguished from each other by saying (as is often done) that one has these *but* the other has those properties, for this presupposes that there is a *meaning* in asserting all these properties of both types. But from this it follows that, at best, these properties may be types, but certainly not the objects of which they are asserted. [*Cf.* 4.1241.]

At a pinch we are always inclined to explanations of logical functions of propositions which aim at introducing into the function either only the constituents of these propositions, or only their form, etc. etc.; and we overlook that ordinary language would not contain the whole propositions if it did not need them: However, e.g., "not-*p*" may be explained, there must always be a meaning given to the question "what is denied?"

The very possibility of Frege's explanations of "not-p" and "if *p* then *q*", from which it follows that "not-not-p" denotes the same as *p*, makes it probable that there is some method of designation in which "not-not-*p*" corresponds to the same symbol as "*p*". But if this method of designation suffices for logic, it must be the right one.

Names are points, propositions arrows—they have *sense*. The sense

of a proposition is determined by the two poles *true* and *false*. The form of a proposition is like a straight line, which divides all points of a plane into right and left. The line does this automatically, the form of proposition only by convention. [*Cf.* 3.144.]

Just as little as we are concerned, in logic, with the relation of a name to its meaning, just so little are we concerned with the relation of a proposition to reality, but we want to know the meaning of names and the sense of propositions—as we introduce an indefinable concept "A" by saying: "'A' denotes something indefinable", so we introduce e.g. the form of propositions *a*R*b* by saying: "For all meanings of "x" and "y", "xRy" expresses something indefinable about x and y".

In place of every proposition "p", let us write "${}^{a}_{b}p$": Let every correlation of propositions to each other or of names to propositions be effected by a correlation of their poles "a" and "b". Let this correlation be transitive. Then accordingly "${}^{a}_{b}{}^{-}_{-}{}^{a}_{b}p$" is the same symbol as "${}^{a}_{b}p$". Let *n* propositions be given. I then call a "class of poles" of these propositions every class of *n* members, of which each is a pole of one of the *n* propositions, so that one member corresponds to each proposition. I then correlate with each class of poles one of two poles (*a* and *b*). The sense of the symbolizing fact thus constructed I cannot define, but I know it.

If p = not-not-p etc., this shows that the traditional method of symbolism is wrong, since it allows a plurality of symbols with the same sense; and thence it follows that, in analyzing such propositions, we must not be guided by Russell's method of symbolizing.

It is to be remembered that names are not things, but classes: "A" is the same letter as "A". This has the most important consequences for every symbolic language. [*Cf.* 3.203].

Neither the sense nor the meaning of a proposition is a thing. These words are incomplete symbols.

It is impossible to dispense with propositions in which the same argument occurs in different positions. It is obviously useless to replace ϕ (a,a) by ϕ(a,b).a = b.

Since the *ab*-functions of *p* are again bi-polar propositions, we can form *ab*-functions of them, and so on. In this way a series of propositions will arise, in which in general the *symbolizing* facts will be the same in several members. If now we find an *ab*-function of such a kind that by repeated application of it every ab-function can be generated, then we can introduce the totality of ab-functions as the totality of those that are generated by application of this function. Such a function is $\sim p \vee \sim q$.

It is easy to suppose a contradiction in the fact that on the one hand every possible complex proposition is a simple *ab*-function of simple

propositions, and that on the other hand the repeated application of one *ab*-function suffices to generate all these propositions. If e.g. an affirmation can be generated by double negation, is negation in any sense contained in affirmation? Does "p" deny "not-p" or assert "p", or both? And how do matters stand with the definition of "⊃" by "v" and ".", or of "v" by "." and "⊃"? And how e.g. shall we introduce p | q (i.e. ~p v ~q), if not by saying that this expression says something indefinable about all arguments *p* and *q*? But the *ab*-functions must be introduced as follows: The function p | q is merely a mechanical instrument for constructing all possible *symbols* of *ab*-functions. The symbols arising by repeated application of the symbol "|" do *not* contain the symbol "p | q". We need a rule according to which we can form all symbols of *ab* functions, in order to be able to speak of the class of them; and now we speak of them e.g. as those symbols of functions which can be generated by repeated application of the operation "|". And we say now: For all p's and q's, "p | q" says something indefinable about the sense of those simple propositions which are contained in p and q. [*Cf.* 5.44.]

The assertion-sign is logically quite without significance. It only shows, in Frege and Whitehead and Russell, that these authors hold the propositions so indicated to be true. "⊢" therefore belongs as little to the proposition as (say) the number of the proposition. A proposition cannot possibly assert of itself that it is true. [*Cf.* 4.442.]

Every right theory of judgment must make it impossible for me to judge that this table penholders the book. Russell's theory does not satisfy this requirement. [*See* 5.5422.]

It is clear that we understand propositions without knowing whether they are true or false. But we can only know the *meaning* of a proposisition when we know if it is true or false. What we understand is the *sense* of the proposition. [*Cf.* 4.024.]

The assumption of the existence of logical objects makes it appear remarkable that in the sciences propositions of the form "p v q", "p ⊃ q", etc. are only then not provisional when "v" and "⊃" stand within the scope of a generality-sign [apparent variable].

Fourth MS

If we formed all possible atomic propositions, the world would be completely described if we declared the truth or falsehood of each. [*Cf.* 4.26.]

The chief characteristic of my theory is that, in it, *p* has the same *meaning* as not-p. [*Cf.* 4.0621.]

A false theory of relations makes it easily seem as if the relation of

fact and constituent were the same as that of fact and fact which follows from it. But the similarity of the two may be expressed thus:

$\phi a. \supset_{\phi, a} a = a.$

If a word creates a world so that in it the principles of logic are true, it thereby creates a world in which the whole of mathematics holds; and similarly it could not create a world in which a proposition was true, without creating its constituents. [*Cf.* 5.123.]

Signs of the form "p v ~p" are senseless, but not the proposition "(p). p v ~p". If I know that this rose is either red or not red, I know nothing. The same holds of all *ab*-functions. [*Cf.* 4.461.]

To understand a proposition means to know what is the case if it is true. Hence we can understand it without knowing if it is true. We understand it when we understand its constituents and forms. If we know the meaning of "a" and "b", and if we know what "xRy" means for all x's and y's, then we also understand "aRb". [*Cf.* 4.024.]

I understand the proposition "aRb" when I know that either the fact that aRb or the fact that not aRb corresponds to it; but this is not to be confused with the false opinion that I understood "aRb" when I know that "aRb or not aRb" is the case.

But the form of a proposition symbolizes in the following way: Let us consider symbols of the form "xRy"; to these correspond primarily pairs of objects, of which one has the name "x", the other the name "y". The x's and y's stand in various relations to each other, among others the relation R holds between some, but not between others. I now determine the sense of "xRy" by laying down: when the facts behave in regard to[1] "xRy" so that the meaning of "x" stands in the relation R to the meaning of "y", then I say that the [the facts] are "of like sense" ["gleichsinnig"] with the proposition "xRy"; otherwise, "of opposite sense" [entgegengesetzt"]; I correlate the facts to the symbol "xRy" *by* thus dividing them into those of like sense and those of opposite sense. To this correlation corresponds the correlation of name and meaning. Both are psychological. Thus I understand the form "xRy" when I know that it discriminates the behaviour of x and y according as these stand in the relation R or not. In this way I extract from all possible relations the relation R, as, by a name, I extract its meaning from among all possible things.

Strictly speaking, it is incorrect to say: we understand the proposition *p* when we know that "'p' is true" ≡p; for this would naturally always be the case if accidentally the propositions to right and left of the symbol "≡" were both true or both false. We require not only an

[1] I.e. *sich verhalten zu*, are related to. *Edd.*

equivalence, but a formal equivalence, which is bound up with the introduction of the form of *p*.

The sense of an ab-function of *p* is a function of the sense of *p*. [*Cf.* 5.2341.]

The *ab*-functions use the discrimination of facts, which their arguments bring forth, in order to generate new discriminations.

Only facts can express sense, a class of names cannot. This is easily shown.

There is no thing which is the form of a proposition, and no name which is the name of a form. Accordingly we can also not say that a relation which in certain cases holds between things holds sometimes between forms and things. This goes against Russell's theory of judgment.

It is very easy to forget that, though the propositions of a form can be either true or false, each one of these propositions can only be either true or false, not both.

Among the facts which make "p or q" true, there are some which make "p and q" true; but the class which makes "p or q" true is different from the class which makes "p and q" true; and only this is what matters. For we introduce this class, as it were, when we introduce *ab*-functions. [*Cf.* 5.1241.]

A very natural objection to the way in which I have introduced e.g. propositions of the form xRy is that by it propositions such as (∃.x.y). xRy and similar ones are not explained, which yet obviously have in common with aRb what cRd has in common with aRb. *But* when we introduce propositions of the form xRy we mentioned no one particular proposition of this form; and we only need to introduce (∃x,y).ϕ(x,y) for all ϕ's in any way which makes the sense of these propositions dependent on the sense of all propositions of the form ϕ(a,b), and thereby the justness of our procedure is proved.

The indefinables of logic must be independent of each other. If an indefinable is introduced, it must be introduced in all combinations in which it can occur. We cannot therefore introduce it first for one combination, then for another; e.g., if the form xRy has been introduced it must henceforth be understood in propositions of the form aRb just in the same way as in propositions such as (∃x,y).xRy and others. We must not introduce it first for one class of cases, then for the other; for it would remain doubtful if its meaning was the same in both cases, and there would be no ground for using the same matter of combining symbols in both cases. In short for the introduction of indefinable symbols and combinations of symbols the same holds, *mutatis mutandis*, that Frege has said for the introduction of symbols by definitions. [*Cf.* 5.451.]

It is *a priori* likely that the introduction of atomic propositions is fundamental for the understanding of all other kinds of propositions. In fact the understanding of general propositions obviously depends on that of atomic propositions.

Cross-definability in the realm of general propositions leads to quite similar questions to those in the realm of *ab*-functions.

When we say "A believes *p*", this sounds, it is true, as if here we could substitute a proper name for "*p*"; but we can see that here a *sense*, not a meaning, is concerned, if we say "A believes that '*p*' is true"; and in order to make the direction of *p* even more explicit, we might say "A believes that 'p' is true and 'not-p' is false". Here the bi-polarity of *p* is expressed, and it seems that we shall only be able to express the proposition "A believes *p*" correctly by the *ab*-notation; say by making "A" have a relation to the poles "a" and "b" of a-p-b. The epistemological questions concerning the nature of judgment and belief cannot be solved without a correct apprehension of the form of the proposition.

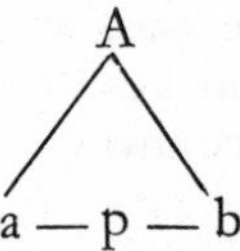

The *ab*-notation shows the dependence of *or* and *not*, and thereby that they are not to be employed as simultaneous indefinables.

Not: "The complex sign 'aRb'" says that *a* stands in the relation R to *b*; but *that* 'a' stands in a certain relation to 'b' says *that* aRb. [3.1432.]

In philosophy there are no deductions: *it* is purely descriptive.

Philosophy gives no pictures of reality.

Philosophy can neither confirm nor confute scientific investigation.

Philosophy consists of logic and metaphysics: logic is its basis.

Epistemology is the philosophy of psychology. [*Cf.* 4.1121.]

Distrust of grammar is the first requisite for philosophizing.

Propositions can never be indefinables, for they are always complex. That also words like "ambulo" are complex appears in the fact that their root with a different termination gives a different sense. [*Cf.* 4.032.]

Only the doctrine of general indefinables permits us to understand the nature of functions. Neglect of this doctrine leads to an impenetrable thicket.

Philosophy is the doctrine of the logical form of scientific propositions (not only of primitive propositions).

The word "philosophy" ought always to designate something over or under but not beside, the natural sciences. [*Cf.* 4.111.]

Judgment, command and question all stand on the same level; but all have in common the propositional form, which does interest *us*.

The structure of the proposition must be recognized, the rest comes of itself. But ordinary language conceals the structure of the proposition: in it, relations look like predicates, predicates like names, etc.

Facts cannot be *named*.

It is easy to suppose that "individual", "particular", "complex" etc. are primitive ideas of logic. Russell e.g. says "individual" and "matrix" are "primitive ideas". This error presumably is to be explained by the fact that, by employment of variables instead of the generality-sign, it comes to seem as if logic dealt with things which have been deprived of all properties except thing-hood, and with propositions deprived of all properties except complexity. We forget that the indefinables of symbols [*Urbilder von Zeichen*] only occur under the generality-sign, never outside it.

Just as people used to struggle to bring all propositions into the subject-predicate form, so now it is natural to conceive every proposition as expressing a relation, which is just as incorrect. What is justified in this desire is fully satisfied by Russell's theory of manufactured relations.

One of the most natural attempts at solution consists in regarding "not-p" as "the opposite of *p*", where then "opposite" would be the indefinable relation. But it is easy to see that every such attempt to replace the *ab*-functions by descriptions must fail.

The false assumption that propositions are names leads us to believe that there must be logical objects: for the meanings of logical propositions will have to be such things.

A correct explanation of logical propositions must give them a unique position as against all other propositions.

No proposition can say anything about itself, because the symbol of the proposition cannot be contained in itself; this must be the basis of the theory of logical types. [*Cf.* 3.332.]

Every proposition which says something indefinable about a thing is a subject-predicate proposition; every proposition which says something indefinable about two things expresses a dual relation between these things, and so on. Thus every proposition which contains only one name and one indefinable form is a subject-predicate proposition, and so on. An indefinable simple symbol can only be a name, and therefore we can know, by the symbol of an atomic proposition, whether it is a subject-predicate proposition.

APPENDIX II

NOTES DICTATED TO G. E. MOORE IN NORWAY[1]

April 1914

LOGICAL so-called propositions *shew* [the] logical properties of language and therefore of [the] Universe, but *say* nothing. [*Cf.* 6.12.]

This means that by merely looking at them you can *see* these properties; whereas, in a proposition proper, you cannot see what is true by looking at it. [*Cf.* 6.113.]

It is impossible to *say* what these properties are, because in order to do so, you would need a language, which hadn't got the properties in question, and it is impossible that this should be a *proper* language. Impossible to construct [an] illogical language.

In order that you should have a language which can express or *say* everything that *can* be said, this language must have certain properties; and when this is the case, *that* it has them can no longer be said in that language or *any* language.

An illogical language would be one in which, e.g., you could put an *event* into a hole.

Thus a language which *can* express everything *mirrors* certain properties of the world by these properties which it must have; and logical so-called propositions shew *in a systematic way* those properties.

How, usually, logical propositions do shew these properties is this: We give a certain description of a kind of symbol; we find that other symbols, combined in certain ways, yield a symbol of this description; and *that* they do shews something about these symbols.

As a rule the description given in ordinary Logic is the description of a tautology; but *others* might shew equally well, e.g., a contradiction. [*Cf.* 6.1202.]

Every *real* proposition *shews* something, besides what it says, about the Universe: *for*, if it has no sense, it can't be used; and if it has a sense, it mirrors some logical property of the Universe.

E.g., take ϕa, $\phi a \supset \psi a$, ψa. By merely looking at these three, I can see that 3 follows from 1 and 2; i.e. I can see what is called the truth of a logical proposition, namely, of [the] proposition $\phi a \,.\, \phi a \supset \psi a : \supset : \psi a$. But this is *not* a proposition; but by seeing that it is a tautology I can

[1] Square brackets round whole sentences or paragraphs are Wittgenstein's; otherwise they mark something supplied in editing.

see what I already saw by looking at the three propositions: the difference is that I *now* see THAT it is a tautology. [*Cf.* 6.1221.]

We want to say, in order to understand [the] above, what properties a symbol must have, in order to be a tautology.

Many ways of saying this are possible:
One way is to give *certain symbols*; then to give a set of rules for combining them; and then to say: any symbol formed from those symbols, by combining them according to one of the given rules, is a tautology. This obviously says something about the kind of symbol you can get in this way.

This is the actual procedure of [the] *old* Logic: it gives so-called primitive propositions; so-called rules of deduction; and then says that what you get by applying the rules to the propositions is a *logical* proposition that you have *proved*. The truth is, it tells you something *about* the kind of proposition you have got, viz that it can be derived from the first symbols by these rules of combination (= is a tautology).

Therefore, if we say one *logical* proposition *follows* logically from another, this means something quite different from saying that a *real* proposition follows logically from *another*. For so-called *proof* of a logical proposition does not prove its *truth* (logical propositions are neither true nor false) but proves *that* it is a logical proposition = is a tautology. [*Cf.* 6.1263.]

Logical propositions *are forms of proofs*: they shew that one or more propositions *follow* from one (or more). [*Cf.* 6.1264.]

Logical propositions *shew* something, *because* the language in which they are expressed can *say* everything that can be *said*.

This same distinction between what can be *shewn* by the language but not *said*, explains the difficulty that is felt about types—e.g., as to [the] difference between things, facts, properties, relations. That M is a *thing* can't be *said*; it is nonsense: but *something* is *shewn* by the symbol "M". In [the] same way, that a *proposition* is a subject-predicate proposition can't be said: but it is *shown* by the symbol.

Therefore a THEORY *of types* is impossible. It tries to say something about the types, when you can only talk about the symbols. But *what* you say about the symbols is not that this symbol has that type, which would be nonsense for [the] same reason: but you say simply: *This* is the symbol, to prevent a misunderstanding. E.g., in "aRb", "R" is *not* a symbol, but *that* "R" is between one name and another symbolizes. Here we have *not* said: this symbol is not of this type but of that, but only: *This* symbolizes and not that. This seems again to make the same

mistake, because "symbolizes" is "typically ambiguous". The true analysis is: "R" is no proper name, and, that "R" stands between "a" and "b" expresses a *relation*. Here are two propositions *of different type* connected by "and".

It is *obvious* that, e.g., with a subject-predicate proposition, *if* it has any sense at all, you *see* the form, so soon as you *understand* the proposition, in spite of not knowing whether it is true or false. Even if there *were* propositions of [the] form "M is a thing" they would be superfluous (tautologous) because what this tries to say is something which is already *seen* when you see "M".

In the above expression "aRb", we were talking only of this particular "R", whereas what we want to do is to talk of all similar symbols. We have to say: in *any* symbol of this form what corresponds to "R" is not a proper name, and [the] fact that ["R" stands between "a" and "b"] expresses a relation. This is what is sought to be expressed by the nonsensical assertion: Symbols like this are of a certain type. This you can't say, because in order to say it you must first know what the symbol is: and in knowing this you *see* the type and therefore also [the] type of [what is] symbolized. I.e. in knowing *what* symbolizes, you know all that is to be known; you can't *say* anything *about* the symbol.

For instance: Consider the two propositions (1) "What symbolizes here is a thing", (2) "What symbolizes here is a relational fact =relation". These are nonsensical for two reasons: (*a*) because they mention "thing" and "relation"; (*b*) because they mention them in propositions of the same form. The two propositions must be expressed in entirely different forms, if properly analysed; and neither the word "thing" nor "relation" must occur.

Now we shall see how properly to analyse propositions in which "thing", "relation", etc., occur.

(1) Take ϕx. We want to explain the meaning of 'In "ϕx" a *thing* symbolizes'. The analysis is:—

(∃y) . y symbolizes . y = "x" . "ϕx"

["x" is the name of y: "ϕx" = ' "ϕ" is at [the] left of "x" ' and *says* ϕx.]

N.B. "x" can't be the name of this actual scratch y, because this isn't a thing: but it can be the name of *a thing*; and we must understand that what we are doing is to explain what would be meant by saying of an ideal symbol, which did actually consist in one *thing*'s being to the left of another, that in it a *thing* symbolized.

[N.B. In [the] expression $(\exists y) . \phi y$, one is apt to say this means "There is a *thing* such that . . . ". But in fact we should say "There is a y, such that . . . "; the fact that the y symbolizes expressing what we mean.]

In general: When such propositions are analysed, while the words "thing", "fact", etc. will disappear, there will appear instead of them a new symbol, of the same form as the one of which we are speaking; and hence it will be at once obvious that we *cannot* get the one kind of proposition from the other by substitution.

In our language names are *not things*: we don't know what they are: all we know is that they are of a different type from relations, etc. etc.. The type of a symbol of a relation is partly fixed by [the] type of [a] symbol of [a] thing, since a symbol of [the] latter type must occur in it.

N.B. In any ordinary proposition, e.g., "Moore good", this *shews* and does not say that "*Moore*" is to the left of "good"; and *here what* is shewn can be *said* by another proposition. But this only applies to that *part* of what is shewn which is arbitrary. The *logical* properties which it shews are not arbitrary, and that it has these cannot be said in any proposition.

When we say of a proposition of [the] form "aRb" that what symbolizes is that "R" is between "a" and "b", it must be remembered that in fact the proposition is capable of further analysis because a, R, and b are not *simples*. But what seems certain is that when we have analysed it we shall in the end come to propositions of the same form in respect of the fact that they do consist in one thing being between two others.[1]

How can we talk of the general form of a proposition, without knowing any unanalysable propositions in which particular names and relations occur? What justifies us in doing this is that though we don't know any unanalysable propositions of this kind, yet we can understand what is meant by a proposition of the form $(\exists x, y, R) . xRy$ (which is unanalysable), even though we know no proposition of the form xRy.

If you had any unanalysable proposition in which particular names and relations occurred (and *unanalysable* proposition = one in which only fundamental symbols = ones not capable of *definition*, occur) then you always can form from it a proposition of the form $(\exists x, y, R)$. xRy, which though it contains no particular names and relations, is unanalysable.

(2) The point can here be brought out as follows. Take ϕa and ϕA:

[1] This paragraph is lightly deleted.

and ask what is meant by saying, "There is a thing in ϕa, and a complex in ϕA"?

(1) means: $(\exists x) . \phi x . x = a$

(2) $(\exists x, \psi\xi) . \phi A = \psi x . \phi x$.[1]

Use of logical propositions. You may have one so complicated that you cannot, by looking at it, see that it is a tautology; but you have shewn that it can be derived by certain operations from certain other propositions according to our rule for constructing tautologies; and hence you are enabled to see that one thing follows from another, when you would not have been able to see it otherwise. E.g., if our tautology is of [the] form $p \supset q$ you can see that q follows from p; and so on.

The *Bedeutung* of a proposition is the fact that corresponds to it, e.g., if our proposition be "aRb", if it's true, the corresponding fact would be the fact aRb, if false, the fact $\sim$aRb. *But* both "the fact aRb" and "the fact $\sim$aRb" are incomplete symbols, which must be analysed.

That a proposition has a relation (in wide sense) to Reality, other than that of *Bedeutung*, is shewn by the fact that you can understand it when you don't know the *Bedeütung*, i.e. don't know whether it is true or false. Let us express this by saying "It has *sense*" (*Sinn*).

In analysing *Bedeutung*, you come upon *Sinn* as follows:

We want to explain the relation of propositions to reality.

The relation is as follows: Its *simples* have meaning = are names of simples; and its relations have a quite different relation to relations; and these two facts already establish a sort of correspondence between a proposition which contains these and only these, and reality: i.e. if all the simples of a proposition are known, we already know that we CAN describe reality by saying that it *behaves*[2] in a certain way to the whole proposition. (This amounts to saying that we can *compare* reality with the proposition. In the case of two lines we can *compare* them in respect of their length without any convention: the comparison is automatic. But in our case the possibility of comparison depends upon the conventions by which we have given meanings to our simples (names and relations).)

It only remains to fix the method of comparison by saying *what* about our simples is to *say* what about reality. E.g., suppose we take two lines of unequal length; and say that the fact that the shorter is of the length it is is to mean that the longer is of the length *it* is. We should then have established a convention as to the meaning of the shorter, of the sort we are now to give.

[1] ξ is Frege's mark of an *Argumentstelle*, to show that ψ is a *Funktionsbuchstabe*. There are several deleted and partly illegible definitions.

[2] Presumably verhält sich zu", i.e. "stands towards." [*Edd.*]

From this it results that "true" and "false" are not accidental properties of a proposition, such that, when it has meaning, we can say it is also true or false: on the contrary, to have meaning *means* to be true or false: the being true or false actually constitutes the relation of the proposition to reality, which we mean by saying that it has meaning (*Sinn*).

There seems at first sight to be a certain ambiguity in what is meant by saying that a proposition is "true", owing to the fact that it seems as if, in the case of different propositions, the way in which they correspond to the facts to which they correspond is quite different. But what is really common to all cases is that they must have *the general form of a proposition.* In giving the general form of a proposition you are explaining what kind of ways of putting together the symbols of things and relations will correspond to (be analogous to) the things having those relations in reality. In doing thus you are saying what is meant by saying that a proposition is true; and you must do it once for all. To say "This proposition *has sense*" means ' "This proposition is true" means . . . .' ("p" is true = "p" . p . Def. : only instead of "p" we must here introduce the general form of a proposition.)[1]

It seems at first sight as if the ab notation must be wrong, because it seems to treat true and false as on exactly the same level. It must be possible to see from the symbols themselves that there is some essential difference between the poles, if the notation is to be right; and it seems as if in fact this was impossible.

The interpretation of a symbolism must not depend upon giving a different interpretation to symbols of the same types.

How asymmetry is introduced is by giving a description of a particular form of symbol which we call a "tautology". The description of the ab-symbol alone is symmetrical with respect to a and b; but this description plus the fact that what satisfies the description of a tautology *is* a tautology is asymmetrical with regard to them. (To say that a description was symmetrical with regard to two symbols, would mean that we could substitute one for the other, and yet the description remain the same, i.e. mean the same.)

Take p.q and q. When you write p.q in the ab notation, it is impossible to see from the symbol alone that q follows from it, for if you were to interpret the true-pole as the false, the same symbol would stand for p v q, from which q doesn't follow. But the moment you

[1] The reader should remember that according to Wittgenstein ' "p" ' is not a name but a description of the fact constituting the proposition. See above, p. 109. [*Edd.*]

say *which* symbols are tautologies, it at once becomes possible to see from the fact that they are and the original symbol that q does follow.

Logical propositions, OF COURSE, all shew something different: all of them shew, *in the same way*, viz by the fact that they are tautologies, but they are different tautologies and therefore shew each something different.

What is unarbitrary about our symbols is not them, nor the rules we give; but the fact that, having given certain rules, others are fixed = follow logically. [*Cf.* 3.342.]

Thus, though it would be possible to interpret the form which we take as the form of a tautology as that of a contradiction and vice versa, they *are* different in logical form because though the apparent form of the symbols is the same, what *symbolizes* in them is different, and hence what follows about the symbols from the one interpretation will be different from what follows from the other. But the difference between a and b is *not* one of logical form, so that nothing will follow from this difference alone as to the interpretation of other symbols. Thus, e.g., p.q., p v q seem symbols of exactly the *same* logical form in the ab notation. Yet they say something entirely different; and, if you ask why, the answer seems to be: In the one case the scratch at the top has the shape b, in the other the shape a. Whereas the interpretation of a tautology as a tautology is an interpretation of a *logical form*, not the giving of a meaning to a scratch of a particular shape. The important thing is that the interpretation of the form of the symbolism must be fixed by giving an interpretation to its *logical properties*, *not* by giving interpretations to particular scratches.

Logical constants can't be made into variables: because in them *what* symbolizes is *not* the same; all symbols for which a variable can be substituted symbolize in the *same* way.

We describe a symbol, and say arbitrarily "A symbol of this description is a tautology". And then, it follows at once, both that any other symbol which answers to the same description is a tautology, and that any symbol which does *not* isn't. That is, we have arbitrarily fixed that any symbol of that description is to be a tautology; and this being fixed it is no longer arbitrary with regard to any other symbol whether it is a tautology or not.

Having thus fixed what is a tautology and what is not, we can then, having fixed arbitrarily again that the relation a-b is transitive get from the two facts together that "p ≡ ∼(∼p)" is a tautology. For ∼(∼p) = a-b-a-p-b-a-b. The point is: that the process of reasoning by which we arrive at the result that a-b-a-p-b-a-b is the *same symbol* as a-p-b, is

exactly the same as that by which we discover that its meaning is the same, viz where we reason if b-a-p-b-a, then *not* a-p-b, if a-b-a-p-b-a-b then *not* b-a-p-b-a, therefore if a-b-a-p-b-a-b, then a-p-b.

It follows from the fact that a-b is transitive, that where we have a-b-a, the first a has to the second the same relation that it has to b. It is just as from the fact that a-true implies b-false, and b-false implies c-true, we get that a-true implies c-true. And we shall be able to see, having fixed the description of a tautology, that $p \equiv \sim(\sim p)$ is a tautology.

That, when a certain rule is given, a symbol is tautological *shews* a logical truth.

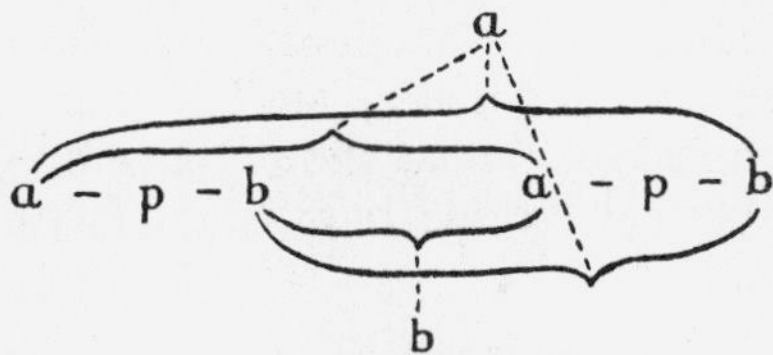

This symbol might be interpreted either as a tautology or a contradiction.

In settling that it is to be interpreted as a tautology and not as a contradiction, I am not assigning a *meaning* to a and b; i.e. saying that they symbolize different things but in the same way. What I am doing is to say that the way in which the a-pole is connected with the whole symbol symbolizes in a *different way* from that in which it would symbolize if the symbol were interpreted as a contradiction. And I add the scratches a and b merely in order to shew in which ways the connexion is symbolizing, so that it may be evident that wherever the same scratch occurs in the corresponding place in another symbol, there also the connexion is symbolizing in the same way.

We could, of course, symbolize any ab-function without using two *outside* poles at all, merely, e.g., omitting the b-pole; and here what would symbolize would be that the three pairs of inside poles of the propositions were connected in a certain way with the a-pole, while the other pair was *not* connected with it. And thus the difference between the scratches a and b, where we do use them, merely shews that it is a different state of things that is symbolizing in the one case and the other: in the one case that certain inside poles *are* connected in a certain way with an outside pole, in the other *that* they're *not*.

The symbol for a tautology, in whatever form we put it, e.g., whether by omitting the a-pole or by omitting the b, would always be capable of being used as the symbol for a contradiction; only *not* in the same language.

The reason why $\sim$x is meaningless, is simply that we have given no meaning to the symbol $\sim\xi$. I.e. whereas ϕx and ϕp look as if they were of the same type, they are not so because in order to give a meaning to $\sim$x you would have to have some *property* $\sim\xi$. What symbolizes in $\phi\xi$ is *that* ϕ stands to the left of *a* proper name and obviously this is not so in $\sim$p. What is common to all propositions in which the name of a property (to speak loosely) occurs is that this name stands to the left of a *name-form*.

The reason why, e.g., it seems as if "Plato Socrates" might have a meaning, while "Abracadabra Socrates" will never be suspected to have one, is because we know that "Plato" has one, and do not observe that in order that the whole phrase should have one, what is necessary is *not* that "Plato" should have one, but that the fact *that* "Plato" *is to the left of a name* should.

The reason why "The property of not being green is not green" is *nonsense*, is because we have only given meaning to the fact that "green" stands to the right of a name; and "the property of not being green" is obviously not *that*.

ϕ cannot possibly stand to the left of (or in any other relation to) the symbol of a property. For the symbol of a property, e.g., ψx is *that* ψ stands to the left of a name form, and another symbol ϕ cannot possibly stand to the left of such a *fact*: if it could, we should have an illogical language, which is impossible.

p is false = $\sim$(p is true) Def.

It is very important that the apparent logical relations v, $\supset$, etc. need brackets, dots, etc., i.e. have "ranges"; which by itself shews they are not relations. This fact has been overlooked, because it is so universal—the very thing which makes it so important. [*Cf.* 5.461.]

There are *internal* relations between one proposition and another; but a proposition cannot have to another *the* internal relation which a *name* has to the proposition of which it is a constituent, and which ought to be meant by saying it "occurs" in it. In this sense one proposition can't "occur" in another.

Internal relations are relations between types, which can't be expressed in propositions, but are all shewn in the symbols themselves, and can be exhibited systematically in tautologies. Why we come to

call them "relations" is because logical propositions have an analogous relation to them, to that which properly relational propositions have to relations.

Propositions can have many different internal relations to one another. *The* one which entitles us to deduce one from another is that if, say, they are ϕa and $\phi a \supset \psi a$, then $\phi a . \phi a \supset \psi a : \supset : \psi a$ is a tautology.

The symbol of identity expresses the internal relation between a function and its argument: i.e. $\phi a = (\exists x) . \phi x . x = a$.

The proposition $(\exists x) . \phi x . x = a : \equiv : \phi a$ can be seen to be a tautology, if one expresses the *conditions* of the truth of $(\exists x) . \phi x . x = a$, successively, e.g., by saying: This is true *if* so and so; and this again is true *if* so and so, etc., for $(\exists x) . \phi x . x = a$; and then also for ϕa. To express the matter in this way is itself a cumbrous notation, of which the ab-notation is a neater translation.

What symbolizes in a symbol, is that which is common to all the symbols which could in accordance with the rules of logic = syntactical rules for manipulation of symbols, be substituted for it. [*Cf.* 3.344.]

The question whether a proposition has sense (*Sinn*) can never depend on the *truth* of another proposition about a constituent of the first. E.g., the question whether $(x)\ x = x$ has meaning (*Sinn*) can't depend on the question whether $(\exists x)\ x = x$ is *true*. It doesn't describe reality at all, and deals therefore solely with symbols; and it says that they must *symbolize*, but not *what* they symbolize.

It's obvious that the dots and brackets are symbols, and obvious that they haven't any *independent* meaning. You must, therefore, in order to introduce so-called "logical constants" properly, introduce the general notion of *all possible* combinations of them = the general form of a proposition. You thus introduce both ab-functions, identity, and universality (the three fundamental constants) simultaneously.

The *variable proposition* $p \supset p$ is not identical with the *variable proposition* $\sim(p . \sim p)$. The corresponding universals *would* be identical. The variable proposition $\sim(p . \sim p)$ shews that out of $\sim(p . q)$ you get a tautology by substituting $\sim p$ for q, whereas the other does not shew this.

It's very important to realize that when you have two different relations $(a,b)_R$, $(c,d)_S$ this does *not* establish a correlation between a and c, and b and d, or a and d, and b and c: there is no correlation whatsoever thus established. Of course, in the case of two pairs of terms united by the *same* relation, there is a correlation. This shews that the theory which held that a relational fact contained the terms and

relations united by a *copula* (ϵ_2) is untrue; for if this were so there would be a correspondence between the terms of different relations.

The question arises how can one proposition (or function) occur in another proposition? The proposition or function itself can't possibly stand in relation to the other symbols. For this reason we must introduce functions as well as names at once in our general form of a proposition; explaining what is meant, by assigning meaning to the fact that the names stand between the | ,[1] and that the function stands on the left of the names.

It is true, in a sense, that logical propositions are "postulates"—something which we "demand"; for we *demand* a satisfactory notation. [*Cf.* 6.1223.]

A tautology (*not* a logical proposition) is not nonsense in the same sense in which, e.g., a proposition in which words which have no meaning occur is nonsense. What happens in it is that all its simple parts have meaning, but it is such that the connexions between these paralyse or destroy one another, so that they are all connected only in some irrelevant manner.

Logical functions all presuppose one another. Just as we can see $\sim$p has no sense, if p has none; so we can also say p has none if $\sim$p has none. The case is quite different with ϕa, and a; since here a has a meaning independently of ϕa, though ϕa presupposes it.

The logical constants seem to be complex-symbols, but on the other hand, they can be interchanged with one another. They are not therefore really complex; what symbolizes is simply the general way in which they are combined.

The combination of symbols in a tautology cannot possibly correspond to any one particular combination of their meanings—it corresponds to every possible combination; and therefore what symbolizes can't be the connexion of the symbols.

From the fact that I *see* that one spot is to the left of another, or that one colour is darker than another, it seems to follow that it *is* so; and if so, this can only be if there is an *internal* relation between the two; and we might express this by saying that the *form* of the latter is part of the *form* of the former. We might thus give a sense to the assertion that logical laws are *forms* of thought and space and time *forms* of intuition.

[1] Possibly "between the Sheffer-strokes".

Different logical types can have nothing whatever in common. But the mere fact that we can talk of the possibility of a relation of n places, or of an analogy between one with two places and one with four, shews that relations with different numbers of places have something in common, that therefore the difference is not one of type, but like the difference between different names—something which depends on experience. This answers the question how we can know that we have really got the most general form of a proposition. We have only to introduce what is *common* to all relations of whatever number of places.

The relation of "I believe p" to "p" can be compared to the relation of ' "p" says (besagt) p' to p: it is just as impossible that *I* should be a simple as that "p" should be. [*Cf.* 5.542.]

APPENDIX III

EXTRACTS FROM WITTGENSTEIN'S LETTERS TO RUSSELL, 1912–20

Cambridge, 22.6.12.

. . . Logic is still in the melting pot but one thing gets more and more obvious to me: The propositions of Logic contain ONLY *apparent* variables and whatever may turn out to be the proper explanation of apparent variables, its consequences *must* be that there are NO *logical* constants.

Logic must turn out to be a *totally* different kind than any other science.

1.7.12.

. . . Will you think that I have gone mad if I make the following suggestion?: The sign "$(x).\phi x$" is not a complete symbol but has meaning only in an inference of the kind: from $\vdash \phi x \supset_x \psi x . \phi(a)$ follows ψa. Or more general: from $\vdash (x).\phi x . \epsilon_0(a)$ follows $\phi(a)$. I am—of course—most uncertain about the matter but something of the sort might really be true.

Hochreit, Post Hohenberg, Nieder-Österreich. (Summer, 1912.)

. . . What troubles me most at present, is not the apparent-variable-business, but rather the meaning of "v" "$\supset$" etc. This latter problem is—I think—still more fundamental and, if possible, still less recognized as a problem. *If* "pvq" means a complex at all—which is quite doubtful—*then*, as far as I can see, one must treat "v" as *part* of a copula in the way we have talked over before. I have—I believe—tried all possible ways of solution *under that hypothesis* and found that if any one will do it *must* be something like this:

Let us write the proposition "from $\vdash$p and $\vdash$q follows $\vdash$r" that way: "i(p; q; r)". Here "i" is a copula (we may call it inference) which copulates *complexes*.

Then "$\vdash \epsilon_I\,(x,y).v.\epsilon_I\,(u,z)$" is to mean:

"$\vdash(\epsilon_I\,(x,y),\ \epsilon_I\,(z,u),\ \beta\,(x,y,z,u)\,).\ i[\epsilon_I\,(x,y);\ \epsilon_I\,(z,u);\ \beta\,(x,y,z,u)]$
$\vdash(\epsilon_I\,(x,y),\ \epsilon_I\,(z,u),\ \beta\,(x,y,z,u)\,).\ i[\sim\epsilon_I\,(x,y);\ \epsilon_I\,(z,u);\ \beta\,(x,y,z,u)]$
$\vdash(\epsilon_I\,(x,y),\ \epsilon_I\,(z,u),\ \beta\,(x,y,z,u)\,).\ i[\epsilon_I\,(x,y);\ \sim\epsilon_I\,(z,u);\ \beta\,(x,y,z,u)]$
$\vdash(\epsilon_I\,(x,y),\ \epsilon_I\,(z,u),\ \beta\,(x,y,z,u)\,).\ i[\sim\epsilon_I\,(x,y);\ \sim\epsilon_I\,(z,u);\ \beta\,(x,y,z,u)]$
$\vdash\ (x,y,z,u)$".

If "pvq" does not mean a complex, then heaven knows what it means!!

August, 1912.
... Now as to 'pvq' etc: I have thought that possibility—namely that all our troubles could be overcome by assuming different sorts of Relations of signs to things—over and over and over again! for the last eight weeks!!! But I have come to the conclusion that this assumption does *not* help us a bit. In fact if you work out any such theory—I believe you will see that *it does not even touch our problem.* I have lately seen a new way out (or perhaps not out) of the difficulty. It is too long to be explained here, but I tell you so much, that it is based on new forms of propositions. For instance: $\sim\!|\!\sim$ (p,q), which is to mean 'the complex p has the opposite form of q's form'. That means that $\sim\!|\!\sim$ (p,q) holds for instance when p is ϵ_1 (a,b) and q is $\sim\epsilon_1$ (c,d). Another instance of the new forms is Ψ (p,q,r) which means something like: "The form of the complex r is composed of the forms of p and q in the way 'or'". That means that Ψ (p,q,r) holds for instance when p is ϵ_1 (a,b), q is ϵ_1 (c,d) and r is ϵ_1 (e,f)v ϵ_1 (g,h) etc. etc. The rest I leave to your imagination.

1912.
I believe that our problems can be traced down to the *atomic* propositions. This you will see if you try to explain precisely in what way the Copula in such a proposition has meaning.

I cannot explain it and I think that as soon as an exact answer to this question is given the problem of "v" and of the apparent variable will be brought *very* near to their solution if not solved. I now think about "Socrates is human" (Good old Socrates!).

IV Alleegasse 16. Wien. 26.12.12.
... I had a long discussion with Frege about our theory of symbolism of which, I think, he roughly understood the general outline. He said he would think the matter over. The complex-problem is now clearer to me and I hope very much that I may solve it.

IV Alleegasse 16. Jan. 1913.
... I have changed my views on "atomic" complexes: I now think that qualities, relations (like love) etc. are all copulae! That means I for instance analyse a subject-predicate proposition, say, "Socrates is

human" into "Socrates" and "something is human", (which I think is not complex). The reason for this is a very fundamental one: I think that there cannot be different Types of things! In other words whatever can be symbolized by a simple proper name must belong to one type. And further: every theory of types must be rendered superfluous by a proper theory of symbolism: For instance if I analyse the proposition Socrates is mortal into Socrates, mortality and $(\exists x,y)\ \epsilon_1 (x,y)$ I want a theory of types to tell me that "mortality is Socrates" is nonsensical, because if I treat "mortality" as a proper name (as I did) there is nothing to prevent me to make the substitution the wrong way round. *But* if I analyse (as I do now) into Socrates and $(\exists x)$. x is mortal or generally into x and $(\exists x)\ \phi x$ it becomes impossible to substitute the wrong way round because the two symbols are now of a different *kind* themselves. What I am *most* certain of is not however the correctness of my present way of analysis, but of the fact that all theory of types must be done away with by a theory of symbolism showing that what seem to be *different kinds of things* are symbolized by different kinds of symbols which *cannot* possibly be substituted in one another's places. I hope I have made this fairly clear!

Propositions which I formerly wrote ϵ_2 (a,R,b) I now write R(a,b) and analyse them into a,b and $\underbrace{(\exists x,y)\ R(x,y)}_{\text{not complex}}$

June, 1913.

. . . I can now express my objection to your theory of judgement exactly: I believe it is obvious that, from the proposition "A judges that (say) *a* is in a relation R to *b*", if correctly analysed, the proposition "a R b.v.∼a R b" must follow directly *without the use of any other premiss*. This condition is not fulfilled by your theory.

Hochreit, Post Hohenberg, Nieder-Österreich, 22.7.13.

. . . My work goes on well; every day my problems get clearer now and I feel rather hopeful. All my progress comes out of the idea that the *indefinables* of Logic are of the general kind (in the same way as the so-called *definitions* of Logic are general) and this again comes from the abolition of the real variable.

. . . I am very sorry to hear that my objection to your theory of judgment paralyses you. I think it can only be removed by a correct theory of propositions.

Hochreit, Post Hohenberg, N.-Ö.

(This letter seems to have been written sometime near to that of the letter dated 22.7.13.)

Your axiom of reducibility is

$$\vdash : (\exists f) : \phi x \equiv_x f!x;$$

now is this not all nonsense as this proposition has only then a meaning if we can turn the ϕ into an *apparent* variable. For if we cannot do so no general laws can ever follow from your axiom. The whole axiom seems to me at present a mere juggling trick. Do let me know if there is more in it. The axiom as you have put it is only a schema and the real Pp ought to be

$$\vdash :. (\phi) : (\exists f) : \phi (x) \equiv_x f!x,$$

and where would be the use of that?—

5.9.13.

I am sitting here in a little place inside a beautiful fiord and thinking about the beastly theory of types. There are still some *very* difficult problems (and very fundamental ones too) to be solved and I won't begin to write until I have got some sort of a solution for them. However I don't think that will in any way affect the bipolarity business which still seems to me to be absolutely untangible.

c/o Draegni, Skjolden, Sogn, Norway. 29.10.13.

. . . Identity is the very Devil and *immensely important*; *very* much more so than I thought. It hangs—like everything else—directly together with the most fundamental questions, especially with the questions concerning the occurrence of the *same* argument in different places of a function. I have all sorts of ideas for a solution of the problem but could not yet arrive at anything definite. However, I don't lose courage and go on thinking.

30.10.

I wrote this[1] letter yesterday. Since then quite new ideas have come into my mind; new problems have arisen in the theory of molecular propositions and the theory of inference has received a new and very important aspect. One of the consequences of my new ideas will—I think—be that the whole of Logic follows from one Pp only!! I cannot say more about it at present.

[1] The foregoing letter; the present extract is a postscript. [*Edd.*]

1913.

Thanks for your letter and the typed stuff![1] I will begin by answering your questions as well as I can:

(1) Your question was—I think due to the misprint (polarity instead of *bi*-polarity). What I mean to say is that we *only* then understand a proposition if we know *both* what would be the case if it was *false* *and* what if it was *true*.

(2) The symbol for ∼ p is a-b-p-a-b. The proposition p has two poles and it does not matter a hang where they stand. You might just as well write ∼ p like this:

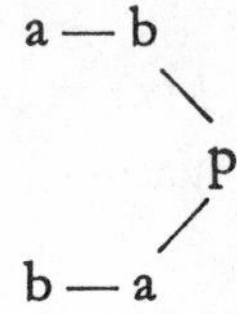

or b — a — p — b — a etc. etc. All that *is* important is that the new *a*-pole should be correlated to the old *b*-pole and vice versa *wherever these old poles may stand.* If you had only remembered the WF scheme of ∼ p you would never have asked this question (I think). In fact all rules of the ab symbolism follow directly from the essence of the WF scheme.

(3) Whether ab-functions and your truth-functions are the same cannot yet be decided.

(4) "The correlation of new poles is to be transitive" means that by correlating one pole in the symbolizing way to another and the other to a third we have *thereby* correlated the first in the symbolizing way to the third, etc.. For instance in a-b-a-bpa-b-a-b, a and b are correlated to *b* and *a* respectively and this means that our symbol is the same as a-bpa-b.

(5) (p) p v ∼ p *is* derived from *the function* p v∼q but the point will only become quite clear when identity is clear (as you said). I will some other time write to you about this matter at length.

(6) Explanation in the typed stuff.

(7) You say, you thought that Bedeutung was the "fact", this is quite true, but remember that there are no such things as facts and that therefore this proposition itself wants analysing. If we speak of "die Bedeutung" we seem to be speaking of a thing with a proper name. Of course the symbol for "a fact" is a proposition and this is *no* incomplete symbol.

[1] Presumably the 1913 *Notes on Logic.* [*Edd.*]

(8) The exact a-b indefinable is given in the manuscript.

(9) An account of general indefinables? Oh Lord! It is too boring!!! Some other time! — Honestly — I *will* write to you about it some time, if by that time you have not found out all about it (because it is all quite clear in the manuscript I think). But just now I am *so* troubled with Identity that I really cannot write any long jaw. All sorts of new logical stuff seems to be growing in me, but I can't yet write about it.

... The following is a list of the questions you asked me in your letter of the 25th.10.:

(1) "What is the point of 'p.≡. "p" is true'? I mean why is it worth saying?"

(2) "If 'apb' is the symbol for p, is 'bpa' the symbol for ∼p? and if not, what is?"

(3) "What you call ab-functions are what the Principia calls 'truth-functions'. I don't see why you shouldn't stick to the name 'truth-functions'."

(4) "I don't understand your rules about *a*'s and *b*'s, i.e. 'the correlation of new poles is to be transitive'."

(5) (Is obvious from my letter) so is (6).

(7) "You say 'Weder der Sinn noch die Bedeutung eines Satzes ist ein Ding. Jene Worte sind unvollständige Zeichen". I understand neither being a *thing*, but I thought the Bedeutung was the *fact*, which is surely not indicated by an incomplete symbol?"

I don't know whether I have answered the question (7) clearly. The answer is *of course* this: The Bedeutung of a proposition is symbolized by the proposition—which is *of course* not an incomplete symbol, *but the word "Bedeutung"* is an incomplete symbol.

(8) and (9) are obvious.

Nov., 1913.

... I beg you to notice that, although I shall make use in what follows of my ab notation, the meaning of this notation is not needed; that is to say, even if this notation should turn out not to be the final correct notation what I am going to say is valid if you only admit—as I believe you must do—that it is a *possible* notation. Now listen! I will first talk about those logical propositions which are or might be contained in the first 8 chapters of Principia Mathematica. That they all follow from *one* proposition is clear because *one symbolic* rule is

sufficient to recognize each of them as true or false. And this is the *one* symbolic rule: write the proposition down in the ab notation, trace all connections (of poles) from the outside to the inside poles: Then if the b-pole is connected to such *groups of inside poles only as contain opposite poles of one proposition*, then the whole proposition is a true, logical proposition. If on the other hand this is the case with the a-pole the proposition is false and logical. If finally neither is the case the proposition may be true or false, but it is in no case logical. Such for instance (p).~p —p transmuted to a suitable type, of course—is not a logical proposition at all and its truth can neither be proved nor disproved from logical propositions alone. The same is the case—by the way—with your axiom of reducibility, *it is not a logical proposition at all* and the same applies to the axioms of infinity and the multiplicative axiom. *If these are true propositions they are what I shall call "accidentally" true and not "essentially" true.* Whether a proposition is accidentally or essentially true can be seen by writing it down in the ab notation and applying the above rule. What I—in stating this rule—called "logical" proposition is a proposition which is either essentially true or essentially false. This distinction of accidentally and essentially true propositions explains—by the way—the feeling one always had about the infinity axiom and the axiom of reducibility, the feeling that if they were true they would be so by a lucky accident.

Of course the rule I have given applies first of all only for what you called elementary propositions. But it is easy to see that it must also apply to all others. For consider your two Pps in the theory of apparent variables * 9.1 and * 9.11. Put then instead of ϕx, $(\exists y).\phi y.y = x$ and it becomes obvious that the special cases of these two Pps like those of all the previous ones become tautologous if you apply the ab notation. The ab Notation for Identity is not yet clear enough to show this clearly but it is obvious that such a Notation can be made up. I can sum up by saying that a logical proposition is one the special cases of which are either tautologous—and then the proposition is true—or self-contradictory (as I shall call it) and then it is false. And the ab notation simply shows directly which of these two it is (if any).

That means that there is *one* method of proving or disproving all logical propositions and this is: writing them down in the ab notation and looking at the connections and applying the above rule. But if *one* symbolic rule will do, there must also be *one* Pp that will do. There is much that follows from all this and much that I could only explain vaguely but if you really think it over you will find that I am right.

Norway, 1913.

... Ich will dasjenige, was ich in meinem letzten Brief über Logik schrieb, noch einmal in anderer Weise wiederholen: Alle Sätze der Logik sind Verallgemeinerungen von Tautologien und alle Verallgemeinerungen von Tautologien sind Sätze der Logik. Andere logische Sätze gibt es nicht. (Dies halte ich für definitiv). Ein Satz wie "$(\exists x).x = x$" zum Beispiel ist eigentlich ein Satz der Physik. Der Satz "$(x) : x = x . \supset . (\exists y).y = y$" ist ein Satz der Logik; es ist nun Sache der Physik zu sagen, *ob es ein Ding gibt*. Dasselbe gilt vom infinity axiom; ob es $\aleph_0$ Dinge gibt, das zu bestimmen ist Sache der Erfahrung (und die kann es nicht entscheiden). Nun aber zu Deinem Reductions-Axiom: Stell' Dir vor, wir leben in einer Welt, worin es nichts als *Dinge* gäbe und außerdem *nur noch eine Relation*, welche zwischen unendlich vielen dieser Dinge bestehe und zwar so, daß sie nicht zwischen jedem Ding und jedem anderen besteht, und daß sie ferner auch nie zwischen einer endlichen Anzahl von Dingen besteht. Es ist klar, daß das axiom of reducibility in einer solchen Welt sicher *nicht* bestünde. Es ist mir aber auch klar, daß es nicht die Sache der Logik ist darüber zu entscheiden, ob die Welt worin wir leben nun wirklich so ist, oder nicht. Was aber Tautologien eigentlich sind, das kann ich selber noch nicht ganz klar sagen, will aber trachten es ungefähr zu erklären. Es ist das eigentümliche (und *höchst* wichtige) Merkmal der *nicht*-logischen Sätze, daß man ihre Wahrheit *nicht* am Satzzeichen selbst erkennen kann. Wenn ich z. B. sage "Meier ist dumm", so kannst Du dadurch, daß Du diesen Satz anschaust, nicht sagen ob er wahr oder falsch ist. Die Sätze der Logik aber — und sie allein — haben die Eigenschaft, daß sich ihre Wahrheit bezw. Falschheit schon in ihrem Zeichen ausdrückt. Es ist mir noch nicht gelungen, für die Identität eine Bezeichnung zu finden, die dieser Bedingung genügt; aber *ich zweifle nicht*, daß sich eine solche Bezeichnungsweise finden lassen muß. Für zusammengesetzte Sätze (elementary propositions) genügt die ab-Bezeichnungsweise. Es ist mir unangenehm, daß Du die Zeichenregel an meinem letzten Brief nicht verstanden hast, denn es langweilt mich *unsagbar* sie zu erklären!! Du könntest sie auch durch ein bißchen Nachdenken selber finden!

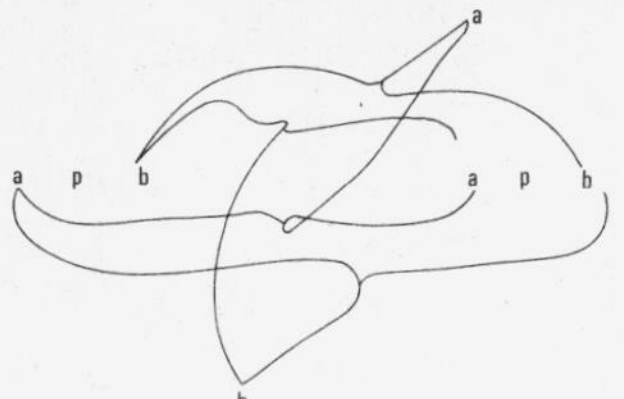

Dies ist das Zeichen für $p \equiv p$; es ist tautologisch weil *b* nur mit solchen Polpaaren verbunden ist, welche aus den entgegengesetzten Polen eines Satzes (nämlich p) bestehen; wenn Du dies auf Sätze anwendest, die mehr als 2 Argumente haben so erhälst Du die allgemeine Regel,

wonach Tautologien gebildet werden. Ich bitte Dich denke selbst über die Sache nach, es ist mir *schrecklich* eine schriftliche Erklärung zu wiederholen, die ich schon zum ersten Mal mit dem aller*größten Widerstreben* gegeben habe. Die Identität ist mir — wie gesagt — noch gar nicht klar. Also hierüber ein andermal! Wenn Dein Axiom of Reducibility fällt, so wird manches geändert werden müssen. Warum gebrauchst Du als Definition der Klassen nicht diese:

$$F[\hat{x}(\phi x)] =: \phi z \equiv_z \psi x . \supset_\psi . F(\psi) \text{ Def.} \qquad ?$$

. . . Die große Frage ist jetzt: Wie muß ein Zeichensystem beschaffen sein, damit es jede Tautologie *auf eine und dieselbe Weise* als Tautologie erkennen läßt? Dies ist das Grundproblem der Logik!

. . . Ich will nur noch sagen, daß Deine Theorie der "Descriptions" *ganz zweifellos* richtig ist, selbst wenn die einzelnen Urzeichen darin ganz andere sind als Du glaubst.

Translation of the above:

I want to repeat what I wrote about logic in my last letter, putting it in a different way: All propositions of logic are generalizations of tautologies and all generalizations of tautologies are propositions of logic. There are no logical propositions but these. (I consider this to be definitive.) A proposition like "$(\exists x) x = x$" is for example really a proposition of physics. The proposition "$(x) : x = x . \supset . (\exists y) . y = y$" is a proposition of logic: it is for physics to say *whether any thing exists*. The same holds of the infinity axiom; whether there are $\aleph_0$ things is for experience to settle (and experience can't decide it). But now for your reducibility axiom: Imagine our living in a world, where there is nothing but *things*, and besides *only one relation*, which holds between infinitely many of these things, but does not hold between every one and every other of them: further, it never holds between a finite number of things. It is clear that the axiom of reducibility would certainly *not* hold in such a world. But it is also clear to me that it is not for logic to decide whether the world we live in is actually like this or not. However, I can't myself say quite clearly yet what tautologies really are, but I'll try to give a rough account. It is the peculiar (and most important) characteristic of *non*-logical propositions, that their truth cannot be seen in the propositional sign itself. If I say for example 'Meier is stupid', you cannot tell whether this proposition is true or false by looking at it. But the propositions of logic—and they alone—have the property of expressing their truth or falsehood in the very sign itself. I haven't yet succeeded in getting a notation for identity which satisfies this condition; but I *don't doubt* that such a

notation must be discoverable. For compounded propositions (elementary propositions) the ab notation is adequate. I am upset that you did not understand the rule for the signs in my last letter, since it bores me *unspeakably* to explain it! You could get at it for yourself if you would think a bit!

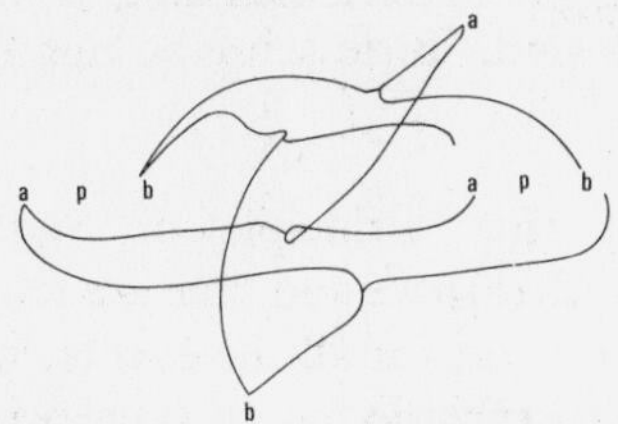

This is the sign for p ≡ p; it is tautological because *b* is connected only with such pairs of poles as consist of opposed poles of a proposition (p); if you apply this to propositions with more than 2 arguments, you get the general rule according to which tautologies are constructed. Please think the matter over yourself, I find it *awful* to repeat a written explanation, which I gave the first time with the *greatest reluctance*. So, another time! If your Axiom of Reducibility fails, various things will have to be altered. Why don't you use the following as a definition of classes:

$$F[\hat{x}(\phi x)] =: \phi z \equiv_z \psi x . \supset_\psi . F(\psi) \text{ Def.} \qquad ?$$

. . . The great question is now: How should a notation be constructed, which will make every tautology recognizable as a tautology *in one and the same way*? This is the fundamental problem of logic.
. . . The only other thing I want to say is that your Theory of Descriptions is *quite undoubtedly* right, even if the individual primitive signs in it are quite different from what you believe.

Skjolden, 15.12.13.
. . . Die Frage nach dem Wesen der Identität läßt sich nicht beantworten, ehe das Wesen der Tautologien erklärt ist. Die Frage nach diesem aber ist die Grundfrage *aller* Logik.

. . . The question of the nature of identity cannot be answered until the nature of tautologies is explained. But that question is the fundamental question of *all* logic.

Skjolden/Januar, 1914/.
. . . Jetzt noch eine Frage: Sagt der "Satz vom zureichenden Grunde" (Law of causality) nicht einfach, daß Raum und Zeit relativ sind? Dies scheint mir jetzt ganz klar zu sein; denn alle die Ereignisse von denen dieser Satz behaupten soll, daß sie nicht eintreten können, könnten überhaupt nur in einer absoluten Zeit und einem absoluten

Raum eintreten. (Dies wäre freilich noch kein unbedingter Grund zu meiner Behauptung.) Aber denke an den Fall des Massenteilchens, das, allein in der Welt existierend, und seit aller Ewigkeit in Ruhe, plötzlich im Zeitpunkt A anfängt sich zu bewegen; und denke an ähnliche Fälle, so wirst Du — glaube ich — sehen, daß *keine* Einsicht a priori uns solche Ereignisse als unmöglich erscheinen läßt, *außer eben in dem Fall*, da Raum und Zeit relativ sind. Bitte schreibe mir Deine Meinung in diesem Punkte.

. . . Now another question: Doesn't the "Principle of Sufficient Reason" (Law of Causality) simply say that space and time are relative? At present this seems to me to be quite clear; for all the events, whose occurrence this principle is supposed to exclude, could only occur at all in an absolute time and an absolute space. (This would not of course quite justify my assertion.) But think of the case of a particle, which was the only thing in the world and had been at rest from all eternity, and then suddenly begins to move at a moment of time A; and of similar cases: then you will see—or so I believe—that *no a priori* insight makes such events seem impossible to us, *except in the case* of space and time's being relative. Please write me your opinion on this point.

Cassino, 19.8.19.[1]

(1) "What is the difference between Tatsache and Sachverhalt?" Sachverhalt is, what corresponds to an Elementarsatz if it is true. Tatsache is what corresponds to the logical product of elementary props when this product is true. The reason why I introduce *Tatsache* before introducing *Sachverhalt* would want a long explanation.

(2) ". . . But a Gedanke is a Tatsache: what are its constituents and components, and what is their relation to those of the pictured Tatsache?" I don't know *what* the constituents of a thought are but I know *that* it must have such constituents which correspond to the words of Language. Again the kind of relation of the constituents of the thought and of the pictured fact is irrelevant. It would be a matter of psychology to find out.

(3) "The theory of types, in my view, is a theory of correct symbolism: a simple symbol must not be used to express anything complex: more generally, a symbol must have the same structure as its meaning." That's exactly what one can't say. You cannot prescribe to a symbol

[1] Wittgenstein had sent Russell a copy of the *Tractatus* by the hand of Keynes, and the following letter is a reply to Russell's queries about the book. [*Edd.*]

what it *may* be used to express. All that a symbol *can* express, it *may* express. This is a short answer but it is true!

(4) "Does a Gedanke consist of words?" No! But of psychical constituents that have the same sort of relation to reality as words. What those constituents are I don't know.

(5) "It is awkward to be unable to speak of Nc^cV[1]." This touches the cardinal question of what can be expressed by a prop, and what can't be expressed, but only shown. I can't explain it at length here. Just think that, what you want to *say* by the apparent proposition "There are 2 things" is *shown* by there being two names which have different meanings (or by there being one name which may have two meanings). A proposition e.g. $\phi(a,b)$ or $(\exists\phi,x,y).\phi(x,y)$ doesn't say that there are two things, it says something quite different; *but whether it's true or false, it shows* you what you want to *express* by saying: "there are 2 things".

(6) Of course no elementary props are negative.

(7) "It is necessary also to be given the proposition that all elementary propositions are given." This is not necessary because it is even impossible. There is no such proposition! That all elementary propositions are given is *shown* by there being none having an elementary sense which is not given. This is again the same story as in No. 5.

(8) I suppose you didn't understand the way how I separate in the old notation of generality what is in it truth-function and what is purely generality. A general proposition is a truth-function of *all propositions* of a certain form.

(9) You are quite right in saying that "$N(\bar{\xi})$" may also be made to mean $\sim p \vee \sim q \vee \sim r \vee \ldots$ But this doesn't matter! I suppose you don't understand the notation "$\bar{\xi}$". It does not mean "for all values of $\xi \ldots$". But all is said in my book about it and I feel unable to write it again.

9.4.20.

Besten Dank für Dein Manuskript.[2] Ich bin mit so manchem darin nicht ganz einverstanden; sowohl dort, wo Du mich kritisierst, als auch dort, wo Du bloß meine Ansicht klarlegen willst. Das macht aber nichts. Die Zukunft wird über uns urteilen. Oder auch nicht — und wenn sie schweigen wird, so wird das auch ein Urteil sein.

[1] In Russell's symbolism, the cardinal number of the universal class, i.e. of all objects. [*Edd.*]

[2] Russell's *Introduction* to the *Tractatus*. [*Edd.*]

Many thanks for your manuscript. I am not quite in agreement with a lot of it: both where you criticize me, and where you are merely trying to expound my views. But it doesn't matter. The future will judge between us. Or it won't—and if it is silent, that will be a judgment too.

6.5.20.

. . . Nun wirst Du aber auf mich böse sein, wenn ich Dir etwas erzähle; Deine Einleitung wird nicht gedruckt und infolgedessen wahrscheinlich auch mein Buch nicht. — Als ich nämlich die deutsche Übersetzung der Einleitung vor mir hatte, da konnte ich mich doch nicht entschließen, sie mit meiner Arbeit drucken zu lassen. Die Feinheit Deines englischen Stils war nämlich in der Übersetzung — selbstverständlich — verloren gegangen und was übrig blieb, war Oberflächlichkeit und Mißverständnis. Ich schickte nun die Abhandlung und Deine Einleitung an Reclam und schrieb ihm, ich wünschte nicht, daß die Einleitung gedruckt würde, sondern sie solle ihm nur zur Orientierung über meine Arbeit dienen. Es ist nun höchst wahrscheinlich, daß Reclam meine Arbeit daraufhin nicht nimmt (obwohl ich noch keine Antwort von ihm habe).

. . . Now, however, you will be angry at what I have to tell you: your introduction will not be printed, and in consequence probably neither will my book. For when I got the German translation of the introduction, I couldn't bring myself to have it printed with my work after all. For the fineness of your English style was—of course—quite lost and what was left was superficiality and misunderstanding. Now I have sent the treatise and your introduction to Reclam, and have written to him that I did not want the introduction to be printed, but that he should just use it to orientate himself about my work. It is now extremely likely that in consequence Reclam will not take my work (although I have not had an answer from him yet).

APPENDIX IV*

$$\varphi(x)(\varphi)\psi = (x)\varphi\psi(y) = (x)R(y) = xRy$$

$$\varphi(\hat{z}(\psi z)) \overset{\text{Def}}{=} \varphi x \equiv_x \psi x . \supset_\varphi . \phi\varphi$$

Von zwei Klassen zu sagen sie seien identisch sagt etwas. Von zwei Dingen dies zu sagen sagt nichts. Dies schon zeigt die Unzulässigkeit der Russellschen Definition.

6.9.14.

$$a\varepsilon\hat{z}(\psi z) \overset{\text{Def}}{=} \varphi(x) \equiv_x \psi(x) . \supset . a\varepsilon\varphi$$

7.9.14

19.9.14.

$$aRb . bRc . cRd . dRe = \varphi(a,e)$$

$$(\exists R^0)\, aR^0e$$

$(\alpha\beta\gamma)$ $\varphi(\alpha \ldots)$

Wie kann sich eine Funktion <u>auf</u> einen <u>Satz</u> <u>beziehen</u>???? Immer die uralten Fragen!

23.9.14.

$$\varphi(a), \psi(b), aRb, (\exists x,y): \varphi x . \psi y . xRy$$

$$aRb . \varphi a . \psi b \overset{\text{Def}}{=} (\varphi,\psi)(aRb) = \Omega(x)$$

aRb $a\sigma c$, $b\sigma d$

cSd

* See Preface.

$F(\hat{x}(\varphi x)) . = . \varphi \equiv \psi \supset_{\psi} F\psi$

$\phi \equiv \psi . \supset_{\psi} \left[F(\hat{x}(\psi x)) = \psi \equiv \chi \supset_{\chi} F\chi \right] =$

$= \left[F(\hat{x}(\psi x)) = (\exists\hat{x})\phi z \equiv \chi z \supset_{\chi} F\chi \right]$

17.4.16.

$\varphi x . \psi y = x \varphi \psi y = xRy$

$Fx . Fy . xRy = F(xRy)$

$F(xRy) = Fx . Fy . \varphi x . \psi y$

$\sim(\exists x) . \varphi x \qquad \psi z \equiv_z \varphi z . \supset_{\psi} \sim(\exists x) \psi x$

6.5.16

21.5.16.

$(\exists x) . (y) . \varphi(x, y) . \; (y) . (\exists x) . \varphi x y ; (x)(\exists y) . \varphi x, y ;$
$(\exists y)(x) \varphi(x, y) . \; (\exists x) . (\exists y) \varphi x y ; (x) . (y) \varphi x, y)$

24.5.16.

$F_0(x, y, z \ldots)$

25.5.16.

11.7.16.

Das aber ist der richtige Ausdruck für $(\exists x).\varphi x$

$(\exists\alpha)\cdot[\varphi\alpha|\psi\beta\ldots]$

~~$\cdot\varphi x\cdot\psi y$~~ $\qquad |(\xi,\eta)\ldots = \varphi_0(x,y,\ldots)$

$(\exists x)\cdot\varphi_0(x,y,\ldots)\;,\quad(\exists y):(\exists x)\cdot\varphi_0(x,y\ldots)$

$(\exists x)::(\exists\alpha):(\exists\alpha)\cdot\varphi_0(\alpha,\alpha,\alpha,\ldots)$

$(\exists\alpha)\{\varphi_0(\alpha\ldots)\}\ldots$

16.7.16.

$xRy.$ $\qquad --\xi\cdot\xi R\eta$

$xRy.yRz$

$xRy.yRz.zRu$ $\qquad \cdot\xi R\eta(--R\xi)\ldots$

– – – – – – – –

20.7.16.

Meine ~~Die~~ alte Erklärung aller Satzformen war im Grunde richtig und das erste andere Art der Allgemeinheit benötigt wird.

Jetzt noch das Abwechseln zwischen $(\exists x)$ und (x) ausdrücken. Dann aber die Allgemeinheit der Form wie z.B. der Ancestral Relation!

$aRx \cdot xRy \cdot yRz \ldots uRb$

$\cdot xRy \{aRx\} \ldots$

15.7.16.

$(\exists (aRx \cdot xRy \ldots zRb))$

$aRb \vee aRx \cdot xRb \vee aRx \cdot xRy \cdot yRb \vee \ldots \vee aRx \cdot xRy \cdot yRz \ldots uRb$

Hier kann vernünftigerweise nicht von einer Existenz von Dingen die Rede sein, da auch der Satz aRb schon den Bedingungen entspricht.

Nichts scheint einfacher zu sein als ein Satz wie „a ist ein Nachkomme von b“!

INDEX

The publishers wish to extend their gratitude to Professor E. D. Klemke and Mr. Ali Enayat for preparing this index.

Numbers not in parentheses indicate page numbers of the English translation. (In all cases the letter 'e' which appears on translated pages is omitted.) Numbers in parentheses indicate paragraphs. Thus "52(6)" indicates the sixth paragraph on page 52. Each indented line is considered as beginning or as being a new paragraph. If a paragraph is continued from a previous page, it is considered as the first paragraph on the page in which it is continued. For the three appendices, the following abbreviations are added to the numbers:

L: "Notes on Logic"
M: "Notes dictated to G. E. Moore in Norway"
R: "Extracts from Wittgenstein's Letters to Russell."

In some cases I have indexed a word or sign with regard to its concept rather than the actual word or sign. For example, citations for '∼' and 'not' are listed under 'negation'. Citations for 'all' are listed under 'generality'. I have tried to keep these departures to a minimum. Also I have included references to the plural under the singular. Thus 'object' includes citations of 'objects' as well as 'object'. Where relevant, I have tried to indicate the context in which a term is used. Thus for a passage in which simple objects are discussed, I have cited it under the heading of 'object, simple', rather than 'object'. Comments which are made by the editors of the book are not indexed.

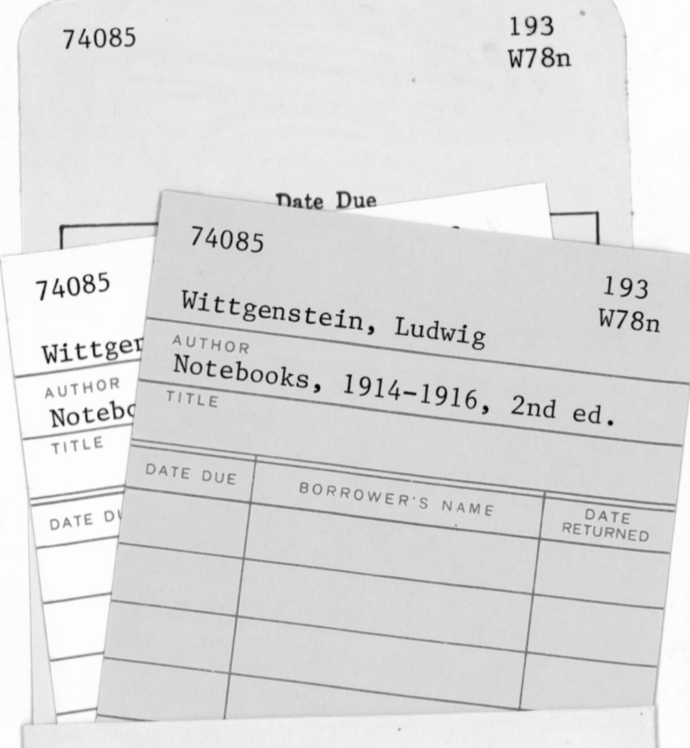
74085
193
W78n
Date Due
74085
Wittgenstein, Ludwig
AUTHOR
Notebooks, 1914-1916, 2nd ed.
TITLE
DATE DUE
BORROWER'S NAME
DATE RETURNED